relations. Please accept the enclosed book which resumes my point of view diametrically opposed, if I may say so, to the position expressed by Professor Samuel Huntington.

Finally, I would like to mention as well that your article about Romania in the preceding issue of the Review, was very much appreciated by Hungarians all over the world. I read it in the Review of which I am a regular subscriber, but later received it by e-mail sent across the continents by the network of the Hungarian diaspora, especially to those who are of Transylvanian origin (the city of Segesvár of which I bear the name is called today Sigishoara).

I went back to Transylvania in 1999, 55 years after I left Kolozsvár, and hope to organize there, together with some friends in Hungary, a meeting of representatives of Transylvanian cultures -- Romanian, Hungarian and Saxon -- next year. This has to be an exclusively cultural encounter because political debates do not lead, unfortunately, very far.

With my best regards,

Victor Segesvary, PhD, D.D.
330 East 39th Street, Apt. 21 E
NEW YORK, N.Y. 10016
E-mail: segesvary@un.org
Phone: (212) 949-1450

INTER-CIVILIZATIONAL RELATIONS AND THE DESTINY OF THE WEST

Dialogue or Confrontation?

Victor Segesvary

University Press of America, ® Inc.
Lanham • New York • Oxford

Copyright © 2000 by
University Press of America,® Inc.

4720 Boston Way
Lanham, Maryland 20706

12 Hid's Copse Rd.
Cumnor Hill, Oxford OX2 9JJ

Library of Congress Cataloging-in-Publication Data

Segesvary, Victor.
Inter-civilizational relations and the destiny of the West : dialogue or
confrontation? / Victor Segesvary.
p.   cm.
Includes bibliographical references and index.
1. Comparative civilization. 2. East and West. 3. Intercultural communication. 4.
Philosophical anthropology—Cross-cultural studies. 5. Ethics, Comparative. 6. Social
history—1970-7. Culture conflict.   I. Title
CB251.S42 2000   909.82—dc21   00—041769 CIP

ISBN 0-7618-1724-7 (pbk: alk. ppr.)

⊖™ The paper used in this publication meets the minimum
requirements of American National Standard for Information
Sciences—Permanence of Paper for Printed Library Materials,
ANSI Z39.48—1984

UXORI MEAE DILECTISSIMAE

TABLE OF CONTENTS

PART TWO

Disjunction Between the Western and Other Cultural Worlds

CHAPTER FOUR

From Utilitarian to Meaningful Rationality and Ethics . . 115

CHAPTER EIGHT

Modernization As Framework of Economic Development 231

CHAPTER NINE

Conclusions 251

PREFACE

This book is the result of a decades-long "inner conversation" with a large number of thinkers, biologists, social scientists, and other intellectuals of the twentieth century, in order to try to find a way out of the culture clash and civilizational decay. During my two decades of work in the field of international cooperation and technical assistance, I realized, through an encounter with other cultures and populations, and through the discovery of the immense richness of the human worlds belonging to various civilizations, that all efforts toward Western-inspired economic and social modernization in the sphere of non-Western civilizations represent an ineffective way to make them benefit from the West's modernity. I am, myself, rooted in a threefold world: in the lands and culture of Europe, the Old Continent, more specifically in *Mitteleuropa* or Central-Eastern Europe; in the worlds of other civilizations which I learned to understand, to respect and to love not only through interest and close contact, but through a sensitivity to their particular lifeworlds anchored in both cosmic and immanent reality; and, finally, in the world of the unforeseeable future already shaped, I felt, by the ever-increasing phenomena of inter-civilizational encounters, and through the discovery of the unmistakable signs of growing troubles in our own civilization.

I spoke above of an "inner conversation" to describe how this book came into being because I have had few chances to discuss its themes with many people, mostly similarly-minded practitioners in the largest sense of the word, but much less with those who are specialists of such questions in academia. The only person who closely followed the progression of my thought, reading, and writing, was my wife to whom I extend, again and always, all my gratitude for her endless patience during this long and sometimes tedious work. I also extend the expressions of my gratitude to all those with whom I had this decades long "inner conversation" -- thinkers and writers -- whom I never knew personally but whose thinking I eagerly absorbed.

I never looked for any financial support during the preparation of this book. I worked as part-time senior advisor in matters of technical assistance and economic and social development within the United Nations system (of which I was a staff member during a good part of my professional career). I have tried to do my work of personal interest without help from any source, in order to avoid any possible interference with my endeavor. Therefore, all ideas expressed, all conclusions made in the following reflections, are my own, and I am alone responsible for them.

I should, finally, clarify three things: first, that any and all references made in the text to persons as 'he', 'him', and the like, are a matter of convenience and should thus be understood as gender-neutral terms. Second, in respect of the transliteration of names and terms in non-Western languages, I avoid to use diacritics because the study is neither linguistic nor highly specialized in such fields that make necessary to follow the rules of transliteration; it is on contemporary problems, and its aim is not a philological or literary examination of classical and historical texts. Third, rather than encumber the study with a full scholarly apparatus and render the reading of a complex text even more difficult, I have reduced the footnotes to the minimum, and made references to authors and their writings in the text.

INTRODUCTION

The need to examine the possibilities of dialogue or conflict between co-existing civilizations of the contemporary world as well as of the reasons for which many people belonging to other cultural worlds oppose extension of the Western civilization to their areas, is an urgent and unavoidable task in the present age. This urgency results from the gradual collapse of the universalistic worldview. The collapse of the West's universalistic modernity is, however, not complete as modern science and technology continue to be applicable everywhere and give the impression, if not of the triumph of the universalistic worldview, but of the "globalization" of Western ways of life. Nevertheless, universalism is fading away, and even the most enthusiastic advocates of the superiority of Western modernity have begun to recognize the advent of pluralistic worlds of culture.

This recognition is essential, as it becomes gradually apparent that the destiny of the West itself depends, to a great extent, on the course inter-civilizational relations will take in the near future. Globalization, the well-known phenomenon of many interdependencies in all fields of human activity defines the crucial role inter-civilizational relations will play in the West's future. It is also necessary, however, to envisage the problem of inter-civilizational dialogue or conflict from the angle of the West's own cultural crisis, because a mutual exchange of views with other cultural worlds and, perhaps, the selective adoption by the West of some of their ideas and practices, may contribute to the correction of the fateful direction of development adopted in Western modernity during the last two centuries.

In the following two sections of this Introduction, I shall, first, define the meanings and reciprocal relations of culture and civilization in the overall framework of the lifeworld, then trace some approaches to worlds of culture. Finally, I shall indicate major methodological problems in the domain of the social sciences and summarize the methodological principles I have followed in the text.

1. *The Concepts of Culture and Civilization*

The definition of culture as a concept is an extremely difficult task, especially if one intends to avoid all misinterpretations that result from one's particular cultural context and conditioning. This is evident from the well-known study of two great American anthropologists, Kroeber and Kluckhohn (1963), in which they cite 400 authors and at least 130 definitions of culture. Without discussing at length culture's definition, I accept the definition given by Clifford Geertz [1973: 144], in which culture is "an ordered system of meaning and symbols, in terms of which social interaction takes place," whereas the social system is "the pattern of social interaction itself."

Culture, then, is not the property of an individual, or a subjective orientation, behavior, but a complex whole shared by a human community. If culture is a complex whole shared by a human community, then two essential characteristics of it must be made evident. The first is that a culture is an organized, coherent whole, not a mere ensemble of isolated elements because its variables are interdependent [Kroeber-Kluckhohn 1963: 374]. Culture patterns, explicit or implicit, are acquired and transmitted through symbols which contain and reflect the distinct way of life of the human community, the bearer of a particular culture. The overall framework of a cultural community or of a specific human society's way of life constitutes the civilization centered on this cultural core.

One misunderstanding has to be avoided in this context. It relates to the technical-descriptive nature, inherited from anthropological studies, of culture as a concept. In fact, a culture is not sufficiently characterized by tools, artifacts, and social habits such as marriage customs, as evoked in these studies. The core of a culture consists of belief and value systems, including ideas relative to the ontological/cosmic context, historically derived and appropriated through their internalization by successive generations of the community. This core of a culture was conceived by Hegel as *Sittlichkeit* (based on his analysis of the Greek *polis*), meaning that the cultural dimension of life constitutes the structures of consciousness through which men identify themselves with their society and its institutions [Taylor, Ch. 1979a: 125]. Hegel called the opposite attitude, the non-identification with the community, *alienation*. He believes that no free society can be sustained if people do not identify themselves with their community or do not share the ethical, *sittliche* dimension of their inherited culture.

All great cultures known in history from antiquity to the present day can be identified with particular belief and value systems, ethical dimensions, cosmic perspectives, creative functions, and technical procedures. The following terminology will therefore be used throughout this book: *culture* as the meaningful and symbolic core of people's life, belonging to a given civilization, and *civilization* is the totality of the way of life of determinate human populations or societies. In accordance with this differentiation of the two terms, *lifeworld* will be understood in an even more inclusive way, encompassing the non-civilizational or environmental and cosmic components of human existence.

The birth and evolution of cultures and civilizations, as we shall see in the first chapter, is brought forth through interaction between gene mutations and variations of the environment, through interaction between already existing cultures, and, finally, through the innovations and creative power of individuals and particular cultures. I prefer to speak of cultural worlds than of cultures or civilizations in order to indicate the global interactive processes of individual and community, culture and environment, genetic evolution and cultural evolution, and to call attention to the influence of various cultures on the life of men and societies they profoundly influenced and modified. The multiplicity of worlds of culture led to enormous difficulties in the interpretation of past cultures, but this temporal dimension raised still less problems than the co-existence, in space and in time, of disparate cultural entities turning, most frequently, from dialogue to domination, suppression, persecution, and war.

2. *Approaches to Worlds of Culture*

(a) UNDERSTANDING CO-EXISTING WORLDS OF CULTURE

The multiplicity of worlds of culture signifies, for most people, not cultural pluralism but a strong relativism of traditions, values, principles, ethos, behavior, and worldviews, the fragmentation of the reality of life in all its aspects, and, of course, even of truths. If everything is relative, there can be no truth of overall validity and no reality that appears the same to everyone. For this reason, philosophers, scientists, and the common man who instinctively believe in objective reality and universally accepted truths either endeavor to ignore cultural differences, or deny the possibility of communication between divergent cultures. Others regard cultural differences as successive stages on the road of progress towards the highest cultural level ever reached, or the highest humanity ever possible, our present Western civilization. I am definitely opposed to the theory of successive stages of the evolution of different cultures. Indeed, one of the objectives of this study is to find the right way to explain the simultaneous existence, or the succession in time, of worlds of culture, and to search for the foundations of their dialogue, not only desirable, but indispensable in the present state of our world at the end of the twentieth century.

Man's existence reveals sometimes unbearable tensions between the individual and the community, the immediately available and the potential, the finite, immanent world and the infinite, cosmic universe (a tension which marks man's existence through his "death-awareness," emphasized by Dobzhansky). All these tensions are felt, known, analyzed, and explained in the framework of the cultural world in which men happen to live. Culture conditions all of man's perceptions and apperception, his cognitive and emotional functions, his belief and value systems, and, consequently, is the foundation of the immense diversity of human existence. Still, despite this underlying diversity, human beings strive incorrigibly towards unity with other men and with the cosmos: the universe of other organisms, of natural forces, and of elements entirely external to his immanent world. This tension between the unavoidable diversity or plurality of different lifeworlds and the longing for unity of all men which overshadows all other essential tensions and is the main motivating force of cultural evolution. This means the understanding and interpretation of oneself, of the human community and of the unity of cosmos.[1]

To facilitate the understanding and interpretation of different, interrelated worlds of culture, I shall now endeavor to depict how concepts of different worlds are viewed by some contemporary philosophers who accept that culture patterns are not universal, but are highly particular in their form and, to a large extent, in their content at certain historical periods and in certain circumstances.

Some of these views appear too limited as they formulate their understanding of the multiplicity of cultural worlds only in cognitive and/or linguistic terms. Nelson Goodman, in his work *Ways of Worldmaking* [Goodman 1985: 2-5], admits that versions of interpretive schemes as well as actual worlds are many and that reality is contextual. Possible worlds may result from divergent systems of description to which frames of reference belong, or to shifting emphasis and relative consideration of the same entities, objects or acts, or to ratings of relevance, value, and utility leading to hierarchies and not to dichotomies. In consequence, truth or untruth becomes irrelevant, and the only validity claim that can be made in respect to the rightness or wrongness of the referential function is what was verbally or not verbally communicated. For Goodman understanding of these cognitively formulated multiple worlds is not only possible, but also the effort of comprehension is the real link between them. His understanding is inventing and imposing patterns; comprehension and creation are inseparable.

Donald Davidson in his essay "On the Very Idea of a Conceptual Scheme" [Davidson 1984: 183-198], criticized the view of different conceptual schemes, related to various languages, and, in particular, the efforts of conceptual relativism, the dualism of scheme and content. He considers that the failure of linguistic intertranslatability makes it impossible to understand, from one's own standpoint other conceptual schemes. He therefore emphasizes the interdependence of belief and meaning and, in consequence, of the interdependence of the attribution of belief and the interpretation of sentences.

These cultural differences explain that no ground for comparing differing conceptual schemes is feasible. For such a purpose, one should have a meta-world, lying outside all possible schemes (or worlds), a neutral standpoint from which to understand attitudes and interpret speech. The lack of such a 'common coordinate system' between representatives of different conceptual schemes -- those living in different civilizations -- makes even a partial translatability impossible because there seems to be no intellectual means at our disposal to decide when others think differently from us, that is, whether the difference lies in beliefs or in concepts not shared with them. Davidson did not find an intelligible basis on which the difference of schemes could be established; if there are different conceptual schemes but no shared ontology and common coordinates, then even the unity of all schemes cannot be affirmed. No dialogue between different worlds is imaginable. Therefore, he recognizes that there is no uninterpreted reality (though he defends a certain notion of objective truth which cannot be scheme-related), but returns to the "unmediated touch with the familiar objects whose antics make our sentences and opinions true or false" [ibid. 198].

Ian Hacking's concept of "styles of reasoning" [Hacking 1985][2] relates the difference between conceptual schemes or cultural worlds to the fact that a style of reasoning may determine the very nature of the knowledge it produces. Conceptual schemes are, in his view, a range of possibilities whose linguistic formulation is a class of sentences which can be as true as false. Different styles of reasoning cannot be sorted out by an independent criticism, because "the very sense of what can be established by that style depends upon the style itself" [ibid. 155], there is no common coordinate system in the Davidsonian sense. The key distinction, therefore, in respect to styles of reasoning is the one between truth-and-falsehood as opposed to truth; different styles may determine possible truth-values that can be objectively true in the framework of a given style of reasoning. That means that styles of reasoning open up new possibilities for reflection, or generate new classes of possibilities. As styles arise from historical events, their possible being-true is a consequence of historical or cultural developments. The issue, then, is not of translation but of understanding, thinking, and reasoning, in one way or another. A style is not a scheme that confronts reality, but is part of reality itself. Thus, Hacking's solution is only partially relativistic, as he recognizes that there are not only biological universals about all things human, but there is also a "common human core of verbal performances" characterized by a "loose fit" [ibid. 159]. This "loose fit" makes it possible to share in styles of reasoning, to participate in more than one style; if this is not the case, then a complete dissociation of the cultural worlds in question excludes understanding [Hacking 1983: 70-71].

Hacking's concept of styles of reasoning, although still remaining on the cognitive level, and couched in terms of the linguistic philosophy in vogue, is important for the possibility of inter-civilizational dialogues for two reasons. First, the recognition that, except for the "common human core" of life experiences (including biological universals), worldviews and discourses depend on the style of reasoning, though the common core constitutes a basis for the dialogue. Second, the abandonment of the logical alternative of truth or falsehood, for that of possible, alternatively posited truths-or-falsehoods, contribute to the breakdown of dogmatic opposition to, and refutation of, inter-cultural understanding.

Jürgen Habermas presents a view in which he distinguishes between the world and lifeworld, the latter not being identical with but underlying the threefold scheme of objective, subjective and social worlds. The three worlds, considered together, constitute a system of several equally primordial worlds "mutually presupposed in communication processes" [Habermas 1984-1989, Vol. I: 84], depicted by Habermas through the metaphor of looking at worlds of culture as if looking at a portrait from various angles [ibid. 82-83]. His views are mainly influenced by the Weberian tradition, as he replaced the one-sided, cognitivistic interpretation of the concept of objective mind with a concept of cultural knowledge or, rather, cultural framework, differentiated according to several validity claims. Accordingly, all cultural domains are autonomous. It still is indispensable to find out what validity means for the noncognitive components of culture, without denying to them the possibility of correlation with the physical world (the first world).

Of Habermas' three worlds, only the first, the objective world, stands for the cognitive totality of true propositions and for the ontological totality of entities. Habermas explains that the demythologization of worldviews led to the desocialization of nature and to the denaturalization of society which, in turn, led to the formal positing of intersubjectivity as an objective standpoint. The foregoing enabled individuals to refer not only to the one objective world identical for all observers, but also to intersubjectively shared values in the social world. Consequently, truth signifies that the asserted states of affairs exist in the objective world, and the rightness of a behavior or of an action in respect to an existing normative context is the acknowledgment that it was based on a legitimate element of the social or cultural world.

Probably Clifford Geertz [Geertz 1973] is correct in his distinction between the ethos of a culture, comprising its evaluative elements, moral and aesthetic expressions, and even social norms, and the worldview, reflecting its cognitive and existential aspects. The problem of all philosophical approaches to the multiplicity of worlds of culture is that they are mostly conceived in terms of worldview though giving a more or less restricted place to the ethos, beliefs, values, subjective expressions or common lore of cultural heritage, because they tend to preserve, in accordance with the philosophical and scientific tradition of the West during the last centuries, the pre-eminence of the cognitive apperception of human existence expressed through the established linguistic structures. Habermas' *Lebenswelt* is, in this sense, the notion which expresses in the most appropriate way what a world of culture means, referring to the differences among the plurality of these *Lebenswelten*, reflecting the diversity of Hacking's patterns of reasoning -- the simultaneously present common human core as well as the relativizing effects of variable styles of reasoning.

The plurality of worlds means the different lifeworlds in which man lives. This plurality is experienced several ways: in stellar and cosmic differences; in the temporal perspective and the huge discrepancies between past, present, and future worlds; in the spatial perspective, in the diversities of cultural, national, traditional, and other characters, phenomena, and events; and, finally, in the individual's life as he changes with age, contextual situations and destinies independent of his will. This all is expressed by the *Leitmotif* of this study: the plurality of human worlds.

The history of the world teaches us that until the second half of the seventeenth century, the great cultural systems of the world co-existed each having its sphere of influence in which they governed human life and gave it its intellectual and social framework indispensable for man's existence. Contacts between these civilizations, especially of those incarnated in powerful states and societies, were generally restricted to the exchange of diplomatic messages or conclusion of alliances, and consisted much more in trade and frequent large-scale wars or local skirmishes between armies. People living in mythical cultural worlds, in tribal societies, and in parts of the world remote from the main centers of activity, have continued to exist since time immemorial. From the point of view of the West, the painful realization of the existence of different civilizations, beliefs, societies and political powers started with the wars against Muhammad's armies, the Crusades, and with the devastating campaigns of the Ottomans, particularly under Sulejman the Magnificent, which brought hostilities to European territories. If we include in the Western cultural period the whole span of more than two thousand years since the Greek culture, the confrontation with different worlds began with the wars against the Persians by the Greeks and with the invasion of Rome by the barbarians, accompanied by the vast influence of alien cultures during the period of twilight between classical Antiquity and the Middle Ages.

However, during the last four centuries, European culture and civilization witnessed the scientific revolution and its ensuing technological progress. This process resulted in unprecedented advances in adapting to and controlling its natural environment, and economic development which gave to its peoples previously unknown wealth and richness, as well as the most efficient social organization, political and military power. The developments since the age of Galileo and Newton represent one of the greatest achievements of mankind and are to be credited entirely to the capabilities and hard work of people who lived in the European world. Their inventiveness and elaborate discipline in life, particularly in work, together with the formulation of a necessary moral framework underlying all the achievements in the other domains, are inexplicable in other but evolutionary terms. All people on earth, though favorably or unfavorably conditioned by their physical environment and by their cultural heritage, were and are capable of achieving the same scientific and technological successes as those living in the European cultural sphere. Why crucial changes took place in this culture and not in another can only be understood if one takes into account the random character of genetic variations in individuals and populations, the random character expressed in cluster like cultural developments (as in the Renaissance or in the German philosophical awakening at the end of the eighteenth century), or the random character in the interaction of cultural and social factors with genetic and environmental phenomena. It is therefore necessary to discard, once and for all, such nonsense as that which attributes the economic, social and cultural advancement of the West to the European colonial expansion, and exploitation of peoples living in other cultural worlds, because these were the result and not the cause of the Western scientific, technological, and economic evolution.

The extraordinary achievements which took place in the Western cultural world led to the belief in the idea of progress, evolutionary or cultural, with two results: that humanity is progressing in every aspect of life from lower to higher stages, grades, or levels of capacity, competency, activity and achievement; and that as man is the highest complete and final product of natural evolution, Western civilization represents the highest, complete and final stage or level of the cultural evolution and progress of mankind. In fact, both theses on progress are creeds, that is, axioms of the modern scientific and technological worldview which, by definition, cannot be supported by any evidence and therefore cannot be falsified.

(b) DISJUNCTION BETWEEN WORLDS OF CULTURE

The key word, therefore, widely used in today's literature to characterize the present state of Western civilization in relation to other cultures is *disjunction*. This term has a double meaning: first, the disjunction of Western modernity from its own past occurring over the last four centuries in the Western culture itself; and, second, a consecutive disjunction from the great contemporary cultures. When the modern worldview is characterized by disjunction, the meaning of the term should be understood in the sense Anthony Giddens gives to it, which the essential trait of modernity consists in "placing a *caesura* upon the traditional world, which it seems irretrievably to corrode and destroy. The modern world is born out of discontinuity with what went before rather than continuity with it" [Giddens 1984: 239]. In the same vein, the secularization — de-sacralization, disenchantment, or rationalization — of the world which broke the cosmic unity and communion with nature (though, as Hegel said, man can only be himself with reference to a cosmic order) are all expressions equivalent to the caesura or disjunction mentioned above. This inevitably led to the self-reflexivity of the modern age and to a legitimation of modernity on self-generated principles, as it had "to create its normality out of itself" [Habermas 1987: 7].

To summarize modern conditions following such contemporary thinkers as Bellah or Habermas, one can state that modern conditions are the result of a utilitarian individualism which dominates the lifeworld, in its economic form, capitalism, its political form, bureaucracy, and its ideological form, the absolute rule of science. The internal dynamics of monetarization and bureaucratization penetrates the core of culture and society and, by way of disjunction from belief and value systems, interferes with the mutual understanding, which previously formed the basis of action-oriented human behavior and shared identity within the community. For Habermas, the result is a systematically distorted communication pattern, the domination of external discourse over internal discourse, the gradual loss of intrinsic connections between meaning and validity, intention or action.

The domination of the scientific worldview, or the quasi-absolute rule of science,[3] constitutes a major element of modernity. In addition to the utilitarian orientation of society since the eighteenth century, technical reason was idolized and the Aristotelian practical reason entirely subordinated to purposive rationality as a consequence of the overwhelming successes of the scientific revolution. When rationality is confined not to the technical horizon but overseeing the life of society and dominating the culture of a community, another aspect of the disjunction experienced by modern man is revealed. The scientific-bureaucratic management of man's life has proven not only impractical and ahistorical, but also destructive to the ethical dimension of culture, of its inherited beliefs and values, in the name of value-freedom or ethical neutrality. The thesis of value-neutrality, of course, is one of the great fallacies of our age of disjunction, because far from having achieved a value-free or ethically neutral standpoint in the modern era, technology's own value standards dominate and usurp all other domains of life, replacing, in fact, one value-system with another [Habermas 1973: 270].

The domination of technology and purposive rationality leads directly -- as Hegel predicted -- to a vast homogenization of society where autonomous cultural groups are either progressively eliminated or survive only in the periphery of the lifeworld. This homogenization became an imperative within the modern West as, since the nineteenth century, the population explosion due to improved health care and public health conditions has rendered the scientific-technical control and administration of society impossible if homogenization had not been achieved. Homogenization and elimination of cultural differences is therefore inherent in the culture of modernity; this means also the leveling of individual capacities, competencies and social roles in agreement with the falsely conceived principle of equality.

(c) GLOBALIZATION REPLACING UNIVERSALISM

The tendency of modernity toward cultural and civilizational homogenization is completed by *globalization*, a product of late modernity. Globalization is entirely different from Enlightenment universalism because it refers to the "coming into, often problematic, conjunction of different forms of life," [Robertson 1992: 27] and signifies, simultaneously, differential definitions and interpretations at world level. Diversity is, then, essential for globalization in a dialectic of globality and locality as "space and temporal categories and measures were globally institutionalized" [ibid. 179-180]. Cultural pluralism, consequently, is a constitutive element of "the global circumstance" [ibid. 26] as much as inter-societal constraints or the interaction between various societies and cultures. In Robertson's sense, the globalization process does not signify an extension of world culture in accordance with the global extension of economic and political circumstances; that is, it is different from Von Laue's "world revolution of westernization" [Von Laue 1987] or Fukuyama's end of history, it resembles much more Nelson's "inter-civilizational encounters" [Nelson 1981]. The globalized world does not present a unified picture but is in constant disequilibrium, since such a non-equilibrium is inherent in a world of pluralistic cultures which can only be grasped in a dialectical formulation as when Robertson says that post-modernity witnesses "*the interpenetration of the universalization of particularism and the particularization of universalism*" [Robertson 1992: 100; italics added].

Globalization as well as the population explosion, enormously enhanced, since World War II, the homogenization of people living not only in the orbit of Western civilization, but also those living in the vast continents of Asia and Africa: this was the revolution by means of information and systems of communication. The phenomena of the worldwide demographic explosion, of the homogenization in terms of the technical civilization of the West, and of the unforeseeable extension of communications and information disseminated by the mass media also had unpredictable effects, and met unpredictable challenges and resistances in the countries recently conquered by the civilization of technocratic and bureaucratic power. To mention only three of these unpredictable effects and challenges resulting from science and technology, one can refer, first, to environmental problems, second, to the neutralizing effects of the results of science and technology on the forces of natural selection in the evolution of various species, and, third, to the failure of development policies and assistance proving that other cultures, customs, and traditions resist the onslaught of homogenization and require the recognition of the right to be different.

All this said it is not the aim of these investigations to propose a historically impossible return to the world of yesterday, as the trend toward modernization is irreversible. The existence of a plurality of cultural worlds rather suggests the imperative of the *acceptance of the difference of Others*. Such an attitude is more than simple tolerance because it implies a positive encounter, an interactive dialogue, and a cross-cultural development toward a new synthesis. The common core of expressions and actions, similarities inherent in human capabilities and discernible in all cultures facilitates such an acceptance of difference between worldviews. The acceptance of difference, however, means that the other culture has to be considered as what it is, in its global dimension, and not solely in its aspects that appear divergent from the point of view of Western practices. A new humanism must be situated in the double perspective of the ontological/cosmic framework, — Nature — and of the plurality of human cultural worlds.

3. *Some Methodological Remarks*

(a) METHODOLOGICAL DIFFERENCES BETWEEN NATURAL AND SOCIAL SCIENCES

The study of the role of culture in human life and of the dialogue of cultures in today's world necessarily leads us to briefly consider the debate about methodologies in the natural and social sciences, particularly since the pluralistic tendency of Renaissance and Humanism lost out to the totalizing and universalizing will of modern science. It must be clear from the preceding considerations that perhaps the greatest obstacle to a contemporary dialogue of cultures, at the end of this second millennium, is the Western scientific myth. I call it scientific myth not to attack or to devalue all great results and achievements of modern Western science, but to point to the distortion introduced into our culture by the exclusive validity claim of this science which transforms it into a dominating power. A dominating power not only vis-à-vis other cultures and civilizations, but also towards man, as it strives to exclude from the global richness of human existence everything other than the cognitive domain, which alone is admitted as capable of understanding and explaining the multifarious aspects of nature as well as of man and his cultures.

In contrast to this point of view, I stress the ontological and cosmic character of nature, culture and man, understanding by cosmic not the cosmogonies and related worldviews of archaic societies, but the all-embracing framework accessible only to global, holistic understanding and explanation. This corresponds to the evolutionary view of nature and man, though including not only the physical perspective of evolution, but the mental and spiritual as well. Therefore, the much discussed demarcation line between science and pseudo-science (metaphysics) is displaced to separate true science, without domineering tendencies and recognizing its limits in the overall evolutionary-cosmic perspective, from pseudo-science, which asserts science's universal validity claim and rejects anything psychological, mental or spiritual-emotional as non-empirically falsifiable, placing it within the realm of fantasy, imagination, mob-psychology, false consciousness, or undemocratic political manipulation of man by man.

Again, this does not mean any negation of the value of science and of its enormous technological successes,[4] but aims at placing science in its true context, the cosmic-evolutionary perspective of human existence. This approach makes it possible to integrate Western science in the dialogue of cultures, not imposing it to other worldviews as an apodictic truth but as something to be adapted to, to be built in, or to be partially absorbed by other civilizations.

The debate on the merit and explanatory power of natural versus social science, in terms of methodology between explanation (from the *explanans* to the *explanandum*) and understanding (*Verstehen*), can be summarized in the following. Natural science is the paradigmatic science, based on induction or on hypothetico-deductive reasoning. The results of the latter must be checked against nature, that is, justified or falsified through artificially constructed experiments. In terms of logical positivism, meaningful statements fall into two categories: analytic or synthetic. The first cannot be denied without logical contradiction in its terms or, inversely, the truth of the statement is derived from the meaning of these terms as defined by convention. The second is a statement of fact, the truth of which depends on possible justifying or falsifying circumstances. Analytical statements or tautologies therefore are *a priori*, invented by man independently of empirical assertions and, as a consequence, might be changed by any human being. For conventionalists or some deductive rationalists, the character of analytic statements precludes reference to truth or falsity. On the contrary, observation and induction can only establishe synthetic statements. It is in this sense that the validity of hypothetico-deductive reasoning is conditioned by such limiting considerations as "all things being equal" or *ceteris paribus*, meaning that the confirmation of a statement is solely based on certain assumptions held by the statement's authors.[5] If suitable empirical instances occur, causal laws or confirmed empirical generalizations are established.

In many theories, however, truth or confirmation consists of the prediction of events that take place in the future, and it is consequently considered that the operations of explanation and prediction obey the same rules of logical inference which should guarantee their correctness. When the theory is refuted or falsified either the premises or parts of the theoretical construction have to be modified, or the preliminary (initial) conditions reformulated in accordance with revised background information. This trial-and-error process goes on eternally, reflecting the evolutionary trial-and-error processes leading to natural selection (at least in accordance with the view of the evolutionary epistemologists), as no theory appears to be definitive. This was witnessed by Newtonian physics that became only a limiting case of contemporary quantum theory.

It is, however, evident that all philosophies of science, — the positivist/empiricist, the analytical, the critical rationalist or, more recently, the evolutionary epistemologist — posit axioms on which are based the hypothetico-deductive, nomological explanations and predictions which are not explicable in terms of theory. In order to safeguard the coherence of the theoretical construction, the basic axioms therefore are explicated in terms of meta-theories or meta-languages which permit conceptualization or positing final axioms at another, higher level in order to avoid infinite regress. As far as truth is concerned in the history of science, scientific truths reflect physical reality or express the phenomena as they are, or, in the wake of the Einsteinian and quantum revolutions, truth in science became a regulative idea, not an apodictic, absolute reality.

The concept of natural science as described above justified the application and development of more and more abstract, mathematically formalized methodologies. One of the main characteristics is that they are radically *non-ontological*; that is, objects of the natural sciences do not fall under the category of beings. The identity of a thing (the thing-in-itself) is replaced by its isomorphism with other entities. The object may be defined not by its origin or by its ontological characteristics, *as it is* (the "essence" in the old philosophical language), but by its isomorphism with other objects constructed as such in the models. Isomorphism may be expressed as structural or functional similarity, for example, the theoretically constructed individual instead of the living human being. This development of scientific methodology, it is true, allowed for an extensive unification of scientific conceptualization and experimentation never attained before, though at the price of the complete loss of the pragmatic dimension of knowledge, and one might add, at the price of the complete loss of the temporal dimension of existence: institutions, tradition, and culture.

Without entering the debate and taking position on whether such methodology is justified in the natural sciences,[6] I shall briefly point out the shortcomings of the concept and methodology of natural science whenever applied to the social sciences, and through this, throw light on the methodology used in the present investigations. First of all, the issue of *relevance* of the natural scientistic conception and methodology to the fields, problems, and processes of the social sciences has to be examined. Relevance, of course, is a very difficult concept. What is relevant to what? The answer is naturally conditioned by the axioms, values and knowledge already acquired, the pre-existent framework or context in which the relevance of an idea, concept, approach, or a method can be established. In fact, the answer to the problem of relevance is one of the major themes of this book. Relevance in the social sciences depends on the difference of their subjects from the phenomena in natural science, and the different subjects of the two types of science automatically imply a different method.

The role of one's *values* is equally important; there is no disinterested work in the social sciences, remarked the late Gunnar Myrdal, who clearly saw that

> The fact that we do not reach a base of universal and unchangeable factual relationships and thus a generally valid knowledge, is related to the role of valuations in our research. It is true that, in principle, all scientific work has to be based on value premises. There is no view without a viewpoint, no answers except to questions. In the viewpoint applied and the questions raised our valuations are involved. But in the field of natural phenomena the value premises are simple and mostly *a priori* evident [Myrdal 1972: 1486].

To sum up the striking weaknesses of the scientific-epistemological approach which strives for knowledge from the social-scientific point of view but neglects ontological understanding or the explanation of the existent in man's world, the following points can be made:

(i) *Reductionist ontology* makes it impossible to deal with a dynamic, never-rigid human reality including non-material, mental and spiritual facts and motives. This leads to the unavoidable indeterminacy in every explanation and prediction, because the scientific truth is considered as a regulative idea not always corresponding to the real.

(ii) The *fiction of the objective-observer standpoint* is unrealistic and irrational to adopt for any human being whose life and concepts are deeply embedded in his environmental context, his time, and his culture (as expressed by the quantum theoretical principle that the observer is a participant in his experiments).[7]

(iii) The *founding of the whole approach on ideological creeds not on empirically falsifiable axioms and theorems, for example, the theory of ontological reduction, exclude from reality any aspect of nature not explicable in terms of the (apodictic) axiomatic standpoint.*

(b) HERMENEUTICS: THE METHOD OF UNDERSTANDING AND EXPLANATION

The hermeneutic approach in the social sciences recognizes that understanding, interpretation and explanation are, due to the cultural and temporal dimensions, reliant upon a pre-existing and autonomously developed creative background, and grow out of a communicative, dialogical context. The method is based on Aristotle's ethical vision of human life, which distinguishes between theoretical and practical wisdom. The latter, called by Aristotle *phronesis*, is a reflective attitude, a reasoning that mediates between the universal and the particular: man applies universals (beliefs, principles, ideas, or values) to particular situations. But he distances himself from the concrete situation through this reflective attitude, in order to perceive, with the help of intuitive reason, the unchangeable and first terms of life. Man's standpoint is not that of an observer or outsider, but as a participant in an inter-subjective dialogue in which understanding and explanation of material and non-material reality is ontologically rich and in constant movement.

This understanding is attempted by individuals and communities: temporal (contemporaries), spatial (members of a culture or subculture in a permanent process of fusion into each other), or biological (members of a species encountering ever new environmental conditions in the overall evolutionary process). This approach openly admits that there is no value-free observer's standpoint, but objectivity is reflected by the consensus reached in a communicative dialogue between humans belonging to a biological, temporal and cultural community. *This perspective ensures, dialectically, that in the interaction of various communities to which men belong, a worldview is formulated which simultaneously satisfies the validity claims of a realistic standpoint (based on the ontological interdependence of nature and the human species) and the validity claims of the pluralistic position (corresponding to the temporal and cultural dependence or framework of human existence).* Such dialectic could be designated as the co-presence in the lifeworld of invariant and co-variant elements, which represent the cosmic-natural and the cultural-temporal perspectives of human existence.

The dialectical interplay is also manifested in the hermeneutic understanding and interpretation of the relations of community and individual. Creative acts of the individual are validated by the community, as inter-subjective consensus in a sort of "dialogical imagination" [Bakhtin 1981]; whereas the creative acts of the community, manifested, in the long run, and benefiting the individuals' creativity dialogically validated, is incorporated in cultural heritage, such as tradition and language which the individual appropriates through education and acculturation.

The dialogical-communicative approach in the social sciences means that the binomial relationship between object and subject is completely transformed into a multifaceted relation between all participants in a community. Thus, the typically Western phenomenon of the epistemological paradox, the subject/object dichotomy is eliminated. If we speak here of paradox, it is precisely because the epistemological orientation of modern Western thought, due to the Cartesian primacy of the cognitive or to the absolute primacy given to man in the natural world, completely obscured the ontological/cosmic framework in which the subject/object dichotomy does not make sense at all. This dichotomy is a paradox, as it ignores the transcendental interdependence of subject and object, of observer and observed, not only in human affairs, but even in the natural sciences, as quantum physical observations recently proved it. The replacement of the binomial relationship by a multiple and interdependent network of relations excludes the possibility of the objectification of one observer's standpoint, as dialogue and communication presuppose an intentionality on behalf of all participants.

The first twentieth-century thinker who attempted a solution to the paradox of epistemology was Martin Heidegger. His thinking, although grown out of Husserlian phenomenology, reached a previously unattained stage in the defense of the ontological unity of the world and in the affirmation of the absolute priority of ontology in the founding of existence and knowledge. The enunciation of the ontological premises of "worldhood" (the most comprehensive type of holism, as there is no other kind of a whole which would encompass Being as such) overcame the subject-object dichotomy of Western philosophies.

Heidegger radically eliminates the dichotomy of subject and object because he conceives of man as *Dasein*, whose desire for knowledge is part of his being-in-the-world. The "facticity" of man, his encountering of other entities within-the-world, the world being the same for all men, excludes the possibility of an opposition of subject to object. The Being-in-the-world of man is a "reflexive awareness" or an "immediate consciousness" (Dilthey); in the Heideggerian parlance, it reflects concomitantly man's ontological or transcendent and ontic or this-worldly character. Among our contemporaries, to mention only a few, there are many versions of the effort to eliminate the subject/object dichotomy from Searle's "rationalistic monism" to Mannheim's "conjunctive knowledge."

Habermas presupposes linguistic or symbolic mediation; he is therefore right that the transition from speech in the first or second person to speech in the third (with a "generalized other") was conceived in the natural sciences as authorizing and justifying the observer's attitude of theoretical objectification of the other. For dialogic communication, the intentionality of the other expressing cognitive interests, mental, emotional, and cultural motivations or predispositions, does not allow for any objectification necessary for causal explanations. Objectification in tradition and cultural heritage appears in a diversity of intentionalities as hypothetically assumed premises in understanding the meaning and reason of others' actions, or in opening up the possibility of a reconstruction of self-understanding; therefore, there is a *"fundamental connection between understanding communicative actions and constructing rational interpretations"* [Habermas 1984-1989, Vol. 1: 116; italics in original].

The hermeneutic method (understanding, interpretation, and explanation) excludes the observer's position in favor of the participant's as well as the object-subject dichotomy, as neither fits into the dialogical setting of communicative interaction. This approach promotes a unified vision of human life, action, and community placed in a cosmic and evolutionary perspective. Instead of looking for a unified theory explaining all material/physical aspects of the world and of man's existence in it, human science turns to the cosmic, all-encompassing view of nature in which the physical life of man and his culture (with its mental and spiritual components) are contained as much as fields and forces, micro-structures, and other objects investigated by the natural sciences, without subordinating any of the perspectives to one to another. Such a unifying vision, the ultimate meta-level of explanation, permits the re-ordaining of the fragmented understanding and the interpretation of cosmic inter-relations and of interactions of nature's various elements in human existence. Knowledge becomes "existential knowledge" (Paul Tillich). The feeling of meaninglessness to which the incorrectly understood role of science in human life led mankind after centuries of real progress and of misplaced hopes, can be dissipated as the regulative role of cosmic interdependence and the effective framework of evolutionary processes is fully understood and accepted.

Hermeneutical understanding dealing with cultural disjunction between distinct cultural worlds must follow an appropriate dialectical, heuristic strategy that convinces the bearers of each and every culture to tolerate and accept the others. One of the essential elements of such a heuristic strategy is to recognize that this endeavor is beyond logic, as logic is unable to secure a transition from one universe of discourse to another, from one cultural world to another. Logical continuity is only conceivable within a given structure or world of discourse, whereas hermeneutics (belonging to the transcendental way of thinking) relates these varying worlds of culture and discourse to each other. Again, turning to Heidegger, an understanding of other cultures and civilizations is a disentangling of a "meaning-contexture," as

> Every world-view thus individually formed arises out of a natural world-view, out of a range of conceptions of the world and determinations of the human *Dasein*, which are at any particular time given more or less explicitly with each such *Dasein*... A world-view is related in its meaning to the particular contemporary *Dasein* at any given time [Heidegger 1982: 6].

Hermeneutical understanding is then the moment when meaning comes to light. It is, in addition, an important aspect of the hermeneutic enterprise to comprehend that understanding and tolerance do not and cannot signify the full assimilation of the others' worldview; it is to comprehend that two or more perhaps incommensurable worldviews in contact, and the hermeneutic method does not mean a choice between them. If understanding would mean identification with the other, then the paradox of the cultural relativist -- so often held against advocates of a dialogue between cultures by the philosophical rigorists, would be right, but nobody can see the moon from the position of another or change at will the worldview into which he was initiated during childhood. The openness and integrative power of the human mind enables man to understand other cultures and acknowledge the self-description of other human societies without necessitating the transformation of oneself into another's identity, or to use, as it has been sometimes proposed, a neutral, scientific meta-language which would be instrumental to express realities in both cultural worlds. A supposedly neutral language that is laden with our usual concepts, functional categories, and instrumental-rational intentions, impregnated with a typically-specific thought structure, can only lead to distortion of the belief and value systems and practical reasoning of alien cultures. Heidegger considers that the very essence of language is saying, which means showing. Saying also implies the capacity to listen, and silence can 'say' more than words spoken.

Understanding and interpreting other cultures and civilizations leads, finally, not only to a pluralistic worldview, but also to a sincere and human relativism. Relativism is the explanation of diversity, as diversity has always been a constant in our natural and social world. In addition to the acceptance and explanation of diversity, relativism also means that there is no universal authority, not even that of science, which can determine the proper way to see and understand reality, the right ends in man's life, or the right design for human society. Cultures are different frames of reference; that is, they represent the difference between things-in-themselves and seeing-things-in-relation, without eliminating universals. Universals cannot be decreed, and they are recognized through inclusion into ontological/cosmic frameworks. Therefore, this relativism does not deny the existence of a common rationality between men, though it does not consider that requirements of human rationality and of varying cultural settings have to be convergent and uniform across space and time. If one eliminates all particularities, all possible prejudices or biases, all imaginative projections across the inherent gap between appearance and reality due to the culture's function as action-orienting information-system, no reality intelligible to human beings will remain. The dialogue of cultures must be a meeting with "alterity," a cross-cultural or trans-cultural event, in which the Heideggerian ontological difference is the foundation of the dialogue, as noted by Vattimo [1988: 147-150], and in which alterity and sameness fuse as the hermeneutical circle is completed.

It is probably true that we no longer live in a modern world; we live in a post-industrial or postmodern society defined as a dialogical society marked by the rapid advancement of information systems and technology. It might be more useful to think, then, in terms of a postmodern science which may be a science that accepts the all-embracing, cosmic understanding in a world which, as Stephen Toulmin so aptly described, is a "world that has not yet discovered how to define itself in terms of what it is, but only in terms of what it has just-not-ceased to be" [Toulmin 1982: 254].

PART ONE

Man and His Culture in the Ontological
Perspective

CHAPTER ONE

THE EVOLUTIONARY FRAMEWORK

1. *Biology Versus Culture: The Interactionist View*

It is quite natural to start the description of culture in the ontological/cosmic perspective, placed in an evolutionary framework, as it constitutes a specific form of the evolutionary process of adaptation, creation, and enrichment. Cultural evolution does not occur in a biological vacuum. As much as selection does not operate on individuals, or certain genes, but on organisms, endowed with a particular constellation of genes, cultural evolution and the selection based on it takes place in the form of great civilizations and societies which are, at the same time, the foundations, bearers, and creations of them. Mankind is the only species that is genetically capable of creating culture. However, there is a definite interdependence, a marked intertwining in human existence between the biological and the cultural evidenced through natural selection, and an outcome of an adaptive relationship between environmental conditions and the capacities of the genotypes. Although natural selection permits orderly evolution and harmonious development between co-existing organisms and between organisms and their environment, no human behavior and consequently, no human cultural act is completely defined by genetic determinism.   Nevertheless, the capacity of self-development in humans, including learning and the acquisition of behavioral types, is conditioned by the innate potential offered by the genotype.

Evolution is not programmed to produce man or any other particular species, but until the emergence of culture "the fundamental causes that operated in human ancestry were the same as those of other evolutionary lines" [Dobzhansky-Boesiger 1983: 74]. Many consider that specialization and differentiation represent, to some extent, an evolutionary impasse; non-differentiation is viewed in positive light, not a handicap. Major advances were therefore accomplished through the succession of generalized undifferentiated types, whereas the soft or plastic types, the well-formed species, were destined to further specialize in the direction chosen. Jean Rostand's formula expresses well this aspect of evolution: "Actual progress depends on differentiation, while potential progress is possible only by virtue of non-differentiation" [Rostand 1960: 165-167].[1] This is so because cultural development is cumulative, whereas the biological process is substitutive.

In the course of history there were some vital transitional phases called "transcendence" by Dobzhansky and Boesiger because it transcended the limits of the preceding evolutionary phase — an event that modified the hitherto valid laws of nature. The two major types of transcendence usually noted are from inorganic to organic evolution and from organic to human evolution. Human evolution thus is composed of the biological or organic, and of the cultural and superorganic components, interrelated and interdependent. The essential feature of organic evolution is that among organisms, each genotype, each individual, and each species is unique and temporary; that is, each evolutionary step is a historical event that has never occurred before and will never be repeated.[2] Evolution is then a movement from homogeneity to heterogeneity, and this is mostly evident in human evolution. If a species is a collection of individuals each of which differs from all others, and these individuals do not represent an immutable entity called the species (a typological fiction), then man does not exist apart from those dissimilar mortal individuals called persons who all share a slowly-evolving genetic endowment.

Therefore, it can be said that in the ontogenetic evolution "every individual is biologically unique and non-recurrent" [Dobzhansky 1962: 219] and a result of the natural process composed of biological and cultural evolutions. It is, however, important to realize that the overall description of human evolution given above does not imply a teleological perspective. Though natural selection indicates the general direction, mutations and gene recombinations are random and undirected, blind as to their usefulness to the organism; they are determined by the historically evolved genotype. This is so because all possible phenotypes resulting from the combination of a given genotype with every possible environment cannot be predicted. Natural selection is the process of differentiated reproduction resulting from differential adaptedness to a common selective environment. It thus depends on heritable variation in the genotype, and adopts, systematically, a directional change in the frequency of different phenotypes of a given population. Natural selection uses accomplished gene variations and recombinations; it is, as Mayr wrote, *a posteriori*. Thus, it tends to bring about the most favorable composition of the gene pool, of the gene variants adapted to the environment, and also to each other. It is striving for the formation of a "co-adapted gene system."

There is a unity of the human species, as its members are capable, if normally constituted, to learn symbolic languages and a variety of cultural forms and expressions. This capability is a species characteristic as much as the erect posture, the brain size exceeding that of other primates, the capacity to subsist on diverse diets, and so on. Nevertheless, the genetic variability affecting the cultural abilities of man, such as learning, creation, and representation, does not disappear. Gens do not transmit culture, and cultural conditioning, learning, and training have to be started afresh in every generation [Dobzhansky 1962: 20-21, 211, 233].

Thus, human phylogenetic (species-related) evolution took on a form that distinguishes it, to a great extent, from the evolution of other organisms, such as the animal species. Human evolution is *multilinear*. "Certain basic types of culture may develop in similar ways in similar conditions but... few concrete aspects of culture will appear among all groups of mankind in a regular sequence" [Steward 1972: 4]. If cross-cultural regularities undeniably exist because similar functionally adaptive processes may respond to similar environments, they do not necessarily pertain to all human societies. Historically independent sequences of formal and functionally similar traditions appear not infrequently, but this is due to identical causality in environmental conditioning (for example, the appearance of large-scale irrigation civilizations which ran a parallel course over thousands of years in the Middle East, Asia and America). Interactions between biological and cultural evolution mutually affect each other. The abilities of man and his capacity of "distancing" himself from the world gained through cultural evolution, has an all-embracing modifying influence on its own biological evolution, and on that of other organisms. Man appears even capable of consciously guiding his own evolution and the evolution of nature, as increasing complexity result from "the emergence of successive levels of socio-cultural integration." However, it appears almost certain today that the feed back effect of the cultural evolution produced such changes in man's inorganic, organic and cultural environment that, in turn, it will re-direct the future evolution of man and of his culture [Monod 1971: 162-163; Dobzhansky-Boesiger 1983: 105-106; Toulmin 1982: 174].

A second, essential factor in the evolution of the human species is that group variability is superimposed on individual variability. The human species is *polymorphic*, due to the infinite variability of the environments to which man has to adapt himself. Mankind is subdivided into a multitude of populations that are genetically mingling and overlapping as boundaries between them are shifting in time and space. In addition to this dynamic variability of the human species, which implies emergence and disappearance, expansion or contraction as well as basic modification in composition, gene pools of the different populations usually differ in the frequency with which certain genes appear and, in consequence, differ qualitatively, as well. Within any given human population there is endless variation between individuals exhibiting extreme values, but the intra-population differences are greater than those between the averages of different peoples are. As much as selection operates in the biological sphere, within the genetic makeup of individuals and given populations, evolution in the cultural sphere operates also on groups and tends to create large cultural ensembles, different civilizations, molding the life of great human societies. Speaking of human evolution, it is surely correct to say that the complex interactions of biological and cultural evolutions play their role at both the infra- and inter-specific levels [Rensch 1972: 116].

It should be noted that no correspondence could be established between a particular gene and a particular characteristic of a human organism. In contrast to the biochemical level, where each structural gene codes for only one particular chain of chemical elements, at the level of the phenotype, genetic effects often represent conditioning rather than pre-determination of morphological or physiological aspects, because in the processes of growth and development of the organism, gene products interact with the environment and with effects of other genes. Cultural evolution is therefore the result of genotypic and environmental influences, interactions in society (including learning experiences), as well as freely made, arbitrary decisions of individuals. There are certain definite covariance relations between genotypes and environments that can favor or obstruct cultural development. In fact, there is a Lamarckian feature in cultural evolution as culture is the framework of conservation and transmission of learned heritage, of products of the work of the human intellect from generation to generation, though the individual must always to acquire anew this cultural heritage. Theories of *tabula rasa* and of genetic predestination are both myths. The thesis of interaction between genetic endowment and of the natural and cultural environments in a network of covariance relations is the only way to explain man and his world.

Ecological anthropology [Rappaport 1971: 244], whose standpoint only slightly overlaps with the position taken in this study, acknowledges the importance of the inter-action of nature and culture. The greater "ecological flexibility" of man, as compared to other species is not attributed to ecological factors, for example, the geographical characteristics of any given region, but to the autonomous forces of cultural development. "Cultural ecology," as defined by Steward, is a similar concept which tries to identify the origins of particular cultural patterns prevalent in different areas of the world, placing special emphasis on their different functions which entail different social arrangements in different environments [Steward 1977: 43]. The core features of a culture play specifically important roles, as they are situated on different levels of integration.

What most tenants of the evolutionary theory did not clearly foresee is the complete disjunction between the biological and cultural evolutions over the course of the last centuries. In the past, both evolutions were slow, and biological adaptations to cultural change occurred concomitantly, whereas in modernity the pace of cultural evolution outstripped that of the biological evolution. At present, "culture increasingly creates its own environment" [Steward 1977: 52]. This disjunction results in considerable limitations on natural selection and on the forces of biological adaptation. As a result problems created by cultural evolution can only be resolved and corrective trends can only be induced by a reorientation of tomorrow's cultural developments, in the first place, by the renascent creativity of man.

Certain theories of cultural evolutionism distinguish between "specific" evolution in which new forms become differentiated from old ones, and "general" evolution, in which evolution generates progress. In the latter, emphasis shifts to forms classed in stages or levels of development, established either from the point of view of one's own civilization's perception, or from the point of view of the utilization of the earth's resources in the service of the survival of our species.

"Specific" evolution is viewed as an adaptive specialization constituting a relative advance in respect to changing environmental circumstances.   Phylogenetic evolution then justifies a biological relativism, according to which significant improvements for one species need not be so for another because of radically different environments or different forms of cultural adaptation.   "General" evolution disregards phylogeny or historical sequences of adaptive modifications and shifts the emphasis from species and populations to organisms that are grouped in types representing successive, higher levels of evolutionary progress. According to this view, cultural relativity is abandoned and absolute criteria are applied which, in Huxley's words, means 'all-round adaptability,' that is, a general propensity to adaptability resulting in a greater freedom from environmental limitations.

It is evident that the "specific," adaptive evolutions of various cultures are not comparable, whereas the concept of "general" cultural evolution implies automatically and necessarily their comparability.
It is affirmed in these theories that culture is transmitted in space and in time by non-genetic mechanisms. Consequently, the random factor being eliminated, the trend toward a greater convergence and homogeneity of cultural types, accompanied by a decrease in the diversity of cultures, dominates in contrast to the biological evolution. There appear, then, two simultaneous movements: one towards an increasing heterogeneity of the higher cultures, the other towards an increasing homogeneity of the same cultures and a gradual reduction of the diversity of cultural forms. It therefore is suggested that the trend toward homogenization of world cultures will continue in the future at an accelerated rate.

2. Culture As Action-Oriented Information System

As early as the 1950s, scientists like D.O. Hebb concluded, on the basis of experiments of controlled simulation, that higher animals were less stimulus-bound.[3] For Sir John Eccles, the fact that thought leads to action supports the claim of free-will, though not the denial of causality: it signifies a true interaction of the mental and the physical. Mental events are considered as causal agents that influence the pattern of neuronal activities — expressing willed movements. Thus, at higher stages of phylogenetic development, a sort of "free will" became apparent, which Clifford Geertz interpreted as proof of the fact that a "high degree of generality of the information [is] intrinsically available to the organism from genetic sources" [Geertz 1973: 79]. Therefore, a sense of "directive reasoning" [ibid. 78], in the form of public symbolic structures [ibid. 45-50], for discovering and selecting environmental stimuli was needed to carry on man's activities permitting an autonomous pattern of activity.

What seems to be the main element in Geertz' thought is the emergence, synchronically and not serially, of the larger human brain and of human culture, filling the gaps left by the higher degree of generality of information intrinsically available from genetic sources. Hence, the role of cultural symbols in 'directive reasoning' toward man's adaptation to his manifold environment.

The individual behavior patterns and the social organization of all species other than the human race are more narrowly specified genetically under selective pressures. Thus, *culture can be defined as the totality of conscious information, belief and value systems, symbolic universes, language and communication — and of behavioral patterns that are transmitted from individual to individual, from generation to generation, through instruction and learning, and through example and imitation.* Although culture ultimately depends on genetic endowment, human genes only transmit the potentiality for the acquisition of culture, not culture itself. This possession of a genetically assured potentiality for the acquisition of culture therefore makes *Homo Sapiens* biologically unique. Adaptation through cultural change ("guided variation") became more important to man than adaptation by genetic change as "new inventions are more significant than new mutations" [Dobzhansky-Boesiger 1983: 65].

Human nature is thus endowed with an extraordinary plasticity and is largely open to environmental influences, cultural traditions, learning, and creative self-development. But it is also true that culture is man's own creation, it could not exist without man as being-in-the-world. In fact, cultures represent shared belief and value systems that include classifications in the environmental fields of nature and society in accordance with traditional and arbitrary perceptions of reality. Specific groups or societies sharing such systems each develop related emotional attitudes, sets of rules for action, and explanatory frameworks for the cosmic world's realities that are inexplicable in terms of the perceptions on which the cognitive system was based. When ideas are translated into effective behavior and the feedback effect from the environment shapes the range of choices available to act upon to a situation, the dialectical process of adaptation and selection has started. In this respect, there is a similarity between the processes of genetic and cultural change. In biological evolution, mutations or gene recombinations are random, but once an adaptive trend is established it tends to continue just as long as possibilities in the variation are inherent but not exhausted. Although evolution in the cultural field has favored a trend toward increased capacity for learning and flexible behavior, history has shown that established cultural adaptive forms and processes continued to survive until the complete exhaustion of their possibilities, contrary to environmental changes, which required an innovative approach.

As much as in biological evolution, randomness plays a great role in cultural evolution, in the whole realm of learning, creativity, and art. Genetic change as well as cultural variations being stochastic processes, require that "a supply of random appearances must be available from which new information can be made" [Bateson 1980: 51]. Sequences of events, although random in certain aspects, are combined with fixed selective processes, which result in longer survival of some of the random occurrences. The random component in the case of natural selection is genetic change and mutation among members of the population. In the case of cultural variation the mutable component is the interaction of the phenotype and the environment. Therefore, in the course of the evolution of a phenotype, organism and environment together generate unpredictability not excluding, however, the prediction of particular changes, responses, or adaptations.

The randomness in cultural evolution leads to continuous exploratory processes in the endless trial and error of mental activity. According to Boyd and Richerson, in learning processes, individuals establish guiding criteria such as objectives, as well as culturally conditioned assumptions or initial, uninformed guesses, to appraise the outcome of their behavior or the outcome of future decisions, compared to their expectations [Boyd-Richerson 1985: 94]. In evolutionary changes, potentialities become objects of selection as well; in the domain of culture, unfamiliar sequences of events, ideas, innovations, or artistic creations are incorporated or explained in terms of tradition, inherited values, or cognitive systems, replicated from generation to generation. Therefore, Boyd and Richerson speak of "guided variation" as opposed to the biological concept of selection. Ideas expressed and followed by acts, innovations, or events can however be distorted or rejected by the environment, by the society, or by the genetically unresponsive organism. In this sense, randomness implies difference, "information consists of differences that make the difference" [Bateson 1980: 110], and difference plays an exceptionally important role in the life of societies and civilizations. It also means divergence from forces of stabilization and convergence in the non-random selection process such as conservation or conformity.

Donald T. Campbell presents, in the framework of evolutionary epistemology, a theory that summarizes the above [Campbell 1987b]. The *blind-variation-and-selective-retention process*: is the major instrument of man's adaptation to the environment and his acquisition of knowledge. The process consists of three components: mechanisms for introducing variations, consistent selection processes, and mechanisms for preserving and/or propagating selected variations. The word "mechanism" in Campbell's description is not clear and might be replaced by "occurrences" as mechanisms suggest some purposefulness that would contradict their "blind" character. Campbell uses the world "blind" instead of "random" for three reasons: First, "blind" expresses the complete independence of variations from the environments in which they occur, or as Popper expressed randomness presupposes a given order, the *a priori* knowledge of elements of the situation, in respect to which trials are random [Popper 1987a: 117-118]. Second, this term indicates the basic lack of correlation of individual trials, as no trials can be specified as correct or incorrect with reference to an outcome. Third, "blind" expresses the complete independence of one trial from another; a variation does not occur in order to correct a previously unsuccessful trial, benefiting, eventually, from the error committed in the course of the latter.

Campbell conceives the interaction pattern of organism and environment encompassing the overall selection process as hierarchical. At lower levels, it operates in accordance with "settings" or criteria, but subject to natural selection at other higher levels. These higher levels are more fundamental in the trial-and-error process, and the selection criteria are increasingly specific. From this perspective, language and meaning are placed in a communicative context, a social trial and error of meanings (and giving names). But the results of this trial and error process remain indeterminate.

Thus, in the Campbellian view, variation and selective retention processes are characteristic of sociocultural evolution as well. He lists among such processes the survival of social organizations and cultural institutions, selective borrowing between cultures, infra-cultural differential imitation of models, and selective repetition from among a set of temporal variations (learning process), which may explain the ubiquity of simultaneous inventions. All these selective processes, of course, can only be successful if they are occurring in appropriate environments. They prove to be dysfunctional if they are irrelevant in the evolutionary context. At all levels of information adaptive change starts from some given structure. On the genetic level, the structure is the genome or DNA. On the behavioral and cultural levels it consists of the genetically inherited repertoire of possible forms of behavior and of culturally developed rules, perceptions, and attitudes perpetuated by tradition. These received structures are always transmitted by instruction: the genome is replicated as template, the tradition is carried over by direct instruction and imitation. New adaptive changes happen at all levels by way of natural selection, the elimination of unfit tentatives; adaptation, based on information, proceeds via trial mutations and variations, and selection. This process is an active one, especially at the behavioral and cultural levels where changes are not completely random as there is a relatively constant background knowledge comprising preference and expectation-structures inherent in the mind.

Culture is then an action-oriented information system in the evolutionary perspective

> Between what our body tells us and what we have to know in order to function, there is a vacuum we must fill ourselves, and we fill it with information (or misinformation) provided by our culture... Almost all complex human behavior is, of course, the interactive, nonadditive outcome of the two [Geertz 1973: 50].[4]

It is because of this "information gap" in which we live that man needs extragenetic mechanisms which culture can provide as an action-oriented information system.

Culture patterns, systems and complexes of beliefs, symbols, values, as well as behavioral repertoires guide man not only in the cognitive field as the tangible formulation of notions, embodiment of ideas, abstractions from experience fixed in perceptible forms, and judgements and beliefs, but also in the emotional domain of longings, desires, hopes and despair. Cultural symbols function as templates in the performance of cultural acts (construction, apprehension, and utilization of symbolic forms) as well as in human attitudes, behavior, and action in its largest sense. Human thought and action are characterized (though with the exception of innovative, creative personalities) by use of models in a twofold way: first, the structural congruence or similarity of models of entities, processes, activities, and relations; and, second, models as programs, representing the symbols programmed. These models are conceived as inter-transposable through symbolic formulation.

The concept of culture and its function in an evolutionary framework, as defined above, excludes all discrimination based on racial differences. It also contradicts theories of "primitive" mentality, because it testifies that there are no essential differences in the cognitive and emotional processes between the various races. It is significant that the great French anthropologist, Lucien Lévy-Bruhl, retreated at the end of his life from the conception of "primitive" mentality professed during his professional career

> There is not a primitive mentality distinguishable from the other by two characteristics which are peculiar to it (mystical and prelogical). There is a mystical mentality which is more marked and more easily observable among 'primitive peoples' than in our own societies, but it is present in every human mind [Lévy-Brühl 1975: 101].

If human beings' genetic endowment does not merely enable them to acquire culture but culture is indispensable for the human organism to function at all; if culture is not only supplementing and extending organically-based capacities but constitutes a crucial complement to those capacities, then being human is as much the result of biological as of cultural evolution. Therefore, racism, based on biological givens, is without foundation in whatever form, because, while every individual is genetically unique, cultural conditioning only differentiates human races or populations.

CHAPTER TWO

THE ONTOLOGICAL / COSMIC
FRAMEWORK

The basic thesis of this book is that an examination of man's existential predicament must take into account the ontological/cosmic framework, or the reality of the order of being in the whole universe. This is not the repetition of the idea of the ancient *cosmopolis*, but a *sine qua non* requirement of man's situation and the conditions of his lifeworld. However, the ontological/cosmic perspective does not impose a uniform view of the universe or any kind of monism or dualism, but recognizes the plurality of cultural worlds, the existing diversity and the prevailing differences among human groups, their worldviews and their actions. In Robertson's words, our age is characterized by the universality of particular experiences, but, conversely, by the particularization of universal perspectives, an infinity of differences and Otherness. Consequently, this view of the world is neither monist nor dualist. It cannot be monist because an overall cosmic perspective, an all-embracing ontological foundation, cannot be qualified monist, as it is logically beyond this distinction. It is an empirical reality. In the same vein, it cannot be dualistic because the plurality of distinct worlds is part of the cosmic, ontological unity.

There are four major consequences of this ontological/cosmic thesis. The first is that man and his lifeworld lost their particular, special status in the universe, parallel to the change in the astral perspective, when the earth lost its central place in the cosmos. The idea of man's privileged status in the universe dominated Western thinking after the adoption of Christianity, and especially since the Enlightenment (which secularized the Christian doctrine), when it was definitely formulated by Kant.

The second consequence of the above thesis is that the ontological has an indisputable primacy over the cognitive and the epistemological. Acquiring and possessing knowledge could only gain this primacy because in Christianity sacred knowledge was necessary to benefit from the salvation offered by God's grace within the ontological framework of God's and man's relationship represented by the church, and with the advent of modernity, knowledge was the means through which man could conquer and master nature and subdue the forces of the physical world for his own purposes. Schelling's idea that "the creative life of nature and the creative power of thought were one"[1] became, consequently, obsolete.

The third consequence is that in the ontological/cosmic unity, good and evil are constituent elements (denied by the Greeks as much as by many of our contemporaries) in the simple sense that they exist, and not in the Augustinian sense, in which evil results from man's corruptness, thus safeguarding the belief in a *Deus justus* whose creation was good. Good and evil can be experienced in everything, especially in man's constitution. There is no necessity, therefore, for any kind of theodicy, Leibnizian or otherwise. As evil is fully integrated into the ontological and cosmic perspective, so it is, most naturally, the reality of death.

Fourth, the primacy of the ontological/cosmic view consequently asserts that man cannot handle nature as his own property, because cosmic forces cannot be subdued in a way as man can subdue another man. Man's relation to his physical environment ought to be conceived in terms of a partnership, a relation of mutual respect and cooperation for the benefit of both man and nature. This view does not exclude either the Darwinian concept of natural selection or the necessity of furthering human knowledge of the universe. It shows, however, that there are limits to knowledge set by ontological/cosmic elements which may cause a boomerang effect when human ingenuity and technology exploit and destroy the environment and the timeless cosmic order.

The fateful disjunction at the advent of the modern age was that between man and the cosmos, our natural environment. Yet a new type of the ontological/cosmic perspective appeared during the Renaissance, with the ideas of Nicholas of Cusa ("the Cusan") and Giordano Bruno of Nola ("the Nolan") - two great thinkers who mark the demise of the late Middle Ages and the birth of modernity. Bruno spoke of the "plurality of worlds" and, juxtaposing the variables of the potential and the real, pointed out that if one world deserves to exist, all other worlds should be able to exist potentially. Or, "If anything at all exists, everything that is possible exists" [Blumenberg 1983: 569]. The Nolan probably built upon the theories of Nicholas of Cusa, who, in his *Docta ignorantia*, asserted that the earth could not be the center of the universe. More importantly, the Cusan took again up Epicurus' idea of the equivalence of worlds and reached a quasi-modern, scientific outlook through his implicit admittance of the limitations inherent in an observer's standpoint, limited by space and time.

Nicholas of Cusa saw in the concept of infinity the reality of the indefiniteness of the universe, reflected in the limitations of human empirical knowledge of this world. These limitations assured an inexhaustible potential for the cognitive efforts of man.

Bruno went further with his theory of infinity as the identity of possibility and reality, following the Cusan's famous principle of *coincidentia oppositorum*. This appears particularly interesting in the light of modern physical theories and speculations. Against the reigning Aristotelian philosophy, he affirmed "that the purposefulness of movement is directed both from possibility toward reality and from reality toward possibility" [ibid. 580], thereby making motion between these two poles the essential element of existence.

In contemporary and future inter-civilizational encounters the question of ontological monism or dualism is of crucial importance: monism in the form of either a unity of the immanent and transcendent worlds, or the recognition of the existence of only one of them; dualism as their more or less pronounced separation. This is so because *all other civilizations but the Western are basically monist, even if tainted sometimes by intermittently apparent dualistic visions*. Such a fundamental difference can be decisive for the conflict or dialogue in inter-civilizational relations in the future. For this reason, this study will examine in detail the principal trends, monistic or dualistic, in other civilizations. The second part of this chapter will explore the mind/body problem which is a particular aspect of the monist/dualist dichotomy. Finally, a detailed presentation of the concepts and of the relational interdependence of Being and experience will examine the complex problem of the ontological/cosmic framework of human existence.

1. *Ontological Monism and Dualism in Different Civilizations*

(a) MONISM AND DUALISM IN THE MODERN WEST

What is well known of Greek cosmology can be said as well of most other ancient cosmologies and worldviews: the conviction that the entire system of the world is integrated in a single unity through the prevalence of universal principles. Humanity and nature were seen as participating in a single, common order. For the Greeks, the rational structure of the astronomical world was reflected in the order of the society (*polis*); this harmonization of human affairs with the natural order, in the Stoic view, gave place to the all-embracing cosmic order, the *cosmopolis*. Therefore, Toulmin asserts that ancient cosmologies were historically a pre-disciplinary, functionally a transdisciplinary (not interdisciplinary), and psychologically (for those who lived at the time) even an antidisciplinary framework of life [Toulmin 1982: 223-229]. It offered, at the same time, an explanation of the world in astronomical, technological and theological terms.

However, an astounding transformation of the cosmic perspective took however, place since the advent of Christianity probably due to Gnosis and other Oriental influences. The monism of Christianity and two other monotheistic religions, Judaism and Islam, is not monism in the sense of the ontological/cosmic worldview, as it is an unquestionable article of faith in a unique God, not the expression of a creed in a cosmic-universal unity of all beings. This monism also implies a certain dualism where God is "Other" than man and the immanent world in its sacredness. The universe, the cosmos, became clearly divided into parts: body as opposed to soul, nature as opposed to man, "good" nature as opposed to "bad" nature. Here, man or the "good," was expected to fight "bad" nature. This dualistic myth, simultaneously ontological and ethical is the basis of all dualism subsequently plaguing Western theorizing. It led to the idea that man has to conquer and dominate nature, making it into its own servant, instead of living with it in harmony through knowledge of its basic elements, structures, functions, and effects. This juxtaposition of an ontological-cum-ethical dualism to the cosmic perspective ignored that the latter makes it absolutely imperative for the human species to strive for knowledge. Knowledge of the physical, chemical, and biological worlds, as well as of the environmental conditions of man's life, is indispensable to humanity's survival.

The belief that man has to stand against a hostile nature to make it subservient also led to a second development which had devastating consequences for him and his lifeworld, the omission of the most fundamental element of earthly existence, its ontological conditioning. The emphasis placed on the acquisition of knowledge necessitated the mastery and domination of the nonhumane world. The distinction between "good" and "bad" nature and the antagonistic juxtaposition of man and nature reached new heights with Descartes. Consequently, in the Enlightenment, the image of nature as savage and man as a similarly "savage" natural phenomenon was weighed against that of the "civilized man" and "civilized society."

It is striking that the philosophers did not see that they adopted a dualistic worldview from the Church against whom they fought a lifelong struggle continuing ever since through successive generations of philosophers and scientists. But, as Stanley Rosen noted, the Cartesian worldview went much further than the medieval dualism because it established the dualism of the abstract, theoretical world against the empirical, everyday world, "the *ego cogitans* is the middle term between mathematics and spatio-temporal particulars" [Rosen 1989: 24-25]. The self-confident rational man, governed by his self-legislated laws, became the master of his thought and action separated from his lifeworld. The homogeneity of rational thought was then guaranteed by abstraction and by the self-assuredness of the *ego cogitans*. Knowledge and practice were divorced because knowledge was not founded on existential realities but on theoretical, abstract considerations. Knowledge became knowing a "reified," "objectified" reality. In whatever sense we look at the Cartesian propositions, it was with Descartes that modern subjectivity was born; the primeval order according to which man's existence was embedded into the ontological/cosmic universe (*sum, ergo cogito*) was reversed, and man became master of his world through his cognitive capabilities and shaped his environment (almost) at his will (*cogito, ergo sum*). The world became the creation of human mind and imagination.

We still live with this dualistic world picture which witnessed a complete reformulation over the course of the scientific revolution. Man no longer has a place in the cosmic Nature (except perhaps as another moving body or a chemical composition) because real nature was identified as empirically testable, valued in a positivistic way in a pseudo-scientific worship. In contrast, the non-tangible, non-materialistic side of nature, the mental world of human communities is rejected with horror as *meta*-physical, as something belonging to the old and condemned tradition. The modern worldview was recently steered by its exponents toward a reductive, monistic position, toward the recognition of only one aspect of the cosmic universe, neglecting the non-material, mental or spiritual aspect.

Developments in the field of science from the seventeenth-century breakthroughs of Copernicus and Newton, and other intellectual accomplishments of the modern West unfortunately led to disciplinary fragmentation as a result of the exclusive recognition of purposive-instrumental rationality. Thus, the integrative function assumed before by the cosmological perspective was abandoned. Science became an aggregate of its component disciplines, instead of an integrated whole representing a comprehensive worldview. This evolution was an outcome of the orientation toward objectivism, characterized by the status of the detached observer (*theoros*) who regarded and examined nature from the outside. Science considered real only what was objectified, "equally accessible to all competent observers," forgetting that as a consequence of the subjectivity of human consciousness, "the ontology of the mental is essentially a first-person ontology" [Searle 1992: 16 and 20]. *Theoria*, corresponding to the Cartesian dualism of the vision of the world and carrying out a rational and (incorrectly understood) reflective enterprise, considers all questions pertaining to the cosmic perspective as "limiting questions" of its own spectator-like approach to the world. To safeguard its rational objectivity, human affairs had to be dealt with in the same manner as things and objects, in order to grasp the facts without being influenced by emotions, beliefs and values. Thus, the fundamental paradox of the standpoint of science is revealed by the isolated spectator-observer's position — isolated from nature and the human world though trying to analyze and explain the first, while belonging to the second or, more correctly, trying to analyze and explain both without acknowledging belonging to both. This striving to attain and safeguard the position of an "objective spectator-observer" ignores the inevitable relativism implicated by

Einstein's thought, as well as the more recent insight into evolutionary improbabilities due to the temporal dimension which points from probable toward more improbable states.

This evolution culminated in the self-centered monism particularly characteristic of late modernity. The integrative force of the ontological/cosmic worldview was replaced by what Anthony Giddens calls the *internally referential system of knowledge and power*, which goes much beyond the mastery of the natural world through an extension of the realm of instrumental reason. This goes much beyond the subjection of natural forces to human reason, and leads to the "end of nature," to the "sequestration" of human life from nature [Giddens 1991: 165-166]. The scientific/technological monism of the modern worldview became thus a ghost of itself, because its orientations are not simply the reduction of all human phenomena to physical elements, but a reduction of all external reference points to the internal referentiality of modernity's abstract systems, its knowledge and technology. These systems constitute the basis of contemporary power structures and induce the sentiment of ontological insecurity and alienation.

A holistic concept of nature excludes all tentatives of dualism or reductionism: those aiming at a unified science, reducing psychology to biology, biology to chemistry, and chemistry to physics (the "mature science"), as well as those trying to reduce the mental to the physical ("physicalism"). These efforts of reductionism were concomitant to the development of the Copernican-Newtonian world picture and were inspired by the real, practical successes of modern science; they led to an existence straight-jacketed in a world of internal referentiality, a sort of ontological vicious circle. The identification of nature with the physical world alone as opposed to its ontological wholeness encompassing the mental as well as the physical appears today as an unjustified assumption. Over the course of the last four centuries, it seems to have been forgotten that mental events are as much empirical facts as physical events.

(b) MONISM AND DUALISM IN THE INDIAN CIVILIZATION

Transcendental Monism

As in Western classical antiquity, the search for understanding the ultimate reality was also the source of metaphysical thought in India. Although in the East, it was always recognized that the limitations of human intellect do not permit definite answers to the problem of Being, and therefore, more emphasis was placed upon grasping the ultimate by direct and immediate apprehension in the search for a fundamental unity underlying the manifold of the universe. The Hymn of the Creation (Verse 4), of the oldest Vedic text the *Rg Veda*, speaks of "the bond of being and non-being" [Radhakrishnan-Moore (eds.) 1957: 27]. The religious core of Hinduism, the transcendental nondualism of the Vedic tradition, is constituted by the symbolism of the eternal yet immanent *Brahman* whose reality represents the eternal Being.[2] The *Brahman* is the indestructible, essential nature, undefinable in terms of any human characteristic (neither this, nor that, or *neti-neti*); it is the Supreme Self, whereas the *atman* is the *Brahman* in this immanent world, the true human self. Beside the *Brahman* the *karma* is the creative force "that brings beings into existence" [*Bhagavad Gita*, 7, 3-4]. This duality, both noumenal and phenomenal, in *Brahman*'s nature becomes a threefold quality in the *Bhagavad Gita* when it explains the signification of the expression *AUM TAT SAT*: absolute supremacy (*AUM*), universality (*TAT*), and the reality (*SAT*) of *Brahman* [*Bhagavad Gita* 17, 23].

Naturalistic, Materialistic or Ethical Dualism

The more materialistic (probably non-Aryan) philosophies such as the *Jaina, Samkhya*, and *Yoga* interpreted the universe in dualistic or pluralistic terms (the infinitely shaded variations of these different creeds, more contemplative than the Vedic action-oriented attitudes cannot, of course, be treated here in detail). Their view insisted on the separation between two spheres or antagonistic principles, *purusa* and *prakrti, jiva* and *a-jiva*, and *jnana* and *jadatva*, the transcendent, immaterial life-monad, on the one hand, and the matter of which even time and space are only aspects, on the other.

Thus, the self is assigned a completely passive role and all action belongs to matter. The life-monad is embedded, through everyday experience, in the thickness of matter, fighting to disengage itself and to obtain its release from this world of illusions. The process of life is the unfolding, ever-ongoing blending of these two entities, their continuous interpenetration and interaction. It is a perpetual procreation and disintegration of unsubstantial elements which necessitates purification, arresting the process of eternal blending of the antagonistic principles in order to become virtuous and to have access to absolute motionlessness in absolute purity. The *Samkhya* and the *Jaina* acknowledge a substantiality in the phenomena of the world; changing states indicate no modification of the ultimate reality of things, but only changes in their contingent conditions (place, time, or form). *Purusa* and *prakrti* are simultaneously independent and interdependent; their differentiation results from their interaction. Cause and effect denote undeveloped (undifferentiated and indeterminate) and developed (differentiated and determinate) states of things. The *Samkhya* agree with the openly materialist *Carvaka*, "that nothing comes out of nothing; that everything must come out of something else" [Riepe 1961: 196]. The *Samkhya* school recognizes two kinds of causes, material and efficient, and two kinds of effects, the simple manifestation and reproduction. One might equate Aristotle's final cause (Prime Mover, rational soul) with the *purusa* that sets in motion *prakrti*. Despite the naturalistic dualism of the above doctrines, it appears that they all tend toward a certain monism in the form of an ethical ideal -- the absoluteness of world renunciation.

The only physicalist monism is the one professed by the *Carvaka*, who taught that the world is composed of uncreated matter out of which all existents were produced. Their doctrine, the *Lokayata*, holds that only this world exists, and there is no beyond, any future life.

In the teachings of the *Bhagavad Gita*, the indestructible life-monad (*purusa*), the essence of the self, is but an infinitesimal part of the Supreme Being. Thus, the transcendental monism of Brahmanism was restored. For the *Bhagavad Gita*, life and death are relative. Physical death is not a unilateral divide, it does not represent a barrier in the infinite continuity of existence because "what really is cannot cease to be; just as death is certain for those who are alive, rebirth is certain for those who are dead."[3] The process of repeated birth and death, the *samsara*, operates as a causal necessity for all existences and in all times. Therefore, freedom for the Hindu is liberation from the eternally recurring of *samsara*, or deliverance from the mechanical necessity of retribution. Weber called this Hindu belief in the transmigration of souls, a "completely connected and self-contained cosmos of ethical retribution," the most complete formalized, rationalized solution of theodicy [Weber 1978, Vol. 1: 524].

A further development of Brahmanism -- the post-Buddhist teachings of the *Vedanta* in *Sankara*'s exposition -- coupled a non-dualistic conception of the universe (and the monistic language of the *Vedas*) with the world as illusion, *maya*, and therefore gave birth to a paradoxical quasi-dualism. It affirmed the sole reality of the self, *atman*, and viewed the cosmos, together with the self, as the product of nescience (*avidya*). Only by eliminating nescience through knowledge, can the release (*moksa*) from the world of illusions be obtained; this knowledge is, however, already present in the core of human existence, in the innermost part of the human being. Consequently, the paradox is this: though *jiva* or *Brahman* is the sole, changeless reality, realizing it depends on temporal human efforts exerted in the world of illusions, even if the fact of ignorance cannot be known, because it constitutes the limit of man's thought. Reality is denied to anything belonging to *maya*, which contains only what is perishable, transient, and becoming.

The Monism of the Immanent in Tantrism

Finally, in *Tantrism* though it submits to the *Vedic* authorities (*Advaita Vedanta*) and rituals, *Vedantic* and *Tantric* traits are intimately intermingled, though the positive aspects of *maya* are emphasized. The world is highly valued, penetrated by intellectual and artistic endeavor lead to enlightenment, because Tantrism insists on the holiness and purity of all things. Social and biological differences are transcended. The Goddess *Kali* represents the active side of *Brahman*, the primordial power, and world renunciation is replaced by world affirmation. The *Tantric* thinking is then basically monistic; it represents an immanent, though not physicalist, monism because it gives unconditionally positive appraisal to earthly life, in all its aspects. It also comes close to the ontological/cosmic perspective advocated in this study, as it contends that man, has to strive for his development through and by means of nature, not in rejecting nature.

(c) No Being but Becoming: Beyond Monism and Dualism in Buddhism

The teachings (*yana*, or vehicle) of *Gautama*, the "silent sage of the *Sakyas*," and the two great doctrinal versions which were derived from his words, the *Hinayana* (Little Vehicle) and the *Mahayana* (Great Vehicle) Buddhism, cannot be subsumed either under the category of monism nor under that of dualism. There are, however, some dualistic tendencies in later developments of *Mahayana* Buddhism. In Hinduism, for example, the *Upanishads* sought to derive the multiplicity of the world from the ultimate Self, *Brahman*, which meant that Being was considered as the fundamental aspect of reality. For Buddha, the universe is an eternal process in which worlds and individuals rise and disappear in an endless succession and in infinite numbers. Present, immanent reality is the only reality, but this reality is one of Becoming, neither Being nor non-Being; it is the complete negation of change. There is nothing permanent in the empirical self, and one thing is dependent on the other (dependent origination). In the momentary flux-in-process which is life, there is no central purpose, no transcendent or immanent goal, but regularities, uniformity, and tendencies. The constitutive elements of the process of Becoming are more real than the totality of the process itself, though in the eternally recurrent phases there are only successive states, not continuity of identities.

This world, then, is a place of suffering, the root of which is ignorance and selfish craving. The attainment of *nirvana* means the elimination of ignorance and of selfishness, and the path that leads to *nirvana* is indicated by the famous five precepts that Buddha gave to his disciples (the Middle Path). It does not appear adequate to say that the view of Buddha reflects a dualism of the world and of *nirvana* (he explicitly rejected any dualism), nor that it represents a monistic position, because the denial of existence and non-existence, the *nirvana*, which has no meaning, cannot be the basis of any conception. In a sense, *nirvana* is true reality, though it is not cosmically creative. It does not effect the universe that is governed by *dharma*, the law of order, and the passing order of things.

In *Mahayana* Buddhism, a monistic philosophy of the Absolute was later developed. The Absolute is the essence of existence, embodied in the *dharmakaya*, personified by Buddha. This reality is called *bhuta-tathata*, the "suchness of beings, the essence of existence" (Zimmer 1974a: 516). However, the *Mahayana* school, even if it recognizes a metaphysical substratum of all phenomena, denies substance to anything existent, to the entire phenomenal world. *Hinayana* Buddhism also developed a metaphysical speculation that maintained the non-existence of substances and individuals while acknowledging the reality of infinitesimal units composing our world of illusion. These are the *dharmas*, brief realities aggregating as pseudo-individuals and giving rise to processes such as cause and effect.

(d) THE CHINESE CIVILIZATION

Some serious conceptual (not only translational) problems must be faced when comparing Indian Buddhist and Western ideas with Chinese philosophical thought. As Staal pointed out, Kant's view that existence is a predicate is unintelligible in Chinese because there is no verb "to be" which functions as copula and expresses at existence [Staal 1988: 149-150]. Therefore, for example, Chinese Buddhists expressed *tathata* (thusness, ultimate reality) by the Taoist term "original non-being," or "pure being" (*pen-wu*), according to Wing-Tsit Chan (1969: 336], and under Neo-Taoist influence concentrated their reflections on the problem of being and non-being. For the Chinese, existence and non-existence are not mutually exclusive concepts. As the excellent parallel given by Wilhelm in his introduction to *Lao-Tzu*'s works [Lao-Tzu 1985: 18] shows they correspond to the negative and positive signs in mathematics. Thus, there is a complete equivalence between positive and negative, being and non-being, coming and not-coming.

The Chinese did resist abstract theorizing for its own sake, as they were not interested in a quest for ultimate foundations. In exploring transcendental perspectives, they preferred the immanent, relational definition of things with one another. Using Chung-ying Cheng's formula, in Chinese culture, "the ontological is revealed in the functioning of the cosmological, and the cosmological is embodied in the framework of the ontological" [Chung-ying Cheng 1989: 175]. Their logic is dialectical and not formal.

Spiritual Monism: Multiplicity in Unity

As is well known, Confucianism, especially the teachings of *Confucius* himself, is ethical in its character, and only became involved in metaphysical questions in its later developments. *Mencius* (IVth century BC) is considered, together with the Taoist school of *Chuang Tzu*, to hold mysticism as the highest spiritual level of human existence. He is also regarded as an idealistic monist. The spirit of the individual is a complete whole in itself ("all things are complete in us"), and as such, it is, in its origins, one with the universe (he speaks of forces flowing "above and below together with Heaven and Earth") [Fung Yu-lan, 1983. Vol. 1.: 129-130].

The spiritualistic-monistic tendency became stronger in Neo-

Confucianism. *Chou Tun-I* (Sung Neo-Confucianism, XIth century) believed in the ultimate unity of the one and the many, each with its own particular state of being. He spelled out the three cardinal principles of Neo-Confucianism: principle (*li*), nature, and destiny which, in his view, were ultimately united.

Among the Ch'eng brothers (also XIth century), *Ch'eng I* followed the line of *Chou Tun-I* and affirmed that "the principle (*li*) is one, but that its manifestations are many," whereas *Ch'eng Hao* emphasized the spirit of life in all things in its perpetual production and reproduction, which in all cases is a new creation, a new origination. Both Ch'eng brothers saw in the principle natural as well as moral elements. They used the expression *T'ien-li*, which may be rendered as Natural Law. Ch'eng Hao went as far as to speak of the creative quality of humanity (*jen*) which binds together the self and the Others, or Heaven, Earth, and man, into a unity. This humanistic monism, as it could be called, was expressed by Ch'eng Hao in his statement that "principle and the mind are one" [Wing-Tsit Chan 1969: 522], but he also added that the inborn nature of man is identical with *ch'i*, the material force, thus reinforcing his rejection of all dichotomies. Ch'eng-I seems to adhere to a weak kind of dualism between material force and the Way (*Tao*), seeing principle and material force as two aspects of the one Way.

For the great systematizer and rationalizer of Confucianism *Chu Hsi* (XIIth century), principle and material force (which he recognized as giving to beings their substance and physical form) are completely different and distinguishable; however, even if he gives the impression of an outspoken dualist, it is more adequate to say that Chu Hsi, like Ch'eng-I, represented a weak dualism because he admitted the interdependence of principle and material force in the universe. In accordance with the law of the universe, principle is the inner law of being; the Principle or *li* of a thing is "the all-perfect or supreme archetype of that thing" [Fung Yu-lan, 1983, Vol. 2: 637], whereas material force is the "thing" to which principle can adhere. He applied this idea of the interdependence or combination of principle and material force to man. The all-embracing unity of principle and material force, of the plurality in the immanent world, is the Supreme Ultimate, which is present in everything *in potentia*. Chu Hsi used a wonderful illustration to depict the relation of the myriad elements of the universe and of the Supreme Ultimate when he said that the latter "is not cut up into pieces. It is merely like the moon reflecting itself in ten thousand streams" [ibid. 541].

Dialectical Dualism: Multiplicity in Unity

Ideas of astrology, the beliefs in the Five Elements or Agents (*wu hsing*) were amalgamated during the difficult period of Warring States (403-222 BC) in a unified cosmology, based on the conviction of interaction between nature and man's world. The *Yin* and *Yang*, the female and male principles, represent a pair of opposites. This doctrine evidently stands for dualism, but a dialectical one, because it also affirms unity in the multiplicity thus nature and man are believed to form one body. For each category of reality, another, opposite or complementary, must be identified. The interaction of the two forces represents a dynamic process that operates according to principles and laws, and results not in chaos, but in an ordered universe. The correlation between man and nature and their mutual influence led to a cyclical view of the world, of historical events as much as of all aspects of evolution, physical and human.

The *Yin-Yang* cosmology imprinted Chinese ethical and social teachings with the perspective of a reality that is in constant transformation. This view was fully developed in the *I Ching* (The Book of Changes), in which the continuous change in the universe is not an aimless fusion and eternal intermingling of things, but evolves in the direction of progress of human society and culture. The transformation moves from the Great Ultimate, through the *Yin* and *Yang*, to the four forms, which connote not only variations of the two elements, but also ideas, symbols, and patterns (*hsiang*). The endless cycle of phenomenal change even applies to worldly reality. Thus, culture, symbols, concepts, systems, are an outcome of the cosmic interaction of natural forces; existences are even assigned numbers (the famous *Trigrams*) to simplify things and make possible a more objective determination and prediction of events.

Mystical Dualism of the Tao

Lao-Tzu and Chuang Tzu (between VIth and IVth century BC) were the great figures of the school, which was called Taoism only after the Han dynasty. They both adhered to a monistic worldview in which the Non-being (*wu*) and the eternal Being (*yu*) are encompassed by the Great Oneness (*t'ai li*). Lao-Tzu was interested, first of all, in the temporal dimension, distinguishing between "what precedes and what follows" [Fung Yu-lan 1983, vol. 1: 173], whereas Chuang-Tzu was interested in the eternal Being, "without beginning and end, beyond life and death" [Wang-Tsit Chan 1969: 202]. But their fundamental conceptions, the Way (*Tao*) for Lao-Tzu, and the Power (*Te*) for Chuang-Tzu had the same meaning. Lao-Tzu transformed the classical meaning of the *Tao*, the Way of moral behavior of man into a metaphysical concept, the all-embracing first principle through which the universe came into being. He believes that certain general principles are invariable in the universe. The root of all existence is the unity of an invariable Non-being (*wu*) which transcends Being; Non-being, at the same time, is opposing the invariable Being and is complementary to it. From Non-being issue all "the ten thousand things." It is "the Mystery of Mysteries" because it produced Oneness which, in turn, produced duality; from duality evolved trinity (the *yin*, the *yang*, and their interaction, resulting in harmony), and from the trinity, the world of infinitely numerous things. Thus, multiplicity is inherent in unity and unfolds progressively in space and in time; it is the eternal return of everything in itself. *Tao* is "Being," the originator of all, the ultimate freedom, the Great Oneness above and beyond time and space.

Chuang-Tzu went a step further beyond the concept of *Tao*. For him, *Te* is not virtue, but power, the underlying principle of each individual thing, which is the "dwelling place of *Tao*." In fact, the two are inseparable; *Te* is the emanation of *Tao*, through which individual things become what they are. But this means also that, through *Te*, life is not limited to the individual. The same existence is shared by all and renders possible mutual understanding or interpersonal communication. The Neo-Taoists extended the concept of non-being into a pure being, the original substance, transcending all distinctions and different descriptions (*Wang Pi*), or replaced (*Kuo Hsiang*) *Tao* by the concept of nature, the ultimate but immanent reality, acting spontaneously. However, they maintained the idea of principle governing each thing and giving it self-sufficiency.

Naturalist Monism

Chang Tsai (XIth century) was the first Neo-Confucian who identified material force (*ch'i*) with the Great Ultimate; *Yin* and *Yang* are only two manifestations of this same force. The material force is, as substance, the Great Vacuity, and, as function, the Great Harmony, both united in the Way (*Tao*). Chang Tsai's naturalistic interpretation of the universe led him to consider existence as a perpetual integration and disintegration through the positive and negative drives of the material force; this happens under the governance of laws and principles that maintain a definite order. There is unity in the plurality of distinct things.

Wang Fu-chih, five hundred years later, continued Chang Tsai's line of thinking and argumentation, but went far beyond him in discussing material force (which he called "indeterminate substance") not only as the order of universe, but rather "the world consists only of concrete things (*ch'i*)" [Wing Tsit-Chan 1969: 693]. It is noteworthy, with reference to the conceptual differences between Chinese and other thought-systems, that *ch'i* as material force and *ch'i* as concrete, tangible objects, structures, or institutions are denoted in Chinese by two different characters. A concrete thing possesses definite contours of an entity corresponding to a principle in it; in fact principle and concreteness are completely interdependent.

In the tradition of the Book of Changes, envisaging *Yin* and *Yang* as phenomenological aspects of a total reality, the *Tao*, from which they are inseparable, Wang Fu-chih conceptualizes the universe as a process of constant concentration and dispersion (integration and disintegration, for Chang Tsai), the first producing being and the second non-being. He, however, understands this continuous movement as a daily renewal of both material force and principle, a process of purposive creativity without repetition, because the transformation of indeterminate substance is life generation. The purpose of the process of creative change is for the universe to evolve into a state of complete differentiation, into a complete display of all varieties of things. Such a progress toward a state of balance and harmony (an infinite order of forms) constitutes indeterminate substance as ultimate reality.

Wang Fu-chih identified mind and reason and his view may be described as rationalist monism. Thus, reason is, objectively seen, the principle of order, or, subjectively seen, the center of cognitive activities. In Wang's very particular dialectics, reason, as well as nature and mind are derived from indeterminate substance, but reason is superior to both, as it is the pattern recognizing and ordering function of the mind. Nature, nevertheless, is the basis of the lifeworld, and man is endowed with natural capabilities in order to carry out activities in this lifeworld. Reason, therefore, represents for *Wang Fu-chih* the tendency in the world toward the creative actualization of indeterminate substance and toward the ordering and patterning of life.

Consequently, even reason is identical with indeterminate substance, but the identity is understood ontologically while empirically, it represents the reality of objects in a totally differentiated (with our expression "thematized") world. In Wang's dialectics between indeterminate substance, nature, and reason, reason becomes entirely linked to nature through its role in patterning the life of man, because reason is recognized in man's mind and mind is part of nature.

Yen Yuan and *Huang Tsung-hsi*, who both lived in the seventeenth century, followed the same line of reasoning as Wang, but developed it in respect to the relations of reason and desire, or the mind and the body. The only determinate physicalist in the naturalistic monist group of thinkers living in the same epoch was *Fanh I-chih*. For him, everything is constituted of physical things (*wu*) including indeterminate substance, nature, mind, and necessity. Reason is a physical characteristic of things as well, and results from the transformation of indeterminate substance as much as nature or the mind.

Weak Dualism and Reductive Monism in Chinese Buddhism

Neo-Confucianism was born out of the efforts of scholars and thinkers to meet the Buddhist challenges that have appeared in China since the VIth century. Chinese Buddhism was characterized by a strong emphasis on the dualism between existence and non-existence, reflected in a series of opposite pairs (law and fact, form and void, pure and polluted, etc.). Nevertheless, this dualism was a weak one, because it was tempered by an idealistic interpretation of reality, which clearly suggests a kind of monism. Already around the turn of the 4th and 5th centuries, *Seng-chao* insisted on the identity of substance and function, but professed that the true nature of things is vacuous, it is emptiness, because they do not exist due to necessity but due to external, illusory causes and conditions. *Seng-Chao* represented a cross-fertilization of Chinese traditional concepts with Buddhist ideas from India combining, for example, substance and function with temporary names and emptiness; thus he stood between Taoism and Buddhism.

The members of the *Three-Treatise School* (4th through 7th centuries) dropped more and more of this Chinese heritage in favor of the Indian metaphysics of Buddhism. Thus, both existence and non-existence are denied, though a dualism of common or relative truth and of absolute truth is affirmed (theory of Two Levels of Truth).

The teachings of the *T'ien-t'ai School* (6th century) propounded a plurality of worlds, located in one universe, that is, they approached a one-is-all and all-is-one monism. But theirs was a curiously restricted monism of the minds, as it was based on the fact that the pluralistic universe is present in every moment of thought, or that all phenomena are manifestations of the "Mind of Pure Nature" in its totality. Their importance, especially in comparison with their contemporary *Consciousness-Only School*, was that as a consequence of their monism they preached universalism, universal salvation.

Another monist tendency in Chinese Buddhism was represented by the *Hua-Yen School* (7th century) whose doctrine was centered on the concept of the Universal Causation of the Realm of *Dharmas* (elements of existence), called objective idealism by Fung Yu-lan. The realm of *dharmas* was the universe in which all elements interact and form a Perfect Harmony signifying a mutual implication by the *dharmas*; this universe of complete concord may suggest, implicitly, an organic conception though never clearly indicated.

(e) COSMIC MONISM IN JAPANESE CULTURE

In Japanese *Shintoism*, nature and man were never separated. Nature occupied a privileged position. Man was perceived as an integral part of the world, as "the Japanese regard this world, with its diverse phenomena, as absolute in itself, and tend to reject viewpoints that seek the absolute in some realm beyond phenomena."[4] This *Shinto* commitment to nature and to the imperfect and changing phenomenal world, what one could designate as cosmic monism, was safeguarded against the Buddhist belief that this world is transcended by the realm of ultimate enlightenment. It is an overwhelming sense of continuity which leads to a sort of phenomenological relativity, an openness to external influences, something which was also called interactive relativism. The *Zen* completes the cosmic monism of the Japanese with the classical belief in the fundamental unity of plurality and diversity in the universe, reinforcing the assimilative potential of Japanese culture.

(f) AFRICAN CULTURES: MONIST/DUALIST SYMBIOSIS

It would not be possible here to review all the various local cultures of Africa and their respective metaphysical concepts, symbolic structures, and rituals. However, it is possible to summarize some of their common traits. African monism is of religious origin as all monism; God, the Supreme Being, simultaneously transcendent and immanent, constitutes the foundation of a global view of the universe. In this framework, an anthropocentrist ontology usually prevails, which does not exclude the existence of either natural or moral evils. However, most African myths about the origin of death, disease, and suffering present a relatively dualistic picture: the division between the earth and the sky, between mankind and the Creator-God. This dualism explains the origins of human mortality in terms of cosmogonic and moral contradictions, in terms of man's resisting God's will. In fact, as in the Baganda cosmogony, the universe is sometimes not composed of only two, but three worlds: the sky (the abode of Gods), the earth (one's land or country), and the underworld (the realm of the dead). In other cases, the triple ontological levels include the universe, the surface of the earth, and the individual psyche. Such a dualism is a kind of theodicy, or the African version of the Augustinian shifting of the burden of evil in the world from God to men. In the Baganda "Story of the Kintu,"[5] it is also evident that the cosmic story of the origin and structure of the universe also depicts the human life cycle, the destiny of each human being. This monistic ontology results in a view of complementarity between life and death, one being corollary to the other, and, therefore, integrates death into earthly existence.

2. The Mind/Body Problem

The return to an ontological/cosmic perspective would eliminate the problem of the mind/body dichotomy haunting so many philosophers of the last hundred years, stated concisely way in Gilbert Ryle's famous treatise *The Concept of Mind*. The mind/body problem constitutes a paradigmatic case illustrating the importance of the choice of a global framework, because in the holistic or cosmic perspective of nature this problem does not exist. There is no question of identity or dichotomy, but of two parts of the same universe, correlated to each other, in constant functional interaction.

Before analyzing recent philosophical efforts to solve the problem of the unity or division of the physical and the meta-physical, it is instructive to refer to a tentative solution of *temporal monism*, undertaken in his study on *Matter and Memory* by the great French philosopher Henri Bergson at the beginning of our century. The divergence between our perception and the non-perceived (or objective) world comes from the immediate intuition, which adapts facts to the interests of the individual, and to the exigencies of his lifeworld; this is the reason why "pure" intuition is "that of an undivided continuity." The Kantian manifold (which mind unifies in a comprehensive picture) is, for Bergson, a refraction of the pure temporal perspective — *la durée* — into space, because absolute space stands for infinite divisibility. The refraction of temporal duration corresponds, therefore, to the rhythmical periods of the individual life, successive moments corresponding to successive acts and events. But how far divisibility will be possible depends on the individual's consciousness. (The imaginary or universal homogeneous time is, in the Bergsonian perspective, a fiction.) Discontinuity in the temporal flux of reality, caused by perception, does not mean that the universe changes; it is a purely mental phenomenon. The perceptual discontinuities are not clear-cut, either. Perceptions shade into each other gradually, through constant reciprocal actions and reactions.

This argumentation shows that there is no reductive tendency in Bergson's philosophy, though the preeminence of the mental is advocated. The real dividing line is, nevertheless, not between perception and matter, but between these two and the temporal dimension, memory. In the temporal perspective, the present is the actuality of immediate action, that is, the state of the body. The past is the possibility of action through insertion of past recollections into the actual. Recollection is thus being transformed into perception. The brain confers materiality on the temporal, on memory, which belongs to the domain of the mental or, using Bergson's expression, the domain of the spirit.

In the recent evolution of the philosophy of science, five proposals have been created, aimed at surpassing the deadlock of the dualistic or reductionist views of mind and body. The first is due to Hilary Putnam as exposed in his 1987 Carus Lectures on *The Many Faces of Realism* [Putnam 1987] and in his 1988 *Representation and Reality*, referring back to the successive stages of his own intellectual evolution. Putnam sums up the fundamental objectivist assumption as the view "that mental phenomena must be highly derived physical phenomena in some way," based on the distinction between properties that things have "in themselves" and properties of things "projected by us," as well as on the pretention of science that it is the only means by which we can learn the properties of things "in themselves" [Putnam 1987: 13].

A central problem of this objectivist materialism remained, however -- the difficulty of explaining the "emergence of the mind." Putnam, in the physicalist phase of his philosophical investigations in the 1950s, formulated the theory of functionalism to explain the emergence of the mental, based on the mind's compositional plasticity by which he understood that mental events could not (perhaps as yet) be explained in terms of physical events. As propositional attitudes, emotions, or feelings cannot be traced back to brain states he therefore tried to explain them as necessary functional aspects of the human organism. Putnam's functionalism thus meant that all sorts of logically possible systems or beings, whatever their material composition, could have the same functional devices or the same functional organization. Later, he proposed that mental states are not only compositionally but also computationally, plastic. Through this changing conceptualization, Putnam sought to show that, in cybernetic language, each human being or group of human beings has an indefinite number of "programs," impossible to compute. Consequently, it would be unrealistic to hold that a given belief could be defined in computational and physical terms, as the mind performs billions of simple computations simultaneously, because it is capable of parallel processing, while machines perform only serial processing. It would then be irrational to think that all human beings, endowed with different bodies of knowledge and different conceptual resources and cultures, have beliefs that could be identified with a common "computational-cum-physical" feature. "The 'intentional level' is simply not reducible to the 'computational level' any more than it is to the 'physical level'" [ibid. 13-15]. The objectivist, scientific rationality tacitly presupposes intentionality, an "open texture" of all notions such as object, reference, or meaning, including even the concept of reason itself.

In his book published in 1988, Putnam criticizes the intimately related ontological and epistemological presuppositions of functionalism. In regard to epistemology, he affirms that reference is a matter of interpretation, an entirely holistic enterprise of knowing people use words because these practices depend on a human group's experience and its whole network of beliefs. From the ontological point of view, he criticizes the functional and objectivist premise that "there is a single system which contains all the objects that anyone could refer to" [Putnam 1988: 120], namely, the organisms and their physical environment. But if intentionality is taken into account as well as cultural and other human differences, things and objects can have different descriptions in different worlds because they are socially and environmentally conditioned.

In the same vein, though remaining more avowedly in the camp of the reductionists, John Z. Young [Young 1988] and David Hodgson [Hodgson 1991] profess that all mental events are associated with change in but not caused by, the brain. Young proposes to speak in terms of brain programs that are directed toward ends. These programs are based on coded instructions (coded in advance in some physical way). They select a mode of action from a large repertoire of possibilities in view of reaching a new state that is the aim of the program. This conception presupposes, of course, a certain correspondence between the range of mental programs and the conditions in the environment, that is, mental programs must, in a sense, represent the world. According to Hodgson, this correspondence is due to the fact that brain and mind are manifestations of the same underlying reality, the quantum reality, as he calls it. He goes, however, much further than Young in acknowledging the integrating power of the mind, whereas the latter only recognizes that no central program that supervises all other mental phenomena is known, and no explanation can be given in scientific theories of the fact that the brain initiates action. Thus, the question of human intentionality, of the purposive mind, remains unresolved.

Another similar tentative, though more daring, was recently formulated by John Searle [Searle 1992] according to which mental phenomena, or consciousness and unconsciousness, are caused by neurobiological processes but still manifest ontologically irreducible phenomenological properties. Consciousness (or mind) always has a definite content, and it is linked to intentionality[6] (which is as much irreducible a phenomenon as consciousness), but its relation to behavior is contingent, not causal. Searle affirms without ambiguity that consciousness is subjective, though a product of biological processes, and precisely for this reason, it does not appear as real; it is itself a way in which man grasps reality, it is a representation.

This subjectivity results in a conscious action or experience as well as intentionality that is always "perspectival" or "aspectual." Everything for a person is represented from his own point of view; on the other hand, any conscious action or experience is structured, seeing is seeing *as*, perceiving is perciving *as*. This structure is derived from what Searle calls the *Background*, or a compact whole of nonrepresentational capacities. The idea of the Background means that the consciousness of a person is located in the "spatio-temporal-socio-biological" complex of this person, a complex that is itself either conscious or intentional, and against which appears consciousness as such.

The function of consciousness is organizing relationships between the human organism and changing environmental conditions. Horizontal consciousness is the short-term temporal dimension of unity, and vertical consciousness the simultaneous awareness of all aspects in a given experience. In addition to this integrative function, consciousness as an evolutionary privilege assures man a much greater capacity of discrimination and creativity than possessed by other species. In Searle's perspective, consciousness becomes self-consciousness when attention is not directed at the object of experience or action, but at the process or state of the consciousness.

Following Brentano, Donald Davidson acknowledges that the distinguishing feature of the mental is not its private, subjective, or immaterial character, but its intentionality as a cultural fact. Davidson's specific variant of the mind/body dichotomy is related to the differences between the physical and the mental due to descriptions, vocabularies, and propositions made in varying languages or meta-languages. This explanation maintains the physicalist worldview, in spite of the fact that mental phenomena and processes do not fit in it. Davidson calls his perception of the mind/body problem as "anomalous monism," because it maintains that "all events are physical," though mental phenomena cannot be explained in purely physical terms [Davidson 1980: 214]. In his view, therefore, there is a curious ontological correspondence between the physical and the mental which interact causally; identity and causality are considered relations between individual events "no matter how described," i.e., they are independent of their linguistic expression. In fact, "events are only mental as described" [ibid. 215], and causal interaction operates independently from the supposed mental-physical dichotomy. From the linguistic point of view, should the events falling under each mental predicate be finite or not, it is possible to suppose that there could be coextensive predicates, one mental and one physical, for each event.

In his argumentation on the nomological or lawlike character of causality, Davidson's considerations are generally compatible with the ontological/cosmic framework exposed here. First, recognizing that the nomological character of causality is not applicable in all cases,

Davidson makes a great leap toward the differentiation of the mental and the physical: he accepts that the mental is nomologically irreducible, true, but affirms that only general statements relating the physical and the mental are *possible*. In attributing a belief, a desire, a goal, an intention or a meaning to a person, one must take into account his total system of concepts determined, partially at least, by his beliefs and desires. That is, we have to discover a coherent and plausible pattern in the attitudes and actions of the agent because his verbal behavior does not indicate the guidelines required for the explanation of his global attitude.

Davidson's theory is complemented by his reliance on the constitutive ideal of rationality. In opposition to the physical, the holistic character of the mental necessarily entails the consideration of conditions of coherence, rationality, and consistency, especially in the cognitive field. The concept of acting on reason implies that reason is a rational cause. Therefore, attributing intelligible attitudes and beliefs to a human agent is to find in his pattern of behavior, beliefs, and desires, a large degree of rationality and consistency. This fundamental idea serves to justify why one can explain human behavior without really knowing how it was caused, without being obliged to single out one of the many causal factors or to avoid testing whether some antecedent conditions hold, as is indispensable in the case of stringent physical laws [ibid. 233-234].

Davidson's reasoning leads to a conclusion vital for the cosmic perspective: the nomological causality in the physical world is derived from the concept of a particular physical domain as a comprehensive, closed system expected to yield a standardized and unique description of every physical event as expressed in a lawlike vocabulary. *The mental world does not constitute a closed, but an open system*, as it is affected by many influences that are not part of it. Its main features are expressed in heteronimic generalizations [ibid. 219]. In consequence, there are no strict laws on the basis of which one can predict and explain mental phenomena.

Roger Sperry proposed another attempt to surpass the deadlock of dualistic or reductionist views. Sperry's concept of the relationship between the brain and the mind (or subjectivity or consciousness), is a particular version of holism. Mind, or consciousness is an "integral dynamic property of the brain process itself,"[7] a central constituent of the brain's action, a causal determinant of the brain's functioning. The regulating influence of mind over the physico-chemical processes of the brain, that is, its causal determinant role, is derived from its power as a whole over its parts. In the hierarchical continuum of the brain structure, operations from subnuclear particles to the brain cells are carried out without any intervention of the mind (this is the mind in physicalist theories), whereas in Sperry's view, cerebral processes are ruled by consciousness.

In this respect, it is helpful to refer to Sherrington's famous example [Sherrington 1947: 262] that sets out to explore what the "I" means when I move my hand. This "I-doing" cannot be a perception, but only awareness. He concludes that my awareness and myself are one: the "I-doing" is awareness of myself in the motor act. The "I" is therefore the self.

Sperry's new approach to consciousness also concerns the latter's relationship to the external world because it implies that the qualitative pattern properties of entities are as real and causally potent as the quantitative data, measurements and abstractions, which are properties of the entities' parts or elements. In consequence, values (*qualia*) and the multiple and differential richness of reality are recognized and preserved.[8]

The last view explaining the mind-body dichotomy in non-reductionist terms is linked to Niels Bohr's complementarity principle in quantum physics. Complementarity, in Bohr's sense, refers to the dual nature of micro-entities, which are both particles and waves, therefore, their precise measurement at the same point in time is not possible; thus, no incompatibility can arise between them. On this basis, Bohr thought to develop an analogy concerning the mind-body problem, explained as the complementarity of the mechanistic and conscious nature of the mind. Testing of the brain as a physical object manifesting physical processes would preclude the observation of its conscious character, and vice versa; the mind's two distinct aspects, as brain, a physical object and as a conscious entity endowed with a free will, cannot be simultaneously displayed. The two separate levels of observation are, in these two modes of description, complementary.[9]

3. *The Ontology of Being and Experience*

The two fundamental elements of the ontological/cosmic framework consist in the concepts of Being and experience. Surprising as it may be, they were most clearly exposed in the twentieth century by two philosophers whose theses are considered stellar years away from each other: in Heidegger's ontology and in the pragmatism of John Dewey.[10] The conjunction of the Heideggerian ontology of Being and beings, of the existence and presence of Being (*Dasein*) and beings in the world, and of the Deweyan philosophy of experience, which expresses the reality of man's existence and of other beings in the world through their experiences, forms the basis of the ontological/cosmic framework envisaged in this study.

(a) THE ONTOLOGICAL FOUNDATION OF THE LIFEWORLD

One of the few philosophers in recent times who restored (although at some points with not as much transparency as required) the ontological/cosmic perspective of existence, was Martin Heidegger. Heidegger's concept of Being expresses a complete unity of all what exists in the cosmos. In examining Being he turns to *Dasein*, man's Being, which is "ontologico-ontically distinctive" [Heidegger 1962: 32],[11] in order to get closer to the meaning of Being in general. Only *Dasein*'s nature as Being-in-the-world is determined in an existential way; it cannot be considered as a subject matter, it can only be defined by being its own Being. The other beings are either entities *Dasein* encounters within-the-world, or such entities *Dasein* comes across within-the-world and whose nature it discovers in their specificity.

The difference between Being and beings is a pre-ontological phenomenon [Heidegger 1982: 319], that is, it is beyond our comprehension. In fact, this distinction, the *ontological difference*, is the reason why any ontological determination is *a priori*, the realization of a possibility. In consequence, any objectification or determination of being is a re-collection, *Dasein*'s remembering of such beings [ibid. 324-326]. Karl Jaspers in his *Philosophy of Existence*, followed a similar line of thinking. For him, Being, which always recedes from us, is encompassing. It never becomes an object and always contains a paradox; whereas objective, determinate appearances are modes of the encompassing being. *Existenz* or *Dasein* is not only a self-being, or a determinate mode of the encompassing, but also transcends its own being through relating to the encompassing Being, -- perhaps not more than a distant remembrance [Jaspers 1971: 17-21].

For both Heidegger and Jaspers, the structure of transcendental Being encompasses nature, the living and inanimate worlds; in this sense, the universe is ontologically transcendent. Being gives sense to all beings. Only man, defined as *Da-sein* takes part simultaneously in the ontological world of Being and in the ontical, factual world. *Dasein's* transcendence is therefore evident in its consciousness, through which it distances itself from the world in which we live, the "worldhood" of the environment. The necessary individuation of *Dasein* is closely related to its transcendence, its uniquely proper perspective. Existence is therefore emergence, an emergence of Being from itself as *Dasein* [Heidegger 1985: 109]. This emergence into existence denotes a being aware of itself, possessing an awareness or consciousness as being.

It would be a mistake to relate Heidegger's characterization of *Dasein's* Being to the object-subject dichotomy. He explicitly says, "subject and object do not coincide with Dasein and the world" [Heidegger 1962: 87]; *Dasein* in his ontic existence is an object as an entity within-the-world. In addition, as concerned with itself, with its own Being and with Being as a whole, it is a transcendental subject belonging to the ontological existence. *To consider the world as subjective means simply that it is the world of Dasein whose being is in the mode of being-in-the-world.* This fundamental statement makes it evident that Heidegger circumvents the Cartesian turn in his ontology by putting aside the question of true being in the sense of certainty. As Hilary Lawson recently pointed out, the transcendental Being, *Dasein's* Being, in Heidegger's description, is entirely reflexive in nature [Lawson 1985: 32]; the reflexivity of understanding — the fore-structure in Heidegger's terminology — is thus expressed in the hermeneutical circle.

If *Dasein* understands itself most of the time in terms of its world, it is necessary to examine what meaning Heidegger gave to the designation "Others"? Beyond the subject-object dichotomy, Others stand for everything else than the *I*, for those against whom the I stands out. Those Being-there-too from whom one distinguishes oneself serve a purpose because from among them, one's *Dasein* emerges too. *Being with Others belongs to the Being of Dasein*; this is an existential characteristic of Dasein, its existence is essentially an existence for "the sake of Others." Self-knowledge is also grounded in the shared existence with fellow humans and is correlate to the understanding of Others. The existential unity with Others excludes all such everyday characteristic relationships such as needing the Others and empathy with Others (empathy comprehended as bridging the distance between two subjects). *Dasein*'s sharing the existence of Others represents an authentic community; they represent part of its worldhood. The grasping of Others as worldhood is described by Heidegger as *Dasein*'s being "circumspectively concerned" with Others in the world; in the case of human relations, between "fellow-*Dasein*" who all have their specific Being, the circumspective concern is transformed into "care." "Care" is a fundamental ingredient of *Dasein*'s essence and it is manifest toward other Beings who are "themselves *Dasein*. These entities are not object of concern, but rather of *solicitude*" [Heidegger 1962: 167; italics in original]. Being-with, of course, excludes Being-alone [ibid. 156], and it automatically implies the understanding of Others, because knowing is a primordial, existential mode of Being. Solicitude and care towards another *Dasein* leads to self-knowledge and to the self-disclosure of the Other, -- toward mutual understanding.

In sum, Heidegger re-established the cosmic unity of nature in the form of universal Being and undertook to heal the dualism developed by the Cartesian and scientific philosophies, eliminating, at the same time, the mind-body problem. In his ontological analysis of the structure of Being he concentrated on man's Being-in-the-world, *Dasein*, and accomplished, in his own way, the task assigned by Toulmin to postmodern science "to reinsert humanity into nature" [Toulmin 1982: 210].

(b) EXPERIENCE AS ONTOLOGICAL/COSMIC REALITY

Experience is used here in the deepest sense of the term, as the ontologically, culturally meaningful, and cumulative interaction of the encounters of man, and of generations of men, with the world, nature, and society. For this reason, experience constitutes the practical aspect of the ontological/cosmic framework in which human existence is encompassed; it involves human intentionality and responsibility embedded in the natural and societal contexts. Hodgson calls man's experiences mental events, which do not entirely reflect the external world [Hodgson 1991 193]; in fact, certain features of the latter never enter a given human experience. As each mental event is unique, it is impossible to predict them or to quantify mental events of different persons for measurement and comparison, because quantitative deterministic laws do not govern them.

Experience, in the Heideggerian perspective, is "a mode of the presence of Being." Experiences happen to beings who endure or suffer them; undergoing these experiences overcomes and transforms these beings as experiences are not of their own making [Heidegger 1970: 57]. However, in his comments on Hegel's concept of experience, Heidegger calls these experiences ordinary or mundane in contrast to the non-mundane or ontological experiences in which, in Hegel's terms, a "reversal of consciousness itself" happens. This reversal means that while ordinary or everyday consciousness does not pay attention to anything but the given, practical aspects of a thing, in ontological experience, attention is turned to the "Being of beings," to the disclosure or appearance of Being which means other *Dasein* [Heidegger 1970: 125-127]. Thus, in the Heideggerian interpretation of Hegel's concept of experience, the latter looses its epistemological connotations; experience is no longer a particular mode of knowledge, it is a communicative act, as Habermas would say, a conversation of beings *qua* beings [ibid. 113-114]. This conception of experience truly is a Hegelian dialectical movement of the consciousness, based on the ontological difference; a journey from the pre-ontological toward ontological knowledge, as it represents *Dasein*'s determinate act.

Our second source of the ontological/cosmic concept of experience is John Dewey's philosophy, although he sometimes shows a certain hesitation between the cosmic and the reductionist/monist worldviews. Dewey was the most explicit in respect to the cosmic perspective of human life based on experience in his *Experience and Nature*. For him, experience is the central phenomenon of the life of man, and experience is embedded in nature. Experience

> recognizes in its primary integrity no division between act and material, subject and object, but contains them both in an unanalyzed totality... Life denotes a function, a comprehensive activity, in which organism and environment are included... [Dewey 1958: 8-9].

The concept of the subjectivity of the human mind is only a necessary instrument to channel natural energies toward the ends of man. This leads to the isolation of scientific experimentation and knowledge from primary experience, setting up opposition between the two. As a result objects of selective preference are erected into exclusive realities. Dewey speaks of natural continuity in the life of the world and man. Yet, continuity, cognitive experience, has to originate within a non-cognitive sort, thus the intellectual or cognitive is secondary or derived as compared to the primary experience.

Dewey clearly emphasized the pervasiveness of Being when he states that all experience is an event, and every event is wholly immediate, self-sufficient, terminal and exclusive, proof of an unknowable existence. This understanding of direct experience is linked to what Clifford Geertz called "experience-near" and "experience-distant" concepts; experience-near concepts are spontaneous, fleeting, "un-self-conscious" [Geertz 1983: 58] in which physical and mental are indissolubly bound together.

The primordial problem in Dewey's philosophy, perceived from this perspective, is therefore metaphysical or existential, not psychological or epistemological. Cause and effect are part of the same historical process. Dualistic distinctions giving, for example, reality to atoms at the expense of mind and conscious experience are not distinctions standing for "kinds of reality," though they might be genuine because they are instrumental. In fact, everything is intertwined; joining events, as joining of parts of space or periods of time, reflects as much reality as their distinction from each other before the act of joining. Each process has its conditions, but the process, conditioned as it is, must lead to an end-event, a conscious experience and an actualization. Events have a temporal quality: direct, immediate, indefinable. This, however, does not influence the end-value of the experience of existence. Dewey juxtaposes this temporal quality of events and the temporal order discovered through reflection. Temporal order is a matter of cognition, whereas the temporal quality of events is an immediate trait of every occurrence, conscious or unconscious. Past, present, and future are entirely interlinked as "an integral part of the character or nature of present existence" [ibid. 111].

In contradiction to Meadian behaviorism,[12] Dewey differentiates between direct meaning and cognitive, intellectual meaning. Direct meaning is experienced in the immediacy of an event or in the use of a tool, whereas cognitive meaning is a derived intellectual significance referring to or giving evidence of a future, potential consequence of an experience. Intellectual or cognitive meanings are, therefore, instrumental. Dewey does not underestimate the importance of intellectual meanings because they affect the meaning of the world and result in existential change. Experience and meaning are interrelated in the immediateness of experience; meaning, act and attitude are undifferentiated. Experience, in the ontological perspective, defines meaning, but meaning does not define the reality experienced.

It therefore becomes clear that in Dewey's ontology dualism was eliminated. The distinction between individual and society or culture is maintained, but in an organic relationship, as the human world is in such a relationship with nature. The double character of the human individual is not represented by the mind/body problem, but in his "opacity of bias and preference" against his "plasticity and permeability of needs and likings" [ibid. 242]. The first of these tendencies induces him to isolation, discreteness, aloofness, solitude; the other directs him toward relationships with Others, continuity in the societal, cultural, and historical framework, and security in the community. Therefore, Dewey speaks not of individuals with minds, but of individual minds. For him, the individual's mind is embedded in the community's culture and tradition, in its systems of beliefs, recognition and omission, acceptances and rejections, expectancies and disillusions. Minds proceed with the appraisal of meanings which are transmitted from generation to generation [ibid. 216-219]. Although the individual is conditioned by his cultural environment, as his experiential framework is partially defined by his society and culture, he nevertheless remains the main actor in his encounter with both the natural and cultural environment. The self is the final instrument of man, "the tool of tools, the means in use of all means" [ibid. 246-247] for achieving its ends-in-view; consequently, man's experience is not solely culturally defined, but culturally defined because it is ontologically embedded in existence.

The ambivalent character of the individual and of human collectivities is rooted in nature. In Dewey's theory, nature is ambiguous as well, showing arbitrariness and intolerance, regularities and flexibility. This conjunction of "whimsical contingency and lawful uniformity" in the natural world makes these properties unavoidable, ineradicable in the human world [ibid. 242]. Dewey's analysis of mind and consciousness, perception and knowledge is consequently permeated by incertitude relative to the natural world and to the human being; both show contingent traits and, in comparison to cognitive expectations, intermittent anomalies.

For Gadamer, experience is related "teleologically to the truth that is derived from it" [All of the following citations on Gadamer's concept of experience are from Gadamer 1985: 310-325]. He affirms the character of process of every experience:

(1) An *essential negativity*: the experience-process is not an "unbroken development of typical universals," but is constituted by "continually false generalizations being refuted by experience." The consequence of this process is then the refutation of what was hitherto regarded as typical. In language, the difference is made between "experience, which fits in with our own expectations" and the experience we simply have. The latter is experience in the real sense, always negative, correcting the preceding experience which provided a non-adequate perspective.

(2) A *dialectical nature*: dialectic leads not to definitive knowledge but to "an openness to further experiences." It represents a radically undogmatic attitude and a readiness to learn from new experiences.

(3) A *dimension of human finitude*: experience inevitably involving many disappointments and the appropriation of new experiences through successive negative instances, revealing in man's historical nature an essential complement to knowledge. This insight is not knowledge, but an escape from deception which held man captive and, therefore, is also part of man's nature forged through experience. Thus, experience is experience of the human finitude; real experience is the one in which man becomes aware of his finiteness. The experience of finitude means that man realizes he is not master of time, that there is no certainty and that all dogmatism reaches an absolute barrier "thus true experience is that of one's own historicality."

The concept of "emergence," an important feature of experience as the basis of existence, was recently revived by Joseph Margolis and constitutes the bridge between ontological Being and ontic realities. Its locus is experience as conceptualized by Heidegger and Dewey, but in a much sharper focus. In Margolis' words

> By 'emergence' is meant the existence, the coming into existence, of phenomena that are not describable or able to be explained in terms restricted to physicalist (or materialist) categories [Margolis 1990: 175].

The ontological "emerges" into the ontical at the moment of experience. Experience is a symbiosis, for Margolis, of the perceived and the percipient, of the real and the known, of the indissolubly intertwined realist and idealist aspects of human existence. In experience "the ascribability of both physical and non-physical properties to the same particular things" [ibid. 171] becomes a fact, because experience is intertvowen with intentionality in human nature. For this reason, experience does not fall under nomological imperatives, and it is entirely contextual. Cultural phenomena, which are intentional and reflexive, emerge as well in individual and collective experience, a formulation that ensures that the physical or natural characteristics and the intrinsic, intentional qualities are congruent.

But precisely this emergent nature of experience, its unforeseeable character due to intentionality, its sometimes revolutionary irruption on the scene of social life as an exceptional event, justifies Giddens' concept of the *sequestration of experience* in modernity and, perhaps even more, in post-modernity. He means by this phenomenon that society intends to "institutionally exclude" from social life the unavoidable, fundamental issues of human existence, the ever-present or recently emerged existential predicaments, in order to safeguard the general feeling of ontological security purchased at the price of day-to-day activities [Giddens 1991: 155-156]. The sequestration of experience therefore is a principal element in the destruction of the ontological/cosmic framework of life in modernity and post-modernity.

The point of departure for the present inquiry thus consists in the ontological/cosmic perspective, a holistic framework of understanding the universe. Nature in a cosmic perspective not only is the physical world, the totality of physical, chemical, biological and neurological processes, but the entire domain of the mental, the totality of the psychological, emotive, cognitive phenomena. Nature represents a holistic concept against all dualism and monism; it is not a mystical or mythological concept but coherent with the evolutionary character of culture spelled out in the preceding pages. Culture is part of nature.

CHAPTER THREE

THE UNIQUENESS OF HUMAN NATURE

In the evolutionary process, the human species occupies a particular place. This special status of man in the universe is the outcome of his multilinear biological evolution interacting with the cultural process, of which man is the only creator and agent. To understand man's cultural role, one must carry out an examination of the uniqueness of human nature with reference to its five fundamental aspects: the self-awareness and transcendence of the human self; its intentionality; the integrative function of its mind; the capacity of human nature for symbolic expression and communication; and the linkage between man, his community and culture or, in other words, the interaction between culture and society. This means, of course, that those from the two elements of the Strawsonian concept of a human person — predicates ascribing states of consciousness and predicates ascribing corporeal characteristics — only the first category of characteristics apply here. The physical description is sufficiently explicable in terms of the biological and neurological sciences. Therefore, the following considerations would fall into the domain of the *meta*-physical. Something beyond the physical stands, therefore, as a fact, an undeniable, *sui generis* reality: man, with all his capabilities and possibilities.

1. *The Self and Its Mind*

(a) SELF-AWARENESS AND TRANSCENDENCE

What is unique in man's biological evolution is his capacity of transcendence, of distancing himself from his environment, as well as from himself. This capacity enables him to create coherent and consistent worldviews. *In one word, transcendence is the foundation of the development of particular cultures, of specific human groups or societies, through individual innovation and collective creative power.* In this conception of transcendence, community and individual are entirely interlocked, as cultural evolution is a resultant of the intertwined activities of both. An individual human being's transcendant abilities are reflected in the cultural creations of their community, of their societies [Ricoeur 1981: 97]. Culture is a symbiosis of man's and his communities' transcendence.

Modern biologists acknowledged quite recently the extraordinary role played by man's transcendence in cultural evolution [Rensch 1972: 60]. Dobzhansky and Boesiger emphasized the extreme importance of *self-awareness* in human beings and have equated self-awareness with the possession of a human mind which "makes the human species biologically unique" [Dobzhansky-Boesiger 1983: 68]. However, their most important contribution to the definition of human transcendence was the linkage of self-awareness with death-awareness:

> Man is aware of his self and therefore of his finitude; self-awareness could hardly exist in any meaningful form without death-awareness. Conversely, it is hard to imagine awareness of the inevitability of death without self-awareness [ibid.]

The appearance of self-awareness-cum-death-awareness is a result of the natural selection process based on genetic endowment; they therefore logically conclude that "the roots of religious quest lie deep in the genetic endowment of our species" [ibid. 69], which, in Robert Bellah's words, means that religion relates man to 'the ultimate conditions of his existence' [Bellah 1964: 359].

Self-awareness is synonymous with self-conscious mind, which cannot be conceived of as only a process or function, because a process or function, or any relational concept for that matter, has to be borne by some entity. As the appearance of the self-conscious mind is an outcome of the evolution of the species, it must represent a survival value or, in other terms, it must serve some purpose. The social theory of self and mind [Mead 1934] does not explain the origin of the mind and of self-consciousness in a plausible way and represents a vicious circle, as there can be no mind without the social group but the constitution of a community of human beings depends on the self-consciousness of the individual (the self in opposition to the "generalized other").

In his essay *The Transcendent Character of Life*, Georg Simmel [1971: 353-374, to which all quotations refer] analyzes the transcendence in human nature, and observes that it is manifest simultaneously in all aspects of human life: biological, cognitive, temporal, and beyond. Transcendence is "reaching out over himself" by the individual. This "reaching out" means, in the biological sphere, procreation and growth; in the cognitive sphere it means the awareness that the world "does not wholly enter our forms of cognition." There is no breaking through to attain the beyond, because the immanent world limits our cognition. In the temporal sphere, it means that "the living present exists in the fact that it transcends the present," because present is nothing else than "unextendedness" of the moment, merely a collision of past and future. Therefore, the present alone represents real time. And, finally, if transcendence is a characteristic of life in an immanent world, the ultimate reaching out and the ultimate stepping out of life beyond itself is death, immanent in life from the beginning. As for Dobzhansky and Boesiger, self-awareness is a projection of death-awareness.

"Transcendence is a fundamental determination of the ontological structure of *Dasein*. It belongs to the existentiality of existence. Transcendence is an existential concept," says Heidegger in *The Basic Problems of Phenomenology* [Heidegger 1982: 162]. *Dasein*'s transcendence means, in Heideggerian terminology (in its literal sense) stepping over, passing over or, sometimes, surpassing, and has nothing to do with otherworldliness. This is similar to Simmel's usage of transcendence — not the object or the world is transcendent but *Dasein*. *Dasein* is not immanent though living in an immanent world; it is through his transcendence in respect to ontic phenomena of the world that he genuinely gets closer to other humans and extant entities. This dialectical conception of transcendence, therefore, is tightly interwoven with Heidegger's concept of worldhood as intuitively-known functionality relations. These relations determine the essence or is-ness of things. Yet, the "functional whole" does not emerge from the conjunction, the simultaneous occurrence of the things, but is prior to them and intuitively known. *Dasein* as being-in-the-world lives in a tightly relational immediateness with his environment, but his apprehension of things existing in the functional whole surrounding it is always optional and variable in certain limits. Thus, *Dasein*'s transcendence is also a limit to the creation of a cultural world.

As, according to Heidegger, existence means that being-in-the-world is a fact that is part of the determination of our own being, transcendence is part of such a determination. Extant entities exist because they are apprehended, determined by the being-in-the-world. For an extant being like nature, intraworldliness does not belong to its being as its determination,[1] but solely as a possible determination; whereas, the being of *Dasein* is not determined as being within the world but being-in-the-world precisely because of its transcendence.

In a parallel vision to the Heideggerian transcendental perspective of the human being, Jaspers also affirms that the awareness of a quasi-separate identity reflects the transcendence of the self-conscious mind [Jaspers 1971: 21]. This transcendence includes a self-reflexive stance towards himself. It is, nevertheless, very important to understand that the relationship of the self to its multiple environments is not an opposition, and it is not identity either; the best way to characterize the links between the self and the world is to conceive it as a dialectical interplay made possible by the self's transcendence in his relationship with the world. But interplay means interdependence as well. The self is molded by the totality of physical and organic phenomena and by the society and civilization in which it lives; in its turn, the self, because it is transcendent, influences the evolution of the natural environment and, especially, the social and cultural life of his age and of future generations.

The dissociation of man from his environment is thus expressed through reflexive thinking which enables the self to distinguish alternative possibilities: in dealing with itself and its environment; in determining its present conduct in accordance with perceived future probabilities; and in delaying action or response to the stimuli it receives. Transcendence in the form of reflexivity is what really distinguishes self-consciousness from consciousness, because a consciously felt phenomenon is attributed, through reflexive thinking, to the self. If thinking is reflection on the world, on existence, on the immanent destiny integrating all aspects of everyday life, then reflection and reflexivity are closely linked to man's transcendence, because they are made possible by the distance he is able to put between himself and the world, between his self-conscious self and his everyday life of monotonous existence, between his self and the "generalized other."

(b) INTENTIONALITY

Heidegger's concept of intentionality is embedded in his denial of the subject-object opposition and in his view on man's transcendence. Both intentionality and transcendence belong to the nature of the *Dasein* that comports itself intentionally, but intentionality is only possible logically if *Dasein* is intrinsically transcendent. Sometimes Heidegger even makes it appear that intentionality and transcendence are almost identical. Both are parts of *Dasein*'s constitution and are grounded in the temporality of human existence.

Among contemporary philosophers, John Searle dealt with the problem of human intentionality in the most exhaustive manner. His definition of intentionality is couched in terms of the Quinean-Davidsonian philosophy. "Intentionality is that property of many mental states and events by which they are directed at or about or of objects and states of affairs in the world" [Searle 1983: 1]. Intentionality, part of man's biological nature, belongs to states and events; it is neither a mental act, nor a linguistic phenomenon. As directedness, it encompasses a much larger field than intending, which is only one sort of possible form of intentionality. Intentionality and consciousness are not identical but are closely connected. In fact, it would be impossible to know about intentionality without being conscious. Searle sharply distinguishes between the intentional state and what the state is directed toward. Intentionality belongs to mental states, such as beliefs and desires, as well as mental events, and always has a normative character, even normative content.

An important concept of Searle's theory of intentionality is the "direction of fit," which means that assertions have a word-to-world direction of fit, whereas committments and directive pronouncements have world-to-word direction of fit. The direction of fit concerns the responsibility of fitting, whether or not truth or satisfaction is attained. This also is the case for beliefs for which the direction of fit is mind-to-world. Therefore, they can be true or false. Or, for desires and intentions with a world-to-mind direction of fit, which cannot be true or false but complied with, they may be fulfilled, carried out, or satisfied. Consequently, in Searle's view, every intentional state partially determines its "conditions of satisfaction" through the specification of its content.

Searle's description of intentionality is linked to two other fundamental insights postulating two conceptual entities. First, specific intentional states are parts of an extended *network* of intentional states of a person and therefore their conditions of satisfaction are related to their position in this network. There is interdependence between various intentional states, as no isolated intentional state could ever determine its conditions of satisfaction. Second, the representative content of an intentional state depends on nonrepresentational mental capacities, and this *background* of nonrepresentational mental capacities conditions the satisfaction of the intentional state

> All conscious intentionality -- all thought, perception, understanding, etc. -- determines conditions of satisfaction only relative to a set of capacities that are not and could not be part of that very conscious state. The actual content by itself is insufficient to determine the conditions of satisfaction" [Searle 1992: 189].

Thus, the network of intentions is part of the background. In fact, Searle identifies the background with the unconscious, with the background presuppositions of discourse, which in turn he defines as an aspect of the brain's neurobiological activity [ibid. 187-188]. However, this background may also be defined as the network of various beliefs, values, and principles appropriated through unconsciously internalized traditions, having the role of an information system complementing genotypic directives.

In Searle's view, perception and action are, biologically, the primary forms of intentionality involving direct causal relations [Searle 1983: 105]. Any perceptual experiences are intentional, and there are no actions that are not intentional; in fact, an intentional action is the condition of satisfaction of an intention. However, there are important differences between intentionality in perception and in action. In the case of perception, the direction of fit is mind-to-world, but the direction of causation is from the object to the visual experience. In contrast, acting has a world-to-mind direction of fit but an opposite direction of causation, mind-to-world, from acting to the occurrence of the event.

The ontic emergence of human reality characterized by intentionality signifies, in Joseph Margolis' view, that causality does not entail law-like regularities in human action-patterns expressible in physicalist terms, not only because there are, in these patterns, discontinuities and discrepancies due to endogenous limitations, but because intentionality implies freedom of action [Margolis, Joseph 1990: 175-177]. There is no contradiction between the simultaneous operations of causality and human freedom. Causality concerns those elements of reality which are recurrent and predictable; therefore, freedom does not exclude predictability but affirms the transcendence of the intentional in respect to the categories of nature. This exemplifies the co-existence of empirical content and creative content in human life, the acceptance of the non-identity of the cognitive and of the intentional/existential fits in the emerging and global cosmic reality.

In the same vein, Arthur Fine insists it is a mistake to consider only the causal explanation, even in the domain of the sciences [Fine 1990: 107-108]. He shows, through the quantum and relativity theories that certain explanations are structural or contextual, and a correlation is not always of a causal nature. Freedom of the intentional human being implies choice between innumerable options and possibilities offered at the ontological/cosmic level. "Choice is therefore the gateway through which finality enters the open-ended and hopeful human existence" [Bauman 1978: 29].

(c) CONSCIOUSNESS AND THE INTEGRATIVE POWER OF THE MIND

Dewey's differentiation between mind and consciousness is placed in an action-oriented framework and is a sound approach toward the explanation of the function of the self through the integrative power of the mind. He considers mind as the totality of meanings "embodied in the workings of organic life" [Dewey 1958: 303], a connected whole the content of which is incomparably wider than that of consciousness. Mind is, in the self the substantial and structural, contextual, and persistent element, a constant "foreground and background" of operative meanings. Consciousness is awareness or perception of meaning (not of sense data), a state of awareness in its immediacy. The perception of events in their meanings, like a light thrown intermittently and with varying intensity on things, is a transitive process in which consciousness actualizes past events, focuses on present events, or projects future events. But the most important effect of consciousness is that in it, inherited or contextual parts of the system of meanings are re-directed, or re-organized under the impulse of a need or a desire for satisfaction of the self as an organic whole.

Action takes place when the organic and environmental are integrated by the self, the meanings are coherent and consistent, and there is no difference between things signifying and things signified. When this organic-environmental integration breaks down due to discrepancies in the perception, actualization or projection of meanings, a re-orientation follows as a consequence of the realization of this discrepancy and the division of perception in consciousness. The change in meaning involves a new action pattern and a new attitude. The unity of this interplay between meaning and action, mind and consciousness, is defined by experience. Therefore, perception or consciousness characterizes a process, not a state of affairs. Intentional change characterizing re-direction or re-orientation of events means change in perception, and in meaning, not the operation of causality [Dewey 1958: 303-304 and 316]. This means that human adaptation to natural and historical contingencies and circumstances is an open-ended process; the constraints appear at several levels, biological and ecological, as well as institutional or social.

Bergson's theory on matter and mind shows many similarities with Dewey's explanation of the operations of consciousness. Bergson, in accordance with his famous concept of temporality, *la durée*, considered pure intuition as "undivided continuity" [Bergson 1991: 183].[2] For this reason, past experience is not remembered as it really was, it is disfigured or distorted by memory due to the fact that many versions of the recollection of past events can be fitted in an actual situation. The ignorance of this phenomenon is the fundamental mistake of empiricism and of dogmatism in the Bergsonian view; consequently, empiricism and dogmatism lead either to determinism or to indeterminism, and these extremes can only be avoided through the acceptance of the continuous flow of time, placing us in the "pure duration." The act of perception reduces, with the help of memory ("a synthesis of past and present with a view to the future") [ibid. 220], the events which in themselves spread and extend over an infinite number of moments into a single intuition; it grasps the multiple effects of repetitive inner evolutions and experiences, discontinuous in their succession, as simultaneously continuous through the reality of the world. As a result, the act of perception through memory liberates man from the rhythm of necessity, from the "movement of the flow of things." The memory of human beings measures their "powers of action upon things" [ibid. 288].

Wilhelm Dilthey, a contemporary of Bergson, also assigned to consciousness a role not only similar to the one given to it by Dewey, but much more extensive and essential because it assumes also the function of the mind in Dewey's conception. Therefore, it must be mentioned here as a "counterpoint" to the Deweyan conceptualization. The key word in Dilthey's philosophy of consciousness is "lived experience" (*Erlebnis*), through which every experience and all objects perceived become "facts of consciousness" — reality. Indeed, the whole world exists for a person only as constituted in a "stream of consciousness" [Dilthey 1989: 330]. However, Dilthey distinguishes appearance from reality, -- curiously but understandably because of his bent toward psychological explanations, -- by the fact that appearance designates the lasting properties of an object, whereas reality can only be inferred when changes in appearances occur in sense perceptions. Knowledge of external reality as such is, by definition, excluded from the philosophy of Dilthey, in which everything must be a "fact of consciousness;" the reality of the external world is molded by conscious perception.

In fact, Dewey's distinction between mind and consciousness is somewhat replicated in Dilthey's distinction of reflexive or direct awareness [ibid. 247 and 300] from representative thought. Reflexive awareness is a disclosure through introspection, ever renewed and without a differentiated content, incapable of disclosing the unified self, which is only assumed. Content and the act of disclosure are identical, or reflexive content and content of consciousness is the same. Thus, reflexive awareness is different from observation or external perception or representation, in which contents are detached from the subject's consciousness and juxtaposed to it. This is the dualism of subject and object. Perception and apperception (integrating actual perceptions into past ones) are related in terms of consciousness, because any representation cannot be defined but as being conscious, that is, being there for someone. A "nexus of facts of consciousness" [ibid. 279] encompasses the totality of psychic life, of lived experiences; it also includes outer experiences integrated with the inner ones. The life process is a continuum of representations changing from moment to moment (like Husserl's internal time-consciousness), simultaneously pointing backward and forward. The unifying self-consciousness selects from the "nexus of facts of consciousness" facts, especially those of inner perception or inner experience, which become part of apperception in any given moment. Self-consciousness proceeds in a holistic way in its apperception of external reality, and, vice versa. Attentive awareness can also use perceptual images for constructing wholes by means of thought-processes.[3]

In the Sixth Dialogue with Professor Popper, Sir John Eccles gave the best summary of an open-minded scientist's view of the mind:

> The self-conscious mind is actively engaged in reading out from the multitude of active centers at the highest level of brain activity, namely in the liaison brain. The self-conscious mind selects from these centers according to attention and interest and from moment to moment integrates its selection to give unity even to the most transient conscious experiences. Furthermore, the self-conscious mind acts upon these neural centers, modifying the dynamic spatio-temporal patterns of the neural events. Thus in agreement with Sperry (1969), it is postulated that the self-conscious mind exercises a superior interpretative and controlling role upon the neural events [Popper-Eccles 1983: 495].

If the specific role of the mind as summarized above is a postulate, it is because in the present status of scientific research, no explanation whatsoever could be given for the brain's ability; for example, the integration into a coherent picture the disparate neuronal events arising in the visual centers as a retinal input.

The integrating function of the self-conscious mind, called cerebral integration by Boesiger, and a unifying interpretation by Eccles is indispensable and complementary to human transcendence. This integrating function proceeds at two levels. First, it proceeds at the level of the experience, integrating all relevant factors: neural events reflecting impulses from the physical environment in the form of ever-changing neural patterns in the brain; cognitive and affective elements; and influences of the cultural and social environment flowing through the central nervous system. This can be viewed as the first-order level of integration. For integration to realize a concerted action, the second-order level of integration, movements of a whole organism, are correlated and organized to give appropriate responses to the stimuli received. This is "teleological" integration in favor organic adaptedness. The self-consciousness of the mind is apparent in its unifying action, reflecting its own interest, attention, or imagination, the selection and integration of various disparate elements which the mind carries out in order to establish oneself as self, as transcendent being, in short to establish its genidentity.

In connection with the mind's integrating function, especially in respect to *a priori* categories of the mind, it will be useful to review some points raised by the advocates of evolutionary epistemology. In the evolutionary perspective, inborn ideas or categories, the Kantian *ipso facto* necessarily valid, synthetic *a priori* categories are, as a matter of course, rejected. Though the necessary *a priori* validity of such mental categories is not accepted, they can be validated as *a priori*, in Campbell's terms, from the point of view of an individual organism. But from the point of view of the history of the species, these are, undoubtedly, *a posteriori* [Campbell 1987a: 79]. Campbell follows in his explication Popper, who considered absurd the supposition of inborn ideas as *a priori* valid and speaks of inborn reactions or responses and inborn expectations. These expectations are not knowledge and are not epistemologically *a priori* valid, but psychologically or genetically *a priori*, that is, prior to all observational experience. In the same vein, Lorenz also noted[4] that the positivist argument that our knowledge is exclusively derived from sensory experience is only applicable to the *ontogenetic* development, but in the perspective of the *phylogenetic* development, man is born with innate knowledge (there is no biological reason why such knowledge could not be passed from generation to generation). Therefore, *a priori* categories or "instinctive" expectations are transmitted to the individual based on the common experience of his cultural group; therefore they are synthetic *a posteriori* from the point of view of the species. Following Lorenz' view, which recognizes that the Kantian *Ding an sich* is only knowable in the knower's categories, not in those of the *Ding an sich*, Campbell also approves Lorenz' idea that forms of intuition and categories are working hypotheses in the adaptation of the human species to its successive environments.

Popper even emphasized that finding regularity or the need or propensity to look for regularities, is the most important of inborn expectations. He considered these as corresponding to the Kantian "laws of causality," *a priori* ingrained in our mental faculties [Popper 1965: 47]. In addition to the idea of regularity or quasi-causation inborn in man as a result of phylogenetic evolution, Popper also introduced the concept of downward causation in relation to upward causation. That means that the substructures of a system, through their joint effects, affect or modify the whole system [Popper 1987b: 147]. In fact, downward causation appears to be nothing else than the feedback effect of the human self and mind on its inorganic, organic, and cultural environments.   If one considers that human cultural activities deeply modify, perhaps irreversibly, man's physical and social surroundings, then the impact of downward causation acquires a crucially important meaning.

2. *Symbolic Communication and Expression*

(a) LANGUAGE AND MEANING

Meaning and the Plurality of Linguistic Worlds

Language and culture co-evolve.   Today it is commonplace to say that man's existence as species started with the appearance of language and the development of cultural activities or expressions, which are based on capacities determined by the genotype.[5]   The history of cultural evolution also shows that a feedback process takes place between the genetic capacity to make and use symbols and the effective utilization of these symbols.   Through this interaction, they mutually reinforce each other, but, at the same time, man also transcends his genetic background by way of culture and language.

In nature, following Dewey's thought, everything is in interaction, this is "a commonplace of existence;" but what characterizes human social relations is not interaction alone but its specificity between men, "the distinctive patterns of human association" [Dewey 1958: 174-175.] Human association is then distinguished, in Dewey's conception, by the transformation of sequence and coexistence into participation and communication.   Human interaction is predominantly symbolic, since man is "Homo depictor" and not "Homo faber" in Ian Hacking's terms, and the most important symbolic expressions is language, which is the means of human communication and the creation of communities of men.   Should a symbol be an act or an object, its meaning is culturally agreed upon or given to it by the community which is the bearer of the culture.   "For language is not complete in any speaker; it exists perfectly only within a collectivity," declared Saussure [Saussure 1964: 55]. The meaning of symbols is as much learned as the meaning of words, although in the case of the former there is a natural, one could say intuitive, basis of reference because symbols do not convey cognitive, conceptual meanings.[6] Linguistic communication therefore becomes an almost unconscious "decoding" process. We can speak of "decoding" because linguistic performance, in addition to already being a comprehensive "code-system" can be further coded in some form of verbal tradition, in written works or artistic expression. Language, consequently, is the instrument of a specific culture to create a time-perspective and to gain a space-extension.

Human language having signaling, descriptive, explanatory and argumentative functions becomes a vehicle of truth or deceit, of critical thinking and debate, of rational and irrational attitudes — always with reference to the cultural framework in which the given language assumes these functions. Communication is always a living process, whatever its form. But linguistic communication is essentially different from any other type of communication, as it discloses a "world," a cultural environment, of those who speak [Whorf 1956; Gadamer 1985: 252; also Dewey 1958: 153-185]. Between speakers of the same language there is interchangeability of words and utterances, and the memorization and anticipation capabilities of the human mind, through the transcendence of the self and the mind's integrative function, makes it possible to speak of objects and acts regardless of their distance in space and time. In his *Philosophical Investigations*, Wittgenstein speaks of natural languages, refuting the concept of an ideal language which can only be a "construct;" words do not have definite referents, but "they are *related* to one another in many different ways" [Wittgenstein 1989: I. 65,3; italics in original]. These relationships constitute the "family resemblance" languages are based on, and he calls these families "language games," the universally accepted element of Wittgenstein's legacy. Despite these family resemblance, even if words evoke the same thing in the mind, their application may still be different because the application is a criterion of understanding. Language is then nothing other than an instrument of communication in accordance with forms of life and with a view to carry out actions corresponding to the constitutive elements of cultural and social backgrounds of different human groups.

Languages, products of the cultural evolution, are genetically conditioned but not transmitted by genes in contrast to the possibilities of animal communication. Language, by its nature, comes to life in conversation, it acquires reality only in the process of communication. For this reason, invented systems of artificial communication, such as Esperanto or mathematical symbols, never become real languages, as they do not have a basis in the lives of communities of men but are used only as tools of understanding. The possibility of penetration into a different linguistic community is certainly facilitated by the phenomenon of imagination, directly linked to human language capabilities. It is a type of active thought process, exploring, rejecting, creating some new understanding, some new synthesis, going much beyond the descriptive or explanatory functions of language. Gadamer suggests, in fact, that language reflects and expresses the lifeworld's underlying reality, which is the same for all men [Gadamer 1985: 405-406]. This, of course, is a widely held view; physicists as well as biologists recognize the role of natural language. For Heisenberg, the concept of natural languages, though vague, contributes more to the progress of knowledge than the much more precise terms of the scientific language, because between reality and natural language terms there is immediacy, an evolving language which represents for man the ever-changing reality. The theoretical concepts and language of science, though derived from experience by complex experimental instruments and refined conceptual tools such as axioms and definitions, lose, through the process of idealization their immediate connections with reality as a whole, although their relevance, their close links with the reality studied, is maintained [Heisenberg 1958: 200-202].

Gadamer points out that words loose their power if they are considered as signs or designators, if they are artificially isolated from the interactive whole through which language comes into immediate contact with reality and with other human beings. He also emphasizes, like Dewey, that concept formation, thinking, and understanding are born from experience, which gives them their unity. Linguistic communication is not extracted from experience by reflection in which language plays an instrumental role; words are not uttered randomly, they correspond to the existential situation in which communication or expression takes place since they are part of the experience in an integral way. Language and thought form an unconscious unity and disclose the world in which we live; this "commensurateness" of language and world (Searle's fit) indicates the objectivity of language. The world of language is a world of understanding and a binding force for all participants in a community in which fundamental experiences, values and actions are shared. Language and world transcend all efforts of objectification. Therefore, Gadamer considers the linguistic experience of the world as an absolute.

As an example of the crucial difference between different linguistic and, consequently, cultural worlds, Chung-Ying Cheng's comparison of the ancient Greek and Chinese languages and cultures is most interesting. He draws a parallel between the phonetic character of the Greek language, oriented to audition and therefore using symbols (signifiers) not having any relationship with the objects (signified), thus separating the "world of meanings from the world of concrete things." Chung-Ying Cheng relates this pattern to the Greek and Western metaphysical orientation and ontological quest for Being. He juxtaposes this separation of the "sensible from the non-sensible," with the pictorial or image-language of the Chinese, in which the cohesion of the sensible and non-sensible is inherent in the language. Here, the association between symbol and meaning results in a metaphysical orientation toward cosmological becoming or, inversely, a non-metaphysical, non-transcendental but practical approach to problems of human life [Chung-Ying Cheng 1989: 167-168]. For this reason, the Chinese language does not have such concepts as "truth," "belief," "meaning," or "propositional knowledge." The lack of separation of the sensible and non-sensible in the Chinese linguistic world excludes, as well, the Western binomial oppositions of knowledge versus action, substance versus function or, most importantly, the separation of fact and value. As a result of this cosmic-practical orientation of Chinese culture, understanding must embrace the totality of experience which, in its turn, cannot be but the experience of total reality.

To show the above described particularity of the Chinese language, Chad Hansen translates into English the Chinese word for "mind" as "heart-mind," which expresses more completely the appropriate meaning of the sign. For him, Chinese language is prescriptive and non-descriptive because associated with social practices such as ritual and music; therefore, learning the language is "as acquiring the ability to follow socially-shared discrimination patterns" [Hansen 1989: 87].

Meaning and Reference: Translation and Interpretation

These considerations lead to the extensive debate in modern linguistic philosophy about reference and meaning. To indicating some elements of this debate Donald Davidson's argumentation is instrumental. Davidson pursues a holistic approach and tries to avoid the pitfalls of introducing the use of meta-languages that can only lead to a reiterative process. He recognizes that linguistic phenomena are "patently supervenient on non-linguistic phenomena" [Davidson 1984: 215], but distinguishes two kinds of relativization of efforts to reach the truth: absolutistic theories such as Tarski's famous Convention T, which must be relativized to a time and speaker, at least; and those which relativized truth to an interpretation, a model, a domain, or possible worlds. Without accepting either of the above variants, Davidson describes what he calls the "paradox of reference": the *building-block* method, building up sentences from simple elements, and the *conceptual* method, starting with complex sentences and reaching their parts through abstraction; neither can be successful. The first is not able to reach the non-linguistic characterization of reference, whereas the second does not offer the means to give a complete account of the semantic features of the sentence's elements; hence, both are unable to explain truth. He therefore proposes a holistic approach, dropping the concept of reference as the link of linguistic expression to reality. In his approach words, meaning of words (meaning being an interpretation of a word or of a sentence), reference, and so on, are posits without empirical basis or any other independent confirmation. However, for Davidson, giving up reference does not mean giving up the ontology of words as each singular term is related to some object or predicate. He remains, *in fine*, a realist.

For Davidson, the empirical basis of understanding meaning lies in the ability to speak and understand a language. In the case of interpretation between different languages, the other's (the alien's) belief system plays a decisive role because what he means depends on what he believes. But how can we know what he believes without understanding what he means? Truth can be related through utterances or speech acts, or, simply, a sentence, a person, and a time; when sets of sentences are relativized to the same speaker and time, ordinary logic applies as usual, but when sentences are spoken by different speakers and at different times new logical axioms are needed [Davidson 1984: 24-35]. Meaning and belief then play interlocking and complementary roles in the interpretation of speech, as utterances are the results of their interplay. Interpretation thus should be based on simple behavioral facts or dispositions because "speakers of a language hold a sentence to be true (under observed circumstances) as prima-facie evidence that the sentence is true under those circumstances" [ibid. 152]. The best guarantee of a more or less correct interpretation will be to take into account not only one individual speaker, but the social group he belongs to, as communities of speakers have the same linguistic repertoire.

Davidson thus satisfies himself with what is a semantic counterpart of Quine's indeterminacy of translation, the indeterminacy of interpretation.   Quine realized that, as Cassirer and Whorf have stressed, a language is not separated from the world but it is part of it. Radical translation is required when there is a clear cultural disruption; indeterminacy of translation comes from the loss of view of the whole as translation proceeds piece by piece and sentences are thought to convey meanings one by one. Indeterminacy of translation excludes "the almost universal belief that the objective references of terms in radically different languages can be objectively compared" [Quine 1983: 28 and 79].

The debate on translation was enriched by MacIntyre on a very important point — the confused linguistic usage of international communication.   MacIntyre differentiates two sets of problems concerning translatability. In one case, translation has to be made from the language of one community with a particularly rich expressive force and having a well-defined belief-system, into the language of another community, whose beliefs in some important matters are incompatible or incommensurable with the belief-system of the first community. In the second case, the translation has to be carried out from a natural language into one of the "internationalized languages of modernity." In both cases, MacIntyre points out, a literal translation or paraphrasing is not sufficient, the translator has to have recourse to linguistic innovation and to a possibly extensive use of interpretive comments and explanations [MacIntyre 1988: 373-374]. One could add, however, that when there is definitive incompatibility or incommensurability between the "background schemes" of two communities, even linguistic innovations or extensive interpretation could not bring much help in Davidson's sense, as understanding of beliefs, concepts, and approaches of the other is prior to translation.

Interactive Meaning and Internal Realism

Hilary Putnam develops an interesting view on the realistic interpretation of meaning conceptually similar to the position of Davidson.   In favor of Davidson's complex arguments regarding meaning without reference, but maintaining the ontological reality of words, Putnam developed his famous thesis on "internal realism." According to this theory speakers, for whom language "mirrors" their environment, construct "*a symbolic representation of that environment*" [Putnam 1981: 123; italics in original]. On the basis of this "internal realism" Putnam strongly criticizes what he calls "functionalism," (his own earlier standpoint), not only from the epistemological point of view but also from the ontological view. For him [Putnam 1988: 120], it is erroneous to consider the world as comparable to a single system ("organisms and their physical environment") containing all possible objects or referents and believe that there is only one relation between a word and the thing referred to (implying that words can be unequivocally defined).   Putnam thinks that "open textures" of reference, meaning, or reason are inter-connected, leading to meaning-holism related to a background network of beliefs in a given community. For Putnam, consequently, "reference is a social phenomenon" [ibid. 22] which is also determined, at least partially, by the environment.

Action-Oriented Generalized Meaning

Dewey's concept of meaning does not take into account the diversity of languages, as he rather conceived meaning in relation to the external world and human experience. Any physical event, the referent, is full of meanings, not only for the present, but also in its potential consequences for the future. Present and future potentialities define a thing, an event, in an overall context of their connections. Potential consequences become part of the nature of a thing, and require contemplation, interpretation, or imputation of consequences in view of the use of these things. This is particularly so as "language is always a form of action and in its instrumental use is always a means of concerted action for an end... It brings with it the sense of sharing and merging in a whole" [Dewey 1958: 184].

In Dewey's action-oriented perspective, meanings are "generic and universal" which are shared by the speaker, the hearer, and the thing referred to. However, shared meaning does not involve validity of reference, meanings being dependent on beliefs. The latter may influence through meanings. For example, in mythical thinking, some existential occurrences are like dramas, where meanings are acted out as reality but without validity of reference to the real world. Perception, or awareness of meanings, enters consciousness through language that grasps past, present and future events in its meaning, but it is mind that integrates the multitude of meanings in a comprehensive whole.   Meanings therefore become operative through the mind's integrative function. Mind is structural, substantial, contextual, and persistent, whereas consciousness is focal and transitive, a process with intermittent illuminations, a series of experienced impressions.

(b) SYMBOLISM: SHARED WORLDVIEWS AND UNITY

Symbolic Representation and Discourse

If man constructs a symbolic representation of his world, human symbolism becomes pervasive, it penetrates all perspectives of human life; language is the most important and most evident aspect of this symbolic representation and communication. Everyday life is interwoven with symbolic content, and thus, meaning is a product of culture, framing the "stubborn fact" in terms of symbolic concepts. Therefore Bellah speaks of symbolic realism [Bellah 1970: 252]. Symbolic forms include not only linguistic but also non-linguistic expression; they are intersubjectively accepted as "meaningful constructs" [Thompson, John 1990: 59]. Symbolism belongs to the conscious self. Symbols in a given cultural world are universal and, at the same time, they condition all thoughts and acts. They aim at communication with other human beings and with the cosmic world.

Signals have a physical or substantial being, whereas symbols have a functional value; the "signal is part of the physical world of being; a symbol is part of the human world of meaning" [Beattie 1984: 242]. From the point of view of evolutionary theory, though relations between symbols and adaptation-producing capabilities are very strenuous, it is recognized that an important adaptive function of symbolism is the facilitation of interpersonal communication and memory organization. Such a functional perspective does not explain, of course, the diversity of symbolic systems; the use of a symbol for a given meaning therefore may be considered as arbitrary but the underlying meaning is not [Boyd-Richerson 1985: 274].

The expressive potential of symbolism is extremely large in its applications in one cultural world or even among worlds of culture. In fact, basic symbolic meanings can be found in all human cultures. In Peircean semiotics, the triad of signs: symbol, icon, and index, and their intersections and combinations lend themselves to multiple representational capacities and communicative functions. These signs constitute a continuum of such capacities, from those used for reference to convey information in a particular context, to those which transmit and communicate sensory and mental messages in a presentational or participatory mode. A correlate to the universal communicative potential of symbols is their variability and flexibility, as they do not have a fixed referent in the existential world. In a given cultural context, symbols can have a fixed meaning for a long period of time, and their changing signification may announce the coming of a new epoch with wide and fundamental inter-cultural exchanges. Even in those cases, however, when symbols appear to be fixed for very long periods, the underlying meaning of the symbol can change in accordance with the modification of belief and value systems. As symbolic thought, the very characteristic of human mental processes, is not tightly linked to reality, it is the most adequate means for man to enter the potential or imaginary world, be it relational, scientific thought, or mythic beliefs and artistic creation [Cassirer 1944: 36-38 and 56-57].

Symbolism is closely related to transcendence or "distanciation" in human existence. In respect to the scientific domain, this became clear when man's efforts of self-distancing, in order to give a true picture of the functioning of the universe, are taken into account. Yet, the interdependence of symbolism and transcendence goes much further in the religious context and the artistic-aesthetic perspectives. In these two spheres, man moves beyond the realities of everyday life in order to communicate with the human and cosmic totality. This communication does not aim at objective, controlling action as in science, but to achieving unity with all men and with the whole of nature — the cosmos. Religious and artistic symbolism therefore tends toward the acceptance of intuitive, non-hypothetical truths, to a commitment to and encounter with realities beyond institutionalized skepticism and hypotheses of critical rationalism.

There is, however, a profound difference between the religious and artistic. The religious, on the one hand, is deeply anchored in the "really real," the everyday actuality of man's life, and seeks to integrate it with the perspective of metaphysical realities representing the totality of mankind and the totality of the cosmic universe. The arts (poetry, drama, music, painting, sculpture, architecture, and handicrafts such as pottery) operate through creative imagination and illusionary symbolism, and go much further towards man's complete self-distancing by "lifting him out" of the usual, or by entirely disengaging him from the real in order to lead him to unity with the totality, in community with other men and with the natural world. In artistic symbolism, possible worlds are actual worlds. The merely possible is, albeit metaphorically, transposed into the actual, "things which never happened but always are" in Sallustius swords fifteen centuries ago. Though artistic creations do not denote the real, do not represent but express or exemplify, they thereby function as symbols of features of the reality which they literally or metaphorically stand for in expressing them in a unifying vision. Artistic activity is coincidental with alternating views of reality, with man's capability, through transcendence, to have his own vision in a unified perspective or even to modify this vision in changing environmental contexts. Art is therefore neither imitation, nor copying reality, but is a discovery of an ever-new perception of it, a personal synthesis expressing a particular vision of the real. Art is a "living form," and has its own, inborn rationality that can only be understood if the overall symbolism of a given art or of a given artist is considered. This rationality has nothing to do with the cognitive instrumental rationality of science and everyday life, nor with the normative, communicatively established rationality of morals. Symbolic art is an autonomous domain in human existence which leads to a particular world with a unified perspective which is perhaps what Aristotle called in his *Poetics* a *katharsis*.

Myth and Ritual

A particular case of symbolic communication and drive towards unity is the myth that played a considerable role in the cultural evolution of man and human societies. Myth is a radical concern with being. All ancient "myth presupposes a break with tradition, a profound shock to an order, a violent intervention with irreversible, long-term consequences. All truly archaic myths deal with such events" [Borkenau 1981: 205]. Mircea Eliade sees myths as the most efficient means to make men aware and sensible to another world, a beyond, the "transcendental;" therefore, myths call for an "eternal return" [Eliade 1965]. This experience of the sacred, "an encounter with transhuman reality," leads man to feel that something really exists, "a perfectly articulated, intelligible, and significant Cosmos" [Eliade 1963: 144-145]. Rituals are reconfirmation of myths, "recollection and re-enactment of the primordial event," and by showing something enduring in the flux of time, they witness the fact that time is not irreversible. Chronological time is replaced by the sacred time, the time of myth.

Lévy-Brühl's explanation of symbolism and of mythical thought shows that in man's thought and action, there are two co-existent mentalities: one which is the mode of practical-instrumental rationality, of science, of objectification, and of postulating causal connections; and the mode of participation, which proceeds by using metaphors and similes as sensory images with metaphysical properties, or through association and identification realizing, in its deepest sense, consubstantiality. Both have their own institutional structure, coherence and rationality; what appear as distinct aspects of reality for the first represent, for the second, a mythical unity in which cause and effect are not mediated by interfering mechanisms, but are simultaneous or immediate, as in the Sanskrit tradition. This view of coexistent modes of thought and action in the human mind can be related to Weber's "world orders" which, in Arnason's words, are not differentiated but co-determined by the same patterns of meaning [Arnason 1990: 229]. Many anthropologists expressed the same idea when they pointed out that the two modes of thought and action, rational and mystical, can coexist as "normative ideational systems" in the same society, and that a human being is endowed with the capability to switch between the two at any time and in specific circumstances. In Durkheimian parlance, these are "collective representations," or, in Malinowski's terms, symbolism, rituals, and ceremonies are linked with social valuations and social imperatives; that is, they are embedded in society's cultural patterns and are co-variant with it.

In this perspective, myth has an ontological structure. Schelling went so far as to consider myths not allegorical or metaphorical, referring to them as another "true" phenomenon, because he considered them representations of the truth [Hübner 1985: 63 and 66]. Myths in modernity are created, according to Kolakowski [1989: 19-26], first, to formulate a holistic explanation of the world, second, to express faith in the permanence of human values, and, third, to establish continuity in the evolution of the world. It is a paradox that while myths must satisfy the latter requirement, any occurrence they relate is excluded from the flow of historical time. It is important that Kolakowski sees myth as limiting people's freedom through its imperative of self-relativization. Value-creation in the mythical context imposes a constraint on each individual, binding each group or community that accepts the myth to abandon divergent values, beliefs, or ways of life, with reference to a primal and non-temporal order. For man living in a mythical world, "the deep conviction of a fundamental and indelible *solidarity of life* that bridges over the multiplicity and variety of all its single forms" [Cassirer 1984: 82; italics in original] is the most fundamental tenet of his existence. Symbolic representations are, for Geertz, culture patterns that give meaning to reality and, at the same time, shape it. *Ritual* is the symbolic fusion of ethos and worldview, ethos designating the moral, the aesthetic, and the emotional, whereas worldview indicates the existential and cognitive aspects of a culture as it embraces the concept of general idea of existence, of the "really real." This fusion means that a single set of symbolic forms and actions reunites the "world as lived and the world as imagined" in one world, the lifeworld. Ritual is essential fusion through shared symbolism and common symbolic action of the participants; it must remain constant and invariable in its modes and procedures. Thus, ritual cannot be rationalized, it loses its importance or changes its character either because it becomes unessential to people, or because its foundation changes with the modification or complete disappearance of the ethos and worldview hitherto believed and maintained [Geertz 1973: 89, 95-96, 113, 126-127].

Ritual, in its widest sense, is not a type of social or cultural activity, but a dimension of all human interactions, as it is not only a symbolic-expressive aspect of behavior, but also a creative process. One therefore speaks of ritualization in everyday life not only because it establishes or reinforces the bond between a person and his moral community, it also assures and develops communication as well as functions, in some cases, as a means of social control. Nevertheless, ritual, in this widest sense, frequently performs differentiation as well. Ritual actions establish culturally or socially specific and privileged status, an implicit hierarchy integrating unity and totality without eliminating the differences, but maintaining them [Bell, Catherine 1992: 108 and 116].

3. *Culture and Society*

(a) INDIVIDUAL AND COMMUNITY

An individual and the community to which he belongs form together an organic whole; there is no identity between the two, but there can be no juxtaposition either. It is necessary here to make explicit this dialectical vision of the relations between individual and community, as the development of modern Western thought was based on the opposition or juxtaposition of the individual and society, or whatever larger entity the individual belonged to. This concept probably evolved from the shift from the notion of human community to the political entity in which a human being may or may not belong; it is the result of the search to find a legitimation for the foundations of the voluntary association (*societas* or *consociatio*) of autonomous human beings or individuals [Dumont 1986: 73] after the disappearance of the feudal order. The "social contract" was the end result, a solution expressed with greatest clarity by Rousseau. It was forgotten that the substitution of *societas* to the medieval *universitas* completely left out of the view that the human community was conceptually and biologically prior to the society founded by autonomous individuals [ibid. 74, 77-78]. Rousseau, of course, realized that shared values are the real cohesive link in and among human groups: "Customs are the moral life of a people, and as soon as they cease to respect them, there is no rule but the passions, no restraint but the laws."[7]

The individual thus is an empirical subject and an independent, autonomous being, bearer of particular values, transcending its contextual reality. Habermas speaks of two aspects of individual identity, namely self-determination and self-realization, both of which presuppose the "Others," the mutual recognition of each other in the community [Habermas 1984-1989, Vol. II: 101]. Scheler stressed emphatically the importance of the co-identity of individual and collectivity, and gave pre-eminence to the latter. One of his formulations is strikingly similar to the ideas of Habermas:

"The basic nexus is this: there can be *no society without life-community* (though there can be life-community without society). All *possible* society is therefore *founded* through community. This proposition holds both for the the manner of 'accord' and for the kind of formation of a *common will*" [Scheler 1973: 531; italics in original].

It is very unfortunate that Tönnies' insight concerning the difference between *Gemeinschaft* (community) and *Gesellschaft* (society) did not serve but to crystallize the conviction regarding the necessity of the juxtaposition of community and society, with the corollary of the (unfortunately) happy conclusion that *Gemeinschaft* disappeared in modernity and was replaced by *Gesellschaft*.

Rom Harré's dualistic presentation of the person and the self should be recalled here. His distinction is one between "the individuality of a human being as it is publicly identified and collectively defined, and the individuality of the unitary subject of experience" [Harré 1989: 388]. Thus, an individual is a person as interpreted within a social or interpersonal framework on the basis of his intentionality declared in acts and speeches. Selves are contingent and nonempirical entities, that cannot be experienced interpersonally but they unify the perceptions, feelings, and beliefs of a person. The "sense of self" is a person's belief system, as related to the "centered" structure of experience; that is, the person is located in a primary structure, the self is located in a secondary structure. In Kant's analysis of the self, as summed up by Harré, human experience is characterized by three realities: being a spatiotemporal manifold; belonging to a world of causally interacting objects; and constituting a coherent field of consciousness. Adopting this Kantian description, Harré consequently expresses the holistic view that only "by virtue of the unity of the sequence of experiences as a series that the singularity of an experiencing self is presented since we are all agreed that it is not presented in itself" [ibid. 386]. Through the concept of agency, defined as acting intentionally, he links moral and social responsibility not to persons, but to the primary structure of culturally divergent moral orders.

Individual and community are constantly interacting in an organic framework, mutually influencing each other in the sense that the community and its shared value and belief systems partially define and articulate the evolution of the individual's life. Conversely, the individual, on the basis of its own unique life experiences, contributes to modifying the evolution of culture, the community's worldview and lifeworld.

(b) THE LIFEWORLD

Schutz defines the lifeworld as the "directly experienced social reality" [Schutz 1967: 142] representing the spatiotemporal community to which one belongs. It is also contiguous with the social world of one's contemporaries, the world of one's possible experiences. Those who "coexist," that is, whose lives have a simultaneous duration constitute the contemporary world. Whereas the subjective experiences of others are part of one's directly experienced world, the subjective experiences of other contemporaries are only inferred from indirect evidence through cultural channels communicated through shared attitudes and approaches. The lifeworld also includes the social world of predecessors and successors. The former are those whom one knows from history, who are part of one's cultural background but with whom only a unilateral interaction can take place, as they have already passed away. The latter are completely unknown and the sole basis of inference as to their individuality and experiences is the belief in the continuity of the cultural heritage, mediated by the transmission of values and beliefs from us to them through channels of tradition and through everyday life's realities.

Schutz' concept of the "directly experienced social world" is based *"on intentional conscious experiences directed toward the other self"* [ibid. 144; italics in original]. In fact, social interaction is derived from the above, as the "directly experienced social reality" is its motivational context, because the object of intentional behavior is, in fact, the expectation of the other being's intentional behavior. In this case, the "intentionally conscious experiences directed toward another self," the "Other-orientation," is first positing the Other's existence; the existence of a transcendental alter ego [ibid. 164]; only later is this positing extended to the particular characteristics, the actualized determination of this other *Dasein*. Giving a sign, for example, becomes an interaction when it aims at affecting the other, when it constitutes an act of communication. Social interaction is therefore taking place when a person acts and expects the other will respond, or, at least, will notice the first person's initiative. These mutually interdependent attitudes are, in Schutz' world, consecutive to the pure, face-to-face relationship with the other, to the immediate and direct understanding of the other's reality.

In the same sense, communicative interaction is based on attitudinal motivations, which lead the self from the genuine intentional action toward the immediate other, to the world of indirectly-known but coexistent contemporaries, to the predecessors and successors in the historical past and in the unfathomable future. Though there is simultaneity of actions and attitudes, the transition from direct to indirect social experience follows the path of "decreasing vividness" in respect to contemporaries, predecessors, and successors. The growing distance between the Thou-relationships and the relationship to contemporaries, predecessors, and successors is proportionate with waning directness and immediateness.

In contrast to the Schutzian phenomenological conception of the social world, Habermas' formulation of the concept of the lifeworld is entirely based on a cultural/linguistic definition, reflecting shared interpretive patterns; the lifeworld of mutual understanding is constituted by culturally pre-interpreted notions of the triple world concept, encompassing objective, social, and subjective worlds [Habermas 1984-1989, Vol. II: 124-126]. Language and culture, as constitutive elements of the lifeworld, according to Habermas, indicate that the situation of man in the lifeworld denotes a certain degree of transcendence in comparison with formal world-concepts. The lifeworld is always in the background, even if it is not consciously taken into account; it can be actualized any time. Therefore, it is logical to say that lifeworld is, as a social *a priori*, built into the language which is the medium of intersubjectivity and mutual understanding.

At this point in the analysis of the lifeworld, the function of meaning has to be addressed. In the Schutzian phenomenological view, meaning is, first of all, the product of one's experience [Schutz 1967: 42], and a selective attitude of the self, based on intersubjectivity, the Thou-experience. Every meaning is embedded in a meaning-structure or meaning-stratification, and intentional acts result in the actualization or crystallization of meaning-structures to which the individual is predisposed. This corresponds to the "preinterpretive" aspect of Habermas' lifeworld. Such pre-interpretation, meaning-structure, and meaning-stratification embodied in a specific culture that link the directly perceived world of the person with the world of contemporaries, predecessors and successors, represent an intersubjective belief and value system, a treasure of intersubjective knowledge and thought. This intersubjective content, an ever newly-emerging world, is apprehended by individuals who not only may modify them in accordance with their experiences, but also relate them to the passage of life, to temporality, or, more properly expressed by Husserl, to one's internal time-consciousness. *Culture is then the depository of meaning-structures deposited over time and space in those communities which are bearer of that culture. These structures therefore are invariant until the culture lives in its bearer-communities, though each meaning-endowing self can inflect or modify them as well.*

A final aspect of the lifeworld is its recent structural differentiation in the West. Durkheim saw this differentiation as that between culture, society, and personality, whereas Habermas suggests that the rationalization in contemporary Western civilization takes the form of structural differentiation, which is extremely important from the point of view of the disjunction of modernity and non-modernity. The structural differentiation of the lifeworld consists essentially of three phenomena: uncoupling of worldviews from the society's institutional system; uncoupling the renewal of cultural value and belief systems from tradition, favoring individuals' innovative initiatives and, thereby, promoting the need for "increasingly variable formal competencies;" and uncoupling cognitive structures and societal orders, such as the legal and moral orders, from the lifeworld through extensive generalization and formalization [Habermas 1984-1989, Vol. II: 145-147].

(c) TEMPORAL DIMENSION AND TRADITION

Temporal Dimension

Schutz' analysis of human interaction, placed within the dialectical interdependence of individual and community, is closely tied to the Husserlian internal time-consciousness and Bergson's *durée*. Bergson juxtaposes *durée*, or the inner stream of consciousness in perpetual movement of emerging and disappearing heterogeneous events, experiences and expectations, with the homogeneous time of the spatiotemporal world, discontinuous, divisible, and quantifiable.

Tying the concept of time to an *a priori* given framework of "pure subjective time-consciousness," expressing the phenomenological content of lived experiences, was best expressed and thoroughly elaborated by Edmund Husserl. He taught that space and temporality were intuited phenomenological data, implying primary intentionality inherent in perception, memory, and expectation; therefore a phenomenological analysis, taking into account only *immanent* time, would give the right perspective on directly experienced concrete duration. Temporal objects, as well as temporally constitutive acts, are both spreading, in their content, over an interval of inner-time; consequently, he excluded all reference to empirically *objective* time and space. "In the object there is duration, in the phenomenon, change" [Husserl 1964: 27]; in this axiom, Husserl refers to the fact that sometimes we can subjectively sense a temporal sequence, when objectively, there is but coexistence of the event experienced. He attributes this difference to the "objectification" of the lived and experienced event, that is, its transfer, due to the unity of experience, into the context of the experience of nature in which objectivity and regularity reign [ibid. 27-29 and 47]. The fading past remains present as "retention," the present is a "now-apprehension," and the future is encompassed in "protensions" corresponding to the intentionality of consciousness.

The content of *retentional consciousness, or memory* is remembrance; it is not a now but a *remembered now* that differentiates it from perception. It is a reproduced content the certainty of which is guaranteed by the coincidence in internal time of the reproductive and retentional processes. Perception and non-perception constitute "a single continuum which is constantly modified" [ibid. 62]. The consciousness of unity is finally due to the intuitive reproduction of the present as a boundary-point between time-intervals; the reproduced past sensations and events are part of a unique chain. In conclusion, every lived experience, in the Husserlian temporal perspective, is either impression or reproduction constituted in temporal consciousness (it's individualizing aspect) and, at the same time, constituted in the objective, real time (its universal, pre-immanent aspect).

In the ontological/cosmic perspective, the juxtaposition of internal time-consciousness and world-time disappears, because the inner-stream of duration, the events, experiences, and expectations apprehended in the *durée*, are all placed in the framework of world-time, which includes all individual *durée*. This oscillation of the human being between inner-time and authentic time is resolved and, at the same time, given unity by the reflexive transcendence of his experiences, expectations and events located in inner-time consciousness but recognized as situated in world-time through the mediating effects of culture and community. The "growing older together" of Schutz' philosophy is simultaneously a happening in the inner *durée* and world-time. The essence of consciousness is thus simultaneously immanent and transcendent.

Reinhart Koselleck developed the modern phenomenological approach in his analysis of experience and expectation. This pair of concepts embodies, for him, past and future from the standpoint of the present. He defines experience as "the present past, whose events have been incorporated and can be remembered" [Koselleck 1985: 272]. With reference to the modern feeling of temporality which, in the name of progress, transfigures history into a diachronic sequence, eliminating all differences, Koselleck speaks of the "contemporaneity of the noncontemporaneous" [ibid. 89]. Experience contains unconscious modes of conduct, not present in the awareness, as well as a reconstruction of past events and occurrences. Expectation, on the other hand, is "at once person-specific and interpersonal...it is the future made present; it directs itself to the not-yet, to the non-experienced, to that which is to be revealed" [ibid. 272]. *The difference between experience and expectation is a consequence of the fact that past and future never coincide; experience made is complete. It is past as an occurrence or event, whereas anticipation in terms of expectation is tied to the multiple possibilities of the unknown, to an infinity of temporal extensions.* Experience is composite. It represents a totality of earlier experiences which are simultaneously present without an indication of their before or after; ignoring chronology, experience leaps over time and does not create continuity. The horizon of expectation promises and ensures new experiences which can only be prognosticated, but never known in advance. The penetration of the horizon of expectations is creative of new experiences. The ever-changing pattern of experience and expectation creates tension in individual and collective life, and generates, in Koselleck's view, historical time.

Thus, human groups fundamentally determine the temporal horizon. Luhmann's definition of time "as the social interpretation of reality with respect to the difference between past and future," therefore means that change "predetermines the universality of time at the cultural level," though each cultural elaboration results "in variations in conceptualization and perspectives" [Luhmann 1982: 274]. As all temporal structures are related to a determinate present, a correlation can be established between a society's temporal framework and other social and cultural variables. Developments in the modern world, characterized by Koselleck [1985: 275] as *the growing distanciation of expectations from experiences and resulting in a coexisting plurality of times* appear to justify Luhmann's hypothesis that "increasing system differentiation correlates with an increasing dissociation between past and the future" [Luhmann 1982: 276]. It is then logically deductible from this dissociation that ever-larger discontinuities shorten human time-perspectives, thus the remote past and distant future both become irrelevant.

Social communication therefore represents one form of nontemporal extension of time,[8] it transforms "remote temporal relevance into present social relevance," in a selective way, replacing one temporal horizon with another [ibid. 306]. In fact, Luhmann defines social systems as nontemporal extensions of time, "making time horizons of other actors available within one contemporaneous present" [ibid. 285]. Complex social systems require abstractions as coordinating generalizations, in order to make it possible for men to relate to, if not integrate into, histories of different systems. This is the reason for abstractly measured dimensions of time and of chronological series; for highly differentiated functional societies, the abstract, generalized time measurements must have the characteristics of homogeneity, reversibility, determinability, and transitivity. This highly abstract, generalized way of visualizing time makes possible a uniform measurement, the simultaneous perception of the running processes of all systems, physical, social, or cultural.

The *iteration of reflexivity of temporal modalities* signifies that one considers the possibility of actualities as much as the actuality of possibilities or the possibility of possibilities. The iteration of the reflexivity of modalities opens up an extremely wide range of visions of time, of future presents, present presents, and past presents because, for example, it is possible to talk about future presents as future presents contain more possibilities than can be realized; or, in respect to past presents, one can envisage them as more than a simple sum of single past presents. Each present's past can be conceived as constituted in a multiple way and future horizons contain, inevitably, their own temporal perspectives.

The perspective of eternity was lost, the one-dimensionality of time makes the temporal space between past and future a *terra incognita*; in modernity, everything becomes historical because the "direction of time is the direction of history" [Luhmann 1992: 282]. Social structures and development condition the arrow of time and the course of history. Luhmann considers that processes in modernity led from progress as the temporal link between different historical phases through social differentiation and complexity to evolutionary improbabilities, in the sense of negative entropy or "increasing artificiality" of societal institutions and collective approaches to resolve common problems [ibid. 281-283]. A further consequence of the dominance of one-dimensional temporality and historical perspective, corresponding to the evolutionary improbability, is that societal change becomes a universal but abstract process; in fact, the process of change is replacing the order within which it took place during past ages, and for modern consciousness change became the normal state.

Gadamer enriched his concept of "effective-historical consciousness" with the important distinction between "situation" and "horizon." In his terminology, "situation" represents a "standpoint that limits the possibility of vision," whereas "horizon" means "the range of vision that includes everything that can be seen from a particular vantage point' [Gadamer 1985: 267]. Therefore, simply living in a "situation" leads to viewing only what is near and the overvaluation of what enters one's vision; contrarily, to have a "horizon" signifies being able to see beyond the immediate and the near, to relativize, to compare, and to make a more balanced judgement [ibid. 269-270]. In fact, Gadamer denies that there are "closed horizons," insurmountable cultural boundaries. Human life is never restricted to one exclusive standpoint. Man moves in a horizon and his horizon moves with him when he changes his environment. Nevertheless, to move together with historical horizons does not mean to abandon one's own world. It does not entail passing into alien worlds, because one's own world and those of Others constitute a single human horizon, hence Gadamer's expression of "fusion of horizons," embracing everything contained in historical consciousness. Various horizons, various cultures, are all rooted in *Dasein*'s existence, in man's Being-there-in-the-world.

As a consequence of man's living in time, both inner and world-time, an action is always a projected act; the action is the process, and the act is the result. From this conclusion, it follows that the meaning of an action is the projected act itself, and that rational action is one, which is defined in accord with the projected goals, final or intermediate. In this case, however, actions bear a temporal character as much as experiences. They can be considered as meaningful or rational in a retrospective glance of recoverable memory through the integrating function of the mind. But the project already exists in the present and its span constitutes the unity between action and act. It is therefore evident that the meaning and rationality of actions are entirely dependent on the temporal context, whether they are based on the intentional grasp of direct experience, inference from formerly lived experiences, or on willed modifications of the self.

Tradition and Values

Tradition and values represent perhaps one of the most controversial issues in contemporary thought, namely, whether traditions and values condition all human, especially mental, activities. The best expression of the modern scientific dogma of objectivity is the ethical postulate of the biologist Jacques Monod [Monod 1972: 176]. He believed that no endeavor can be scientific or objective which is avowedly biased because of traditionally transmitted or self-imposed values not adequate to be tested, experimentally or otherwise, and not corresponding to intersubjectively recognized, recurrent, and explicable phenomena.

Dewey, on the contrary, accepted that "values are values, things immediately having certain intrinsic qualities. Of them as values there is accordingly nothing to be said; they are what they are" [Dewey 1958: 396]. Beliefs convictions, moral, or artistic principles are not to be the subject of discussion, their effects are unforeseeable as they are immediately grasped. They serve to delineate group identity, and constitute the basis of what Bell calls "ritually constructed traditions and communal identities" [Bell, Catherine 1992: 121-123].

A completely different approach to the problem of values is taken by Kenneth J. Arrow, who wrote on the role of values in collective decision-making [Arrow 1951 and 1979]. He admitted that "significant actions involve joint participation of many individuals." Going still further against the current of individualism, Arrow recognized that there is social or group action, distinct from the individual action, and that such an action is a *sui generis* fact in social life, not only the sum of individuals' decisions and actions. From the societal phenomenon of collective or interpersonal actions, he derived the necessity of a public or social value system guiding the collectivity in its choices, though admitting the central role of the individual in the process of social choice between alternative possibilities of action. Thus, he qualified the liberal position (the "principle of limited social preference") as being itself a value judgement. Social choices are second-order evaluations or judgements, and the constitutive social decision process "assigns to any set of individual preference orderings a rule for making society's choices among alternative social actions in any possible environment" [Arrow 1979: 120].

Gadamer launched his attack in favor of cultural prejudgments or traditional values against the Enlightenment's adulation of reason and the subsequent banning of prejudices from human thinking by rationalism. For Gadamer, prejudices are not necessarily erroneous, distorting the truth, they are simply conditions of life for all of who live in our own cultural worlds [Gadamer 1976: 9]. There is no real antithesis between tradition and reason, especially if one considers tradition as an element of freedom and history. Gadamer's image of tradition and prejudice is essentially dynamic. According to his theory, tradition does not survive by inertia, but requires continuous re-examination, affirmation and interpretation, [Gadamer 1985: 250]. Tradition means primarily preservation, in which reason is active, not in an ostentatious but inconspicuous way. He emphasizes the criticism of one of the main illusions of contemporary culture that only what is new, planned or projected through human demonstrative effort is an act of reason.

Among those recognizing the importance of tradition was Heesterman, who defined it "as the way society formulates and deals with the basic problems of existence" [Heesterman 1985: 10]. Yet he completes this definition with the caveat that tradition always has to be bound with the preoccupations of an ever-changing present. This correlation means that tradition shares in culture's adaptability as an action-oriented information system, and not only does not oppose change, but also often legitimizes it.

Hayek, recognizing that values are historically grounded, defined custom and tradition as "both non-rational adaptations to the environment," but points out that social practices such as these will have to prove their beneficial effects for a social group "before selection by evolution can become effective" [Hayek 1988: 136]. Tradition, for Giddens, is the basis for providing people with a sentiment of ontological security, in particular, if combined with routine as ritual [Giddens 1990: 105 and Giddens 1991: 167]. In this sense, traditions always have a "binding," normative character and are part of the "internally referential" life concept of modernity, even assuming a co-ordination between past and present.

Alasdair MacIntyre most recetnly addressed the problem of traditions. For MacIntyre, all forms of social institution, organization, and practice are embedded in traditions. The problem raised by modernity is that traditions presuppose their own type of practical rationality and, therefore, each person belonging to a tradition gives his own motivated answer to problems of society. There is no standard answer based on "universal" rationality which would permit a final judgement, the "common ground" is a condition, not a result, of understanding [MacIntyre 1988: 400]. As thought and language are interdependent, every tradition expresses itself through particular utterances and actions, through particular cultural and symbolic patterns; its essence is embedded in linguistic and expressive forms. Translations from one scheme into another, or understanding people belonging to other traditions, is possible although the indefinite multiplicity of interpretations is paralleled by the indefinite multiplicity of translations, "since every translation is an interpretation" [ibid. 386]. MacIntyre sets forth the most important precondition of any dialogue between representatives of different cultures and traditions when he claims that only a tolerant attitude, renouncing hegemonic intentions, can be the foundation of a true inter-civilizational dialogue.

One of the contemporary philosophers who clearly indicate the changing moods of our times is Hilary Putnam. Putnam attacks the "cultural institution" [Putnam 1981: 127] that affirms that fact and value stand for completely disjointed realms, and that this dichotomy is absolute. For him this distinction is "hopelessly fuzzy" [ibid. 128] because factual statements and the methodology of scientific inquiry decide what is considered or a fact, thus presupposing values. The question then is what are these values? The advocates of the dichotomy recognize the existence of value-presuppositions such as the coherence, simplicity, and, above all, the truth-values of statements based on the equivalence principle. Putnam recognizes that scientific values of coherence or simplicity, among others, "are as historically conditioned" [ibid. 136] as our concepts of kindness, beauty, or goodness; in fact, he puts epistemic values in the same category as ethical and aesthetic values. The greatest underlying problem is therefore which is the most rational concept of rationality. This question poses exactly the same difficulty as judging or evaluating ethical or cultural values, because there is no neutral position from which to judge, no independent frame of reference, no understanding apart from the human condition.

Eric Weil[9] one of the numerous scientists who revised the usual scientific position, considered the problem of values in our modern culture on the basis of the Humean conviction that there is no path from fact to value, but that in a civilization there are coherent value systems, each of which admits a "logical, and thus decidable" debate, a possibility for rational discourse and discussion. However, this is so only for those who share the fundamental axioms of a value system in a given civilization. Applying such a consideration to science, scientific values cannot be proven because "the very idea of proof — the appeal to consistency of discourse — presupposes that these values have been acknowledged beforehand," just as Monod acknowledged the necessity to accept objectivity without proof as a value. For Weil, science as a human activity is based on certain values. It is embedded in a given world, in an existing web of values or axioms, and it is part of a historical evolution ("successive self-interpretations of man"). In fact, exact sciences strive to know and not to understand; man understands and understood before he tried to know, scientifically, the world. "Understanding is an anthropocentric manner, is older than science and more profound." Weil concludes that science became autonomous, "a value in itself" in the modern world, a "universal measuring rod for values." Science, the true science, was overlade by an unscientific ideology.

Tradition and Values in Non-Western Civilizations

The crucial role of traditions and values in all non-Western civilizations is well known. The impact of modernity on the "Otherness" of these age-old but living traditions has been discussed extensively throughout the past two hundred years.

In the case of *Japan*, it is important to remember that in this country modernization did not necessitate a complete overhaul of the symbolic and value spheres, but was embedded in the existing social and symbolic order.   The case of Japan constitutes one of the most intriguing examples of a successful combination of its proper symbolic-traditional heritage and values related to Western structural-organizational differentiation.

Dilworth points out that Japanese modernization did not start with the *Meiji* era, but much earlier, in the seventeenth century; this age is characterized by the Japanese, who distinguish the *kinsei* (Confucian) and *kindai* (Western) stages, which, in fact, meant that the earlier value-system remained the matrix for the later sedimentation of foreign ideas.   The Japanese culture, which at some periods vigorously assimilated foreign ideas and values (for example, in the internalization of the Confucian value system), did not replace the older, traditional value structure, but absorbed the "imported" values in a sort of "stadial" layering into its overall framework. An excellent description of the Japanese modernization process and a good example of Gadamer's "fusion of horizons," was put forth by *Watsuji Tetsuro* in *The Stadial Character of Japanese Culture*. He thought, in Dilworth's words, that

> The synchronistic coexistence of various sediments of Japanese value traditions in a variety of integrative contexts... The Japanese cultural quantum-lattice, as it were, allows for the fact that transcended elements live on as transcended elements, and thus provide for a complex pattern of interflow among stadially inter-present levels and their potential energies, in a given context of integration [Dilworth 1979, 472].

This was due, according to Dilworth's argumentation, to the acceptance of Confucianism under the reign of *Ieyasu*, followed by the adoption of the practical teachings of the *Sung* and *Ming* philosophies, which made possible the appearance of a worldview based on the free development of man's nature and mind. *Shushigaku* functioned under the *Tokugawa* as the central value system that secured the survival of the earlier strata of ethical values in the form of the above described "stadial" coexistence.   Dilworth uses the expression "pluralistic consciousness" to explain this concept, meaning a multiplicity of intentionalities in the cognitive, moral, religious, or aesthetic fields. Robertson writes about different components of the Japanese belief-system catering to different needs, and considers that between these different components an *interlegitimation* takes place [Robertson 1992: 94-95].

Another explanation of the Japanese miracle was given by Bellah, who emphasizes the "'group loyalty" of the Japanese, acknowledging that "value is realized in groups which are thought of as natural entities" (*Gemeinschaften, kyodotai*) [Bellah 1971: 378-380], practically eliminating the tension between universalistic and individualistic tendencies. It is in the nation, and in this framework only, that particularities, for example, loyalty to the head of one's collectivity, take on their real importance. The high marks given to performance are also explicable as a means of goal-attainment, a cultural and social dimension of the integrative values' predominance. This conceptualization explains that modifications in the society's politico-economic value-system do not create social and cultural upheavals, a sudden and radical shift in the goal-content, insofar as the highest authorities authenticate it. It is also evident that the primacy of the integrative value-orientation imposes conformity with all social and cultural conventions, a feature of Japanese society that limited mobility between social classes. To explain the Japanese success in modernizing the nation's economic and political life, Bellah also affirms that its reason is the "contentlessness" of the old Japanese *Shinto* religious framework, which was then filled with successively borrowed systems. However, this view does not seem plausible, as it ignores the Neo-Confucian developments under the *Tokugawa* period, the survival of the old belief and value system even when Confucian thought was internalized in the Japanese mental processes. Watsuji Tetsuro's view is much more convincing. Bellah's conclusion is certainly valid: "The continuity is mainly in the realm of values and the structure of group life. The change is mainly in cultural content and large-scale institutional and organizational forms" [ibid. 385].

Heesterman analyzed *Indian* traditions in great detail, particularly the effect of *dharma* on culture and society in an attempt to explain the difficulties the Indian civilization faces today. He recognizes that *dharma*, inexorable destiny and unbroken tradition during thousands of years, reflects a monolithic, predetermined, and immutable order of things. Reality is then atemporal and not subject to changes which intervene during consecutive world ages. In the *dharmic* system, the essential obligation of man is to avoid any kind of worldly motivation and immanent causation for one's actions and related events. In Heesterman's view, *dharma* poses an insoluble dilemma to people living in the Hindu cultural orbit, but he presumes that precisely because of this dynamic inner tension between the temporal and the atemporal requirements, the Hindu culture shows a certain degree of adaptive flexibility as a tradition. He concludes that the dilemma of *dharma* reflects the inner conflict of the immanent and the transcendent; its immanence in the lifeworld and its transcendence of the latter offering redemption from the sufferings and evils of earthly life.

Albert Hourani's words about the "lost generations" in the Arab world are well-known; he referred to people who were educated in Western ways and, consequently, lost their national, cultural, Islamic heritage without really assimilating Western belief and value systems or being assimilated into a Western-type society. This is all the more striking in that the cognitive and experiential background of Middle Eastern Muslim peoples is similar to that of those who were brought up in the Western culture.   Although these similarities between the Christian and Islamic cultures resulting from a monotheistic faith and the classical Greek heritage appear to be one of the main sources of the antagonism between the two civilizations.

The Moroccan writer Abdallah Laroui distinguishes between "tradition-structure" and "tradition-value" or, simply expressed, traditional value system and traditional social structure. He believes that when the two coincide, the community or society is homogeneous, avoiding fundamental conflicts among its members. This is even more valid for societies in which transmission of fundamental traditional beliefs and values is predominantly oral. Homogeneity is broken when the traditional social structure is modified. Thus, the community is broken; that is, the traditional value-system remains intact, but the corresponding social structure evolves in accordance with the actual experience of people, the "lived tradition" [Laroui 1974: 55-57]. Laroui therefore seeks the convergence of Arab identity and actual authenticity through emancipation from tradition and Western domination as well as through the historic process of integration of Arab identity into a universalistic conception of mankind. He abandons the idea of the reconstitution of a purely Arab authenticity, but accepts the recognition of the European or Western "other" in the perspective of transcendental universalism, as "to recognize the universal is to become reconciled with oneself" [Laroui 1967: 164].

In contemporary Muslim countries the traditional belief and value system, on the one hand, and the societal structure, on the other hand, are not homogeneous any more, though their disjunction is far from complete. This is partly the result of the impact of modernity in the whole Mediterranean basin, the area most exposed to Western influence in the non-Western world. Many thinkers acknowledge that the present backwardness of the Arabo-Islamic civilization in technology, social, economic and political development, as compared to that of the contemporary West, is probably due to the symbolic "closing of the gates of *ijtihad*," the elimination of free reflection, of free individual search for immanent solutions, being bound forever to the hitherto-established verities, values, and norms *taqlid*).

Arabs like *Hasan Saab*, who try to determine how to modernize their countries while safeguarding their basic religious beliefs and cultural values conceive of Islam as a dynamic system, an ideological framework "whose civilization can always be creatively renovated with the help of creative minds"' [Boullata 1990: 68]. Many Muslim thinkers agree with this opinion, among them Indian Muslims, including *Muhammad Iqbal*, who, in *The Reconstruction of Religious Thought in Islam* linked the reopening of the gates of *ijtihad* to contextual relativity, or to the temporal and spatial limitation of the consensus (*ijma*), giving a new historical perspective to the development of Islam. In the same vein, one of the Arab reformers, *Abd al-Wahhab Khallaf*, in view of the disturbances and upheavals in the age when the gates of *ijtihad* were closed, insisted that not personal *ijtihad* should be reopened but a collective *ijtihad*, a collective legislation on the basis of the *Sharia,* an *ijtihad* joining the concept of *ijma*. This would represent the agreed upon opinion (though personally reached) of such learned men who possess the required moral and intellectual qualities.

Muhammad Abduh, employing standard reformist strategy, distinguished between essential and inessential doctrines in Islamic teaching. All the pronouncements related to the fundamental questions of life, such as belief in God, worship, death, morals, and religious life are essential. Living in accordance with the *Quranic* imperatives necessitates following not only the prophetic revelation but reason as well; the latter serves as a sort of interpreter of the more complex doctrines, especially those contained in the prophetic traditions, the *hadith*. If reasoning does not clarify what the sources of revelation say, then one has to submit oneself to the Word of God or to the prophetic commands without searching further.

The main theoretician of the Muslim Brotherhood movement, who paid with his life for the ideas he fought for, *Sayyid Qutb*, followed a different path from that of other Muslim reformists examined above. First, he affirmed that the whole world, being God's creation, the sacred law (*Sharia*) and natural law, or the law of creation (*sharia kawniyya*) cannot but be two aspects of the same reality. Existence is becoming, process, and movement and man understand the world through intuition and representation, expressing himself through intentional action. The fundamental linkage of sacred and natural laws in human life ought to be achieved through what Binder calls "ontological integration," an all-embracing coordination of human motivation and behavior with those of other creatures, including other human beings [Binder 1988: 189]. Man's alienation from the natural and human environment cannot be overcome, according to Qutb, but through the Islamic faith. From this radical standpoint Qutb's second important thesis is derived. This notion rejects all sorts of idealism, essentialism, and intellectualism, and requires from Muslims a total commitment to existential *praxis*, as a life devoted to God. Experience is not phenomenological or discursive but direct and based on God's creation. Islamic faith and Islamic praxis are one. Qutb makes Islamic commitment anti-determinist, contextual or situational, in the sense that a Muslim's consciousness and intentional action are fully integrated into prevailing conditions and circumstances of the community.

A completely different version of Islamic reformism was the conceptual framework worked out by *Ziya Gökalp* for Turkey at the beginning of the century. *Gökalp* was convinced of the applicability of the evolutionary perspective to religious and social matters, understood as differentiation through mutual interaction [Rosenthal 1965: 52]. He traced a simple developmental process from primitive to organic society, where primitive society is dominated by religion, but in an organic society, political and cultural values and customs are important as well. In fact, to these three value orders correspond three distinct social units: the *ummet* is centered on religious practice, the state incorporates the political principles and customs, while cultural beliefs and values create the nation. From this perspective of societal evolution, Gökalp, contrary to the authentic Islamic doctrine of the unity of the spiritual and material in the life of man, deliberately relinquishes Islam's grasp on Turkish society. He purports that religion should be restricted to spiritual institutions invested by the collective conscience of society, but it has no place in organizations and institutions which are active in the material world and in secular matters. Gökalp thus chose an entirely different path of reform from that followed by his Arab and Indian Islamic predecessors, who never doubted the all-encompassing relevance of religion in the life of society, though he also supported a reconciliation of religion and the necessities of contemporary civilization.

In the second part of this study, major areas of disjunction between the Western and non-Western cultural worlds will be highlighted. This is necessary as, in the first part, the evolutionary and ontological foundations of man's nature, capabilities, and culture were analyzed and, consequently, the philosophical-anthropological perspective was traced in which a dialogue or confrontation of contemporary civilizations may take place.

Based on these foundations, the most important points of disjunction from the point of view of structural and cultural characteristics of these civilizations must be examined to enable us to suggest where incommensurable and irreconcilable differences exist, or where a rapprochement is possible between the participants in inter-civilizational encounters. Disjunction in five particular areas of inter-civilizational relations — rationalism, together with ethics and morality, the interactive social order, ethnicity and nationalism, state and democracy, and, finally, economy and development — will be addressed in the following chapters in an effort to indicate those major problems which will have to be dealt with in a future inter-civilizational dialogue.

PART TWO

Disjunction Between the Western and Other
Cultural Worlds

CHAPTER FOUR

FROM UTILITARIAN TO MEANINGFUL RATIONALITY AND ETHICS

A. *Meaningful Rationality*

It is necessary to trace the contours of Western rationalism which evolved since the scientific discoveries of the seventeenth century and the Enlightenment, led to the quasi-inquisitional debates of the last decades (of which Newton-Smith, Hollis, and Lukes were, among others, the main protagonists). The rationalism/relativism debate created, since the time of Locke, a devastating confusion in people's minds, limiting their capacity to understand others; this confusion deepened with the seemingly triumphal progress of technology and instrumentalist reason. The post-war economic upswing and stability, despite the menacing threat of nuclear destruction, did not shake the foundations of this optimism in our rationalism and scientific reason. Paradoxically, an awakening began only in the last two decades following the increasing realization of ecological disaster, of the threatening overpopulation of the globe, and of the unexpected impoverishment of the quality of life at a moment when the global East-West conflict is a thing of the past. Indeed, more and more political and social conflicts have been born due to our "irrationality" in Western societies, as well as in the countries of other cultural worlds.

1. *The Essence of Western Rationalism*

Rooted in the late Middle Ages, modern Western rationalism was born from a profound longing for certitude in the domain of rational inquiry. This foundationalist drive grew parallel to the unexpected development in the natural sciences, and Descartes believed he had found the final refuge with his *"Cogito, ergo sum."* This was an unmistakable error, as thought is not a proof of being but is inherent in human existence as in the evolutionary perspective, especially, ontology precedes reasoning and knowledge. However, the gradually-confirmed predominance of the mathematical in human thought required and justified the search for ultimate and absolutely certain foundations, "a knowledge which becomes founded by knowing itself and allowing only this as known. Knowledge considers itself founded when it is certain of itself" [Heidegger 1985: 30]. The Cartesian *cogito* thus set the whole future development of Western thinking within the framework of foundationalism in cognitive terms and in the locus of the subject, the human person; the mathematical structure of reason was born, determining the structure of Being and striving to control nature, as well as other beings juxtaposed to the subject. Through this development, procedure (or method) also gained a marked predominance over content. Locke's transposition of science's reasoning to rational belief in general, and to problems in human society and culture in particular, carried this further. He identified reason with natural revelation and revelation with natural reason. For him, reason "must be our last judge and guide in everything."[1] Locke's position was only the first step in the gradual severing of relations with any ontological/cosmic worldview other than the one promoted by scientific reason. The religious unity of the world was lost, but it was rescued by the "self-evident validity of the natural order" [Gadamer 1976: 219], conceived in mathematical terms.

The correctness, even the possibility of the so-called foundationalist rationalism (or teleology of truth) depends on "the truth of realism," on the correspondence of rational conclusions to the reality of the physical world, just as results in the empirical sciences depend on the justification or non-falsification of hypotheses by experiment. Realism also means that a particular rational belief is rational because it is part of a whole pattern of rationally held beliefs and practices, or because it is a rationally conceived belief-system based on experientially upheld or non-falsified deductions from "first principles." Kant insisted on reason's universality; after Kant, the universalism of reason and the corresponding rules of inference in hypothetico-deductive thinking became a dogma. A truth and certainty for eternity replaced the ancient dogmas of Christianity.

Newton-Smith, one of the most ardent contemporary defenders of modern rationalism, expressed the fundamental relationship between truth and reasoning with great clarity. His argument against relativism is based entirely on the logic of propositions and inferences, which excludes any variation "in patterns of valid reasoning" [Newton-Smith 1984: 108 and 100]. He, however, recognized that reasons for acting are intertwined within a web of belief, especially in respect to conditions justifying that a belief stands as a reason to another belief. He called this pattern the "conditionalization of reason." Now, the concept of different reasons being conditioned by beliefs were held in a more or less coherent belief-system embedded in a spatial and temporal context. Newton-Smith considers that intelligibility and possible translation between different languages (and cultures) can be arrived at only when truth-conditions such as inferential logic or correspondence to reality, are the same for all interlocutors [ibid. 115-156].

In Donald Davidson's view, rationality and causality are interdependent ("reason is a rational cause"). Knowledge about another's system of beliefs and motives is gained by inference from evidence; we "impose conditions of coherence, rationality, and consistency" [Davidson 1980: 233] on the emerging picture. Rationality, coherence, and consistency in another's behavior makes it possible, in an intelligible way, for us to attribute attitudes and beliefs to him, to explain the other's actions without knowing exactly why and how he was motivated to act as he did.

For Martin Hollis and Steven Lukes the crux of the matter is relativism, as opposed to truth. After reviewing moral, conceptual and perceptual relativism, they relate the existence of incommensurable conceptual schemes to the existence of a common stock of "non-relative observational truths which serve to anchor communication" [Hollis-Lukes 1984 and Hollis 1984: 10-11]. Human thought and communication therefore are based on universal truths. The warrantability of beliefs is guaranteed by the belief system in which they are embedded, and such warranted belief becomes objectively rational whenever it passes the test with a minimum score. The test is presumably the degree of correspondence of a belief to the world, the perceptible reality. The basis of communication with people living in other cultures consists in shared precepts, concepts, judgements, and rules of judgement empirically discovered through encounters. This shared cognitive basis which refers to the empirically known physical world ("Whether or not the world is a fact, it is an indispensable presupposition") [ibid. 74] is Hollis' famous "bridgehead" without which no communication, no interpretation, and no translation is possible. "A massive central core of human thinking which has no history" [Strawson 1959: 10], a universal core of human beliefs, shared cognitive categories, and judgements made by everyone ("which a rational man cannot fail to subscribe to") [ibid.], constitute the "bridgehead." It is striking that nobody thought of the circularity of the argument, though this circularity is evident, as the universal core is required for interpretation and communication, but the core represents beliefs which are characteristic to rational man as conceived by our modern rationalists.

Steven Lukes deals somewhat differently with the problem of alternative standards of rationality; his conclusions oscillate between the dogmatic or context-related concepts, as he still maintained some old "hang-ups" of the empiricist philosophies, such as accepting reality as a simple, unqualified state of affairs or existence-conditions and equating truth-claims with correspondence to that reality ("copy theory of truth"). He recognizes two kinds of rationality: the first having universal validity, relevantly applicable to all beliefs in any context, and the second, context-dependent rationality, discovered by investigating that relevant cultural context. But even though recognizing the dual nature of rationality, Lukes suggests that criteria of universal rationality which simply *are* (supposedly unique and universal, such as logical rules) ought to be applied to evaluating context-dependent beliefs and actions, as well as their specific rationality criteria.

Thus, Lukes establishes a hierarchy of universal and context-dependent forms of rationality in which the latter are *de facto*, parasitic on the former. He derives this position from the perfectly legitimate expectation, an indispensable feature of human nature, that understanding between people speaking various languages and, consequently, growing up in different cultural worlds, can only be reached by reference to a common reality, independent from particular contexts, but shared by all. However, when he adds to this requirement the need of shared, formal, operational rules, our correspondence-truth concepts and logical procedures, to this condition for understanding other people and other cultures, because "these are the criteria of rationality," Lukes makes impossible any approach not only to other civilizations, but even to the normatively regulated or collectively or individually self-expressive domains of our own societies [Lukes 1970: 210].

2. Rationalism in the Social Sciences

In the social sciences, rationalism is still dominant in the form Max Weber formulated almost a century ago. It would be impossible to overestimate the influence of Weber's theory of rationalism and his concept of rationalization in world history. He enumerated four categories of rationality in social action: instrumentally rational, value-rational, affectual and traditional [Weber 1978, Vol. 1: 24]. The most important, in his view, was undoubtedly the instrumentally rational as linked to the value-rational through the expectation of rationally pursued and calculated ends [ibid. 26]. In another categorization, Weber speaks of formal and substantive rationality [ibid. 85] that correspond, however, to those designated above as instrumentally- and value-rational.

There are some remarkable features of Weber's definition of instrumental rationality. First, it is presented as a clearly calculative, probabilistic, amoral, and manipulative stance reflecting the needs of the developing free market and the industrial economy of his times; second, despite its above characteristics, it is not at all contradictory to the Weberian value-rationality, because instrumental rationality depends on and serves the aims of the individual who is rationally considering alternative means and thus the relative importance of different possible ends. Instrumental-purposive rationality is, of course, incompatible with affectual or traditional rationality because, from Weber's point of view, values are always irrational. This, however, is a *non sequitur*, because the concept of instrumental rationality presupposes value-rationality in the definition of self-interest; if the ends that are realized through instrumental action are irrational, then such an action must be irrational too. But the qualification irrational applies, in Weber's mind, only to fundamental, cultural, and ethical values (absolute goodness, beauty, devotion to duty, etc.), not to those which determine the self-interest of individuals. Instrumental rationality orients actions when they aim at the realization of an individual's or a collectivity's everyday physical or material interest.

Paul Ricoeur noted the overall impact of such a conceptualization of instrumental rationality: instrumental action became, from a sub-system of social interaction, a global principle of action-orientation, eliminating simultaneously the sphere of communicative action [Ricoeur 1981: 98]. Rationality motivated by tradition can be pursued self-consciously, in contrast to the "ingrained manner" of everyday practices habitually followed in an unreflective way. In case of such a self-conscious action respecting traditional rationality, the latter shades over into value-rationality. In this case, however, rational action abandons "the unthinking acceptance of ancient customs by deliberate adaptation to situations in terms of self-interest" [ibid. 30].

Weber was aware of the fact that choice between different values cannot be rationally justified (just as the choice of first axioms in deductive logic) because they are intuitively grasped or acquired through the socialization process. Weber therefore called fundamental values irrational. This led him to the conviction that only values generalized into abstract principles and internalized in a formalized frame can be effectively adopted in the modern age, and the process of rationalization is unavoidable. His intention is therefore clear: he posited the rationalization process of the world as *explanans*, in order to explain and justify the institutionalization of the instrumental-purposive rational orientation of action. For this reason, the disenchantment of ontological/cosmic interpretive systems (religions, myths, magic, ritual) is grasped under the universal-historical process of rationalization.

Following Habermas, we can deconstruct the Weberian rationalization of Western culture into the *systematization of worldviews* and the *inner logic of value spheres*. The first, more fundamental element of rationalization through "the formal organization of symbol systems, of religious systems in particular, as well as of legal and moral representations" [Habermas 1984-1989, Vol. I: 174-175], reflects a *sine qua non* requirement of modernity. Human rationality as embedded in an encompassing cosmic/ontological worldview was displaced by cognitive rationality and reduced later to a specific form of such rationality, the rationality of science. The second component of the process of rationalization is the complete differentiation of cognitive, normative/evaluative, and expressive spheres, as a consequence of disenchantment. Their "internal and autonomous logic" could be affirmed, though the overwhelming value of the rationalized cognitive sphere, through the language of science, absorbed more and more parts of the autonomy of the other spheres. It is, thus, not at all clear how Weber could speak of "value enhancing" (*Wertsteigerung*), as against technical progress through instrumental rationality.

Rationalization, or disenchantment, (or secularization, though the term has a narrower meaning than the other two) is a worldwide process in Weber's historical perspective, a movement from concrete, individualized, context- and content-related conceptions of religion, cosmos, world and man to an abstract, formalized, and generalizable representation that led, undoubtedly, to the global rejection of ontologically and cosmically anchored worldviews. This trend produced a double effect in the West: first, the generalization of an ethic based on inner religious faith derived, as pretended by Weber, from Protestantism; second, a strong, indomitable individualism. At the very opposite of this trend, the rationality of the impersonal ("but for this very reason ethically irrational") [Weber, op. cit. 584] took over the economic realm in the form of the logic of purely commercial relationships. Weber thus correctly saw that the degree of differentiation of the economic structure is inverse to the possibility of exercising personal control. In fact, the impersonal rationality in economy is the *par excellence* instrumental or purposive rationality that dominates the modern world. This caused religions as well as other ontological/cosmic worldviews, to be considered as irrational.

Weber's argument on rationality was adopted by almost all social scientists in our century. Parsons clearly adopts the Weberian stance; rationality, in his action theory, is practically identical with instrumentality, but with an epistemic requirement derived from scientific practice. Social theorists like Margaret Archer follow the standard rationalist approach; Archer bluntly states that the problem of translation in anthropological research is virtually non-existent: "If the natives reason logically at all, then they reason as we do... because logic being universal, it also is neutral" [Archer 1988: 110 and 137, note 90].

3. *Recent Changes of the Concept of Rationality in the Social Sciences*

The turnabout in philosophy and the social sciences left aside the exclusively cognitive approach of modern rationalism and took into account the notion that rationality cannot be considered independently of its lifeworld context. Peter Winch, a follower of Wittgenstein, considered that the nature and intelligibility of reality is an aspect of the relation between thought, language and reality. He emphasized that categories of thought, such as meaning or intelligibility, are "*logically* dependent for their sense on social interaction between men" [Winch 1958: 44]. Thus, principles of conduct and meaningful action are interwoven. Understanding an actor of another society is based on the discovery of motives of this actor, understood as analogous to the reasons of an agent who acted in that way (reasons and motives are not synonymous, for Winch). In this sense there cannot be regularities, because events similar in one social or cultural setting are not similar in another where judgements are dependent on the given mode of behavior dominant in that context. The fact of human intentionality makes the prediction of the outcome of actions or events very unreliable; historical "trends are in part the *outcome* of intentions and decisions of their participants" [ibid. 93]. Finally, Winch opposes the attitude that qualifies as non-logical acts or events that do not conform to Western rationality; understanding another *sui generis* mode of discourse is a *sine qua non* condition of being able to qualify some ideas or acts as same or different, which means that reference to a set of criteria established in one's own culture is not reasonable.[2]

Habermas' model of communicative rationality posits the lifeworld as "an intuitively known, unproblematic, and unanalyzable, holistic background" which "both forms the *context* and furnishes *resources* for the process of mutual understanding" [Habermas 1987: 298]. Understanding communicative action and the construction of rational interpretations are completely interwoven in interpretive understanding; the ontological comprehension of the lifeworld necessitates that parties reaching understanding judge their mutual argumentation and criticism, and that the validity claims and potential reasons confronted in the other's discourse are immediately grasped on a commonly shared basis [ibid. 314]. Communicative rationality presupposes an intuitive knowledge of the shared elements of the lifeworld, not thematized and not abstracted from the communicative consensus. This rationality is immanent in speech [ibid. 326]; rational communication, as defined by Habermas, contains universal ideas on truth and rightness which are closer to Weber's substantive or value-rationality than to the purposive-rational one. Participants in a communicative process of understanding are therefore expected to possess a shared cultural background; comprehension of the other's world is the core of communicative rationality. The cognitive, moral, and expressive elements are part of man's own self-description as they are constitutive of his self.

The rationality of actions, for Giddens, represents an individual's causal powers as an agent in social interaction. But Giddens adds two caveats to this concept of rationality. The first recognizes that though the individual reflexively monitors his actions, he is subject to unconscious influences that do not operate through his rational considerations. The second insists on external influences, circumstances that condition the individual's actions which are entirely independent from his conscious rationalizations. Thus he acknowledges that behind the individual's causal powers, there are beliefs which represent mutual knowledge in communicative interaction. This tacit knowledge, the constitutive part of practical consciousness (having reasons but not reasoning consciously), makes it necessary to distinguish "credibility criteria" from the classical "validity criteria" in order to understand reasoning patterns [Giddens 1984: 339 and 346]. Using Giddens' theory to examine contemporary culture, it follows that our Western society became a risk society in which the failure of the techno-scientific rationality, the prototype of instrumental rationality, to recognize the paramount ecological dangers created by its technological processes, represents the true irrational position [Beck 1992a: 54].

4. *The Concept of Rationality Reconsidered*

When reconsidering the concept of rationality from the point of view of a dialogue or conflict of civilizations, we have to start with the evolutionary fact that our intellectual and emotional capacities are biologically inherent in the species, shaped by the evolutionary adaptation to the world surrounding us. But, according to Julian Huxley, our cognitive and other faculties are only tools that can be instrumental for any purpose [Huxley 1989: 132]. If the history of modern Western rationalism is viewed with this caveat in mind, it becomes clear that modern rationalism went astray for specific historic reasons; lifeworld phenomena can neither be contained nor expressed by logical propositions or be justified or falsified in terms of any of the usual kinds of inference, *modus ponens*, or other methodological devices. The "iron cage" of rationalism and foundationalism excludes any differential emphases authorized by the ontological/cosmic outlook. It does not take into account, for example, that myth is a coherent thought, the coherence of which reflects a multidimensionality and a rationality other than the rationality of discursive thinking. Rationality *tout court* tends to globality, to a holistic grasp, but not to the Kantian rational unity or system. The common man does not participate in scientific activity, as he does in myth and ritual. Scientific rationality resides only in a specific methodology and each separate scientific domain has its own rationality, having a purposive-instrumental character. Rationality compartmentalized in accordance with the needs of specific domains break up the hitherto existing unity of the complex human experience.

In reconsidering the concept of rationality, then, one has to eliminate four elements: the utterly formalistic approach — safeguarding it only in the limited domain of logical inference; the seventeenth and eighteenth centuries' legacy of explaining all human behavior and action by man's natural desires as well as his solely utilitarian interests, thus excluding impulses related to his belief and value systems; the Weberian heritage of justifying the quasi-dominant role of purposive-instrumental rationality (which, anyway, was nothing else than the *ex post facto* justification of the prevailing trends in the scientific and market-oriented economic developments); and modern individualism which attributed rationality only to the person who was sovereign in his decisions, irrespective of being genetically endowed through the biological selective process and inextricably enmeshed in his community's accumulated memories and life-expectations. Finally, one has to avoid the complete isolation of rationality from an overall ontological and cosmic view, as if any valid rationality concept could be formulated without linking it to the global framework of life. The right direction of enquiry must be toward intentionality, which is the essential human phenomenon. An understanding that humans are able to grasp the modalities of the actual and the possible in the emergent phenomena is essential, as human experience and action both are envisaged intuitively, but not as formulated empirically.

What is therefore proposed is a *meaningful rationality*, not an empty formalism or a rationality which is linked to the intentional realization of values, beliefs, ideas, a rationality which belongs to a communal setting, expressing personal desires and utilities. The ends-means or instrumental rationality is not eliminated but dethroned; it has its validity only in some spheres of the lifeworld. In the evolutionary perspective, culture is considered as an action-oriented information system and as such, it pertains to the species' adaptive efforts, whatever its particular form and content. Rationality is meaningful if it serves humanity's survival, inclusive of the individual and the community together with their values and particularities.

As the best example of non-meaningful rationality in this ontological sense, one can cite that which engendered environmental problems, and, as culture has also to be considered part of human ecology, the destruction of plurality, of the vibrant variety of mankind's cultures. Environmental damage, the disappearance of cultures, the destruction of human values and degradation of human life over the last two hundred years were the result of this *meaningless*, purposive-instrumental rationality *asserting that any kind of logical inference and other (intellectually exciting) exercises cannot stand for human rationality if their guiding axioms are not deducted from the fundamental values and beliefs of human groups.* Methods of justification or falsification, however empirical, cannot protect this type of rationality from such truly devastating effects.

Meaningful rationality is *relational*. Reasons for acting and judging are contextual and rationality cannot, therefore, be universal; that is, if a reasoning is correct and valid in one circumstance, it is not necessarily applicable in other circumstances. Rationalism's universalistic pretensions were never justified, but simply assumed (Gellner 1992). Reasons relate human intentions to the community's values and beliefs (whether ethnic, national, religious, or other) to which the individual belongs, and to the the physical world which surrounds him. Human intentionality reflects a person's unique genetic endowment, his intuitive knowledge about the world (acquired during his whole existence), and his knowledge obtained through socialization which merges him in the culture, traditions, symbolic patterns and activities of his community. Man's mentally elaborated meaning-structure is derived from these various sources over the course of a life-long experience, and his corresponding rationality therefore reflects a relational web upon which reasons and motivations are based.

Meanings expressed through language, gestures, behavior, expressive creations in art, or through deeply felt emotions, sensations, and feelings, constitute the social and cultural worlds, and even penetrate an individual's views of the physical world of nature. Meaningful rationality gives a causal as well as a possible *and* actual explanation of actions and utterances, as it reflects actual possibilities and the possible actualization of them. Therefore, good reasons for an action cannot be reasons of an instrumental character because their evaluation or judgement by others depends on the meanings conveyed and on the meanings confessed. In other words, judgement is based on the values and beliefs held by intentional individuals, and cultural and social traditions crystallized and institutionalized in their communities during the lifetime of preceding and present generations.

This ontologically based rationality (rooted in intentionality, transcendence and culture) has its cosmic aspects as well. The cosmos represents the infinite space and the inexorable flow of time, and the human being is aware of the limitations these boundaries set for his rational efforts. Man's death-awareness relates him to the cosmos; to live a limited life span is the final determining element of human rationality because the inescapable shadow of death transforms the perspectives, modifies the meanings and their foundations in values, beliefs, feelings, emotions and perceptual sensations. But meaningful rationality placed into the ontological/cosmic framework also secures the famous 'core' of common percepts, beliefs and values that make possible understanding between humans of all cultures. It is not logical formulae, algorithms, or rational standards established by Western science and classical-foundational rationalism that constitute the universals on which understanding or interpretation is based. It is human phenomena, which are like natural phenomena because *they are as they are*, because they are given to all beings of our species as overwhelming reality, which constitute the "core" universals. It is, of course, not meant that these human capabilities, attitudes and norms are constitutive of rationality, but it is certainly essential to consider them as underlying meaning-variances which give sense to rational action and make good reasons to be good reasons. This concept of rationality, therefore, is valid and applicable in all civilizations or cultural worlds and it may even be a factor of understanding between them.

If the above presentation of meaningful rationality is accepted, there is no point in speaking of relativization of the concept of rationality to individuals, as a person's rational decision or act is based on the naturally-given constituents of life and the intersubjective context. The "cunning of reason" nevertheless introduces, through unintended consequences, a definite uncertainty in rational behavior and action because it is hard to read the activities of other minds, though a common foundation of belief and value systems in the same culture allows for some rational expectations concerning the intentions of others as their actions are also, at least partially rule-determined role-playing. Finally, in the classical-foundationalist model rationality and truth are inseparably linked in a one-way direction: false propositions cannot be rationally embraced, and rational thinking is bound to lead to the truth. This was a *sine qua non* requirement of the model that had to hold universally if it was to hold at all, because of the cognitive orientation of that type of rationalism. For meaningful rationality, the fundamental concept is, as for Hacking and Joseph Margolis, not truth as such but truth-or-falsity; it is based on a pluri-dimensional concept of truth defended by Ricoeur. It can lead to truth, to warranted assertability of a state of affairs, or even to a satisfactory accomplishment of a social role or a cultural function. *In fine*, this means that meaningful rationality provides an integrated set of definitions of reality, an all-things-considered view of life embracing man's ultimate concerns in the light of his "death-awareness" or, as Spinoza said, *sub specie aeternitatis*. Meaningful rationality, therefore, necessitates good judgement because such a judgement is the only option available to man leading to rational action. There is, of course, no way to ensure that judgements are correct, as no empirical methods of justification/falsification are at our disposal because, judgements deal with intentional and socially conditioned matters. Searle's considerations on intentionality, Brown's considerations on background knowledge [Brown, Harold 1988: 137], and relevance are perfectly applicable to meaningful rationality, because they justify the evident fact that not everybody does exercise judgement in a similar way; even in the same environment and genetic and cultural atmosphere, everyone does not necessarily possess the elements for a correct judgement, the same perspective of relevance, or the same "style of reasoning."

B. *Meaningful Ethics and Morality*

It might appear strange to the reader (who is not a Kantian) to treat the problem of ethics and morality together with rationality. In effect, this is made with the intent to juxtapose the tenets of the two main pillars in man's life, his rationality and his ethical existence, in a "disenchanted" world. Is it not true that "we cannot know what is rational without deciding what is best" [Hollis 1977: 137]?

1. *The Meaning of Ethics and Morality*

What do ethics and morality mean?   By ethics, I mean the fundamental convictions governing man's life.   Convictions are principles which are intimately linked to a culture's core of belief- and value-systems and, therefore, interrelated as much with religious beliefs as with rationality; whereas by morality I mean the practical aspect of man's behavior corresponding to, and derived from, ethical principles and convictions. Ethics and morality are simultaneously individual and collective, as both are rooted in the individual's mental or inner world and the world of culture in which he lives.   The problem for man is what is good and what is evil, what is right and what is wrong, how to conduct one's own life and the interactive existence in the human community while satisfying individual interests and intentions as well as cultural values and norms.

The Aristotelian "good life" is as much the subject of ethics as the identification of evil in terms of the worldview predominant in the culture of one's time and community; that is, the grasping of destructive forces within one's own the self and inherent in all extant beings. Good and evil are ontologically different from the rational and the irrational, and the two pairs cannot be fused, even if most present-day moralists deploy all possible artifices to do just that. The coercive *ought* is not an outgrowth of the comprehensive, factual *is*, because the two are inextricably linked in the holistic framework and each is constitutive of the other.[3] The difference between the "ought" and the "is" is a difference of modalities, of the possible and of the actual, and of the non-possible and of the non-actual. The possible can be viewed as non-actual and the actual can appear as non-possible. But these modal changes can only take place in the framework of one cultural world, in its core existential tenets such as beliefs and values.

2. The Foundation of Ethics and Morality

(a) RATIONAL ETHICS

The foundations of ethics and morals were derived by the philosophers of the last two hundred years: from reason; from intuition and sentiments; or from the imperatives of public life. Immanuel Kant was the foremost representative of rationalist ethics, David Hume stood for morals based on human sentiments, and George Herbert Mead and John Dewey represented those who determined ethical behavior by its social origins.

For Kant, reason is a faculty of the human mind the function of which is "to produce a *will* which is *good*, not as a *means* to some further end, but *in itself*" [Kant 1964: 64]. He did not deny that reason also has the purpose of producing a will which is good, as a means to happiness (though he compared this function of reason to the role of instinct in animals), but affirmed that human reason represented the highest cognitive level in finite beings, and must produce a will good in itself. Therefore, reason's function has to be entirely unconditioned by empirical reality, even if this was meant to restrain its purpose in the empirical world: the attainment of happiness and of good life. Moral principles derived from reason are known *a priori* by man, since the actions and conduct of human beings can only be judged from the point of view of their goodness if one is already in the possession of reason's ethical guidance. The objective and necessary commands of reason, called imperatives by Kant, operate directly, without any kind of intervening feeling of pleasure or displeasure. The absolute moral law for man is the *categorical imperative* which is apodeictic; that is, it does not refer to some other purpose but being without any further end, and is a synthetic, *a priori*, and practical proposition. It is also universal, as much as universal laws govern nature itself. To be a categorical imperative is a *sine qua non* condition of reason's legislative power, of its power to impose moral laws or principles valid for all rational beings.

Will is a kind of causality in rational man; this is best expressed by the description of man's nature as intentional. Negative freedom as intentionality is completed by the positive aspect meaning that freedom entails submission to laws, immutable laws inscribed *a priori* in the human rational nature; the will, therefore, being free, its laws are necessary and its effect can be lawfully posited. "Thus a free will and a will under moral laws are one and the same" [ibid. 114], freedom is posited as the regulative principle of reason. Kant's ethics, consequently, cognitively posit the existence of two worlds, the world of nature and the world of intelligence.

One contemporary representative of rationalist ethics is R. M. Hare, whose ethics of prescriptivity and universalizability is linked to rationality, and inasmuch, follows in Kant's footsteps. Moral judgements guide conduct, commit one to a line of action, or prescribe them for others. As they are prescriptive they must therefore be universalizable, as a judgement valid for its author must be applicable to all in a precisely similar situation. Prescriptive and universalizable judgements can be rational or irrational, but moral conclusions have to be arrived at rationally, without correspondence to facts.

Ethical rationalism does not presuppose ethical realism. Moral statements are reflected in beliefs and attitudes; though they contain descriptive elements, they are all closely tied to reasoning. Rational considerations are conducted at two levels: the intuitive and the critical. The latter meta-level is for assessing results obtained at the intuitive level and for carrying out arbitration between conflicting cases. It is most intriguing that Hare designates his theory of ethics as a version of utilitarianism, "maximizing preference-satisfactions, in sum, of all those affected by our action, considered impartially" [Hare 1989: 109], which can only be understood in a formal sense, corresponding to his non-realist stance.

(b) ETHICS BASED ON INTUITION AND SENTIMENT

As Kant is the author of the most profound and best known conception of rational ethics and morals, David Hume is, in modern times, the foremost exponent of moral teachings, as based on human sentiments. In fact, this presentation of Hume's ideas is not entirely correct, because he favors a morality in the service of the public good and a sort of utilitarianism aimed toward usefulness of human conduct from the point of view of the community. This public-oriented utilitarianism is, of course, an outcome of a well-conceived utilitarianism of the individual, whose own interests dictate promotion of the public well-being as "every man reap[s] the fruits of mutual protection and assistance." Thus, usefulness becomes a source of moral sentiment [Hume 1966: 49 and 54]. Hume admits that reason has to play a role in ethical decisions or moral actions, but he refuses to see in it alone the source of moral conduct. Virtue is therefore defined as action giving a "pleasing sentiment of approbation" [ibid. 129] to others, that is, the spectators. Hume's attack on rationalism was motivated by his empiricist stand, which could not accept generalities, empty terms, and comparisons as arguments in place of concrete instances, and therefore found the rationalist argumentation unintelligible.

Stuart Hampshire bases his ethical and moral thinking on the Aristotelian two-way interaction between intuition and individual reflection, which modify and revise each other. He does not accept independent or transcendental sanctions for moral restraints nor external moral authority in respect to the inner workings of man's own nature. For him, moral beliefs are man's own intuitions and beliefs, expressed in reflective judgement [Hampshire 1977: 4]. Intuitions are in fact "pre-conscious inferences" guiding actions and conduct; they constitute also the core of regularly and automatically exercised skills as a sort of compressed reasoning without entering conscious mental activities. Consequently, one can have a reason for doing something without knowing that reason. In view of the biologically necessary and individually elaborated (reasoned) moral beliefs, it is inevitable that there should be an irreducible plurality of moral intuitions, virtues, and prohibitions. Now, rational judgement in conflict between these intuitions, virtues or even prohibitions is possible; it can be spelled out and made public.

A balance has to be struck between such divergent orientations, in order to arrive at the best life attainable in a given context. However, such reasoning patterns can never entirely foresee effects of future actions based on moral principles, because the mind is not capable of giving complete descriptions of future moral perspectives; there remains always a margin of uncertainty, of unknown contingencies or chance which make the future uncontrollable and unpredictable. Therefore, Hampshire attacks single-criterion moralities like utilitarianism, as they eliminate creative reflection of possible but not actual aims, as well as not-yet-intended variations in action. On the other hand, he approves the Aristotelian abstract ideal of good as the permanent norm for historically conditioned, and therefore divergent moralities. Conclusions about the abstract ideal give an objective feature to concrete moral action through the validity and relevance of the contrary arguments independent of varying empirical circumstances.

In fact, Hampshire is an advocate of an ethical reflection and moral practice open to the future and open to the world.

Hampshire, in consequence, relates action to thought and intention (thought being an expression of intention) in a holistic framework. Moral virtues depend not only on action, but on thought as well, and intention, thought, and action are tied to each other in the mind [Hampshire 1983: 137]. Conscious moral action is an intended and, therefore, necessary action, but there are many unconscious actions which follow a natural movement or routine behavior patterns. The criterion of an intentional action necessarily linked to consciousness is that it can be openly declared at any time and any place [ibid. 99]; this means that behind the intentional action, there is the conviction that it is mentally anchored within a morally relevant situation. Acceptance of a moral rule or convention is a declaration of intention through adherence to it. Intentions and beliefs are closely linked, as a firm intention reflects a firm underlying belief. Everyone tries to anticipate the actions of others, but this anticipation is uncertain and, therefore, "expectation and decision are two complementary aspects of the notion of action" [ibid. 111]. Thus, intentional action is thoroughly linked to experience and temporal order; rational action is coherent action based on the consistency of intentions and reasons, for action and reasons for belief must be integrated into a worldview.

(c) Ethics and Morality As Products of the Social Order

The most important trend in modern thinking is the one that examines the foundation of ethics and morality in public life; it considers both as the product of the social order. Durkheim emphasized first the social origin of morals against Kant, and Dewey, under the influence of Mead, wrote that "all morality is social" [Dewey 1922: 316]. Crudely stated, this principle appears, however, to be incorrect, as phenomena of human life are the result of an interaction between the individual and the community constituting together a cultural world, as Scheler [1973: 521-522] already had written about the interactive ethical context of a human community. This conception corresponds to Dewey's later arguments acknowledging the possibility of a consciousness of the "enduring and comprehensive whole," of a "sense of encompassing continuities" in the existence of men and communities [Dewey op. cit. 300 and 331]. This confirms the mutually constitutive character of the ethical and moral, on the one hand, and of the social, on the other hand. The concept of a comprehensive whole excludes the possibility of reducing one aspect of man's world to another.

Among recent writers studying ethical problems, Bernard Gert forges a stance in which ethics and morality are publicly based, or interpersonally held. Rationality and irrationality are not human faculties but features of relevant normative judgements commonly or publicly acknowledged; irrationality, therefore, is a more basic normative concept than rationality, as it goes against commonly- held norms. Gert considers a belief irrational when it is held by a person who knows there is overwhelming evidence against that belief, yet is mentally capable of knowing that his belief is false; such beliefs generally lead to irrational action [Gert 1988: 21]. Rational beliefs, i.e., those accepted by everyone with intelligence sufficient to comprehend moral rules and act on them, are divided into two categories: rationally required beliefs and rationally allowed beliefs; the latter are beliefs which can be considered true or false by intelligent persons subject to moral judgement (thus not considered as irrational beliefs). It is therefore evident that all categories of rational/irrational beliefs or actions are logically linked.

In Gert's moral conception, reason is a means of coordination or harmonization of desires, and all desires as such, are rationally allowed. Yet he runs into serious difficulties here, because if "reasons for acting are conscious rational beliefs... determining what counts as a reason for acting does not solve the problem of what counts as an adequate reason" [ibid. 34]; he considers that at this point, the limits of ethical reflection are reached, but understanding of what are adequate reasons could, perhaps, be advanced by exploring the cultural world or context in which the are persons acting. This could be especially useful, for example, in the case of exclusive alternatives in which both are often rationally allowed, but neither rationally required.

Gert's ethics of interpersonally agreed upon principles is based on persons as part of community, and, therefore, not acting exclusively in their self-interest. Following a rule or custom is not a reason for acting; if the subjective belief of the actor certifies that the rule or custom is good, he may follow it for specific considerations. Neither is an adequate reason for action to follow examples or experiences of the past, because all reasons for acting involve beliefs about the present or the future. This is another limit of Gert's moral reflection, as there is no justification given for linking rationality to the future and through the future, to the present.

In fact, Habermas' and Apel's communicative or discourse ethics, based on the distinction between the truth of propositions and the validity of normative evaluations, also belongs to the group of ethics anchored in the public space. This dialogical ethic is discursively redeemable but only norms possess an existence independent of speech acts. Norms are intersubjectively recognized ethical rules whose justification is that they are universally and unconditionally accepted as impersonal and corresponding to a general will. Discourse ethics, an overtly cognitive ethic adjudged by reason, though implanted in the lifeworld through communication, is different from Kantian and similar deontological ethics, as well as the publicly-recognized or socially-anchored moralities in that the required universality is a feature of the communicative dialogue in which there is a plurality of participants. The dialogue or argumentation attests to the universal acceptability of the norms in question. Therefore, it is not less formalistic and abstract than are other modern ethical conceptions. Habermas recognizes that the positions of participants in a moral argumentation are situationally or contextually determined, but believes that in the course of the argumentation, in the course of their discourses, they derive universally valid, impersonal norms from the contents of their practical experiences. Consequently, discourse ethics is not only "demotivated" and "decontextualized" but procedural as well; though it is like any other culturally conditioned ethics because its origins lie in the values of everyday life, values intersubjectively recognized by members of a given community. To render the universally accepted rules applicable in real life, Habermas believes in the necessity of congruence between morals and life's everyday exigencies, meeting halfway through socialization and other cultural forms of integration.

3. *Contemporary Trends in Ethics and Morals: Utilitarianism and the Ethics of Rights*

(a) UTILITARIANISM

Utilitarianism is a single-criterion conception of man's ethical and moral life and action that became more and more dominant in shaping the evolution of Western civilization after the end of the eighteenth century. One major reason for the domination of the utilitarian outlook was its epistemological appeal, as it satisfied the canons of rational validation cherished by the rationalist philosophical and scientific outlook. There were, of course, innumerable studies and analyses written about it and innumerable definitions given, but they all derived from the simplest one, formulated by Bentham, which determined as the only moral objective — the greatest happiness for the greatest number. This means to judge every action (there is no question here of beliefs, intentions, or thoughts) according to its usefulness to society; this is what Harsányi calls social utility, the basic criterion of morality. Among contemporary moralists, Russel Hardin illuminates the utilitarian idea by noting:

> Utilitarianism is the moral theory that judges the goodness of outcomes and therefore the rightness of actions insofar as they affect outcomes -- by the degree by which they secure the greatest benefit to all concerned [Hardin 1988: xv].

In fact, there are two elements here denoting some circularity: the principle of usefulness in view of the realization of an objective, and the Benthamite objective consisting of the utilitarian principle.

The dominant significance of utilitarianism today is three-fold: it is evidently *individualist* (standing for a person's conception of his own well being) though ignoring individual autonomy; it has been re-formulated as a *welfarist consequentialism*;[4] and, is presented as a theory of *maximizing choice*. All forms of utilitarian consequentialism, nevertheless, are characterized by their conviction that moral judgements based on utilitarianism are universal without regard to time, place, or person, and that any and all facts are subject to such moral judgements.

R.M. Hare constructs a formal interpretation of utilitarianism parallel of John Rawls. He based his construction on the moral imperatives of prescriptivity and universalizability, giving equal weight to the equal interests of all parties in a given situation, including himself for sake of impartiality (and to replicate Rawls' concepts of "veil of ignorance" or "reflective equilibrium"). Hare includes in his calculations the reduction of harm as a benefit. He contends that, while giving equal weight to all, he will maximize, in accordance with the classical principle of utility, total benefits over the entire population, which for fixed populations (wherever they exist) will be practically equivalent to average utility. He realizes, however, that this is the most one can do in light of competing interests of different people, but

defends the utilitarian calculus considering that the diminishing
marginal utility of money and commodities will increase equality and,
consequently, will also tend to increase total utility. Hare also thinks
that his prescriptivism is, at least partially, the panacea for the
problems related to interest, defined in terms of states of mind such as
liking and desireing ("assents to prescriptions"), and to solve the
problem of how to balance present against future desires, or actual
states of mind against those resulting from alternative courses of action.
Hare designates his utilitarianism as act-utilitarianism, which is
practically equivalent to rule-utilitarianism, as a consequence of the
universalizability of moral judgements. This rule-utilitarianism would
include rules of various degrees of specificity, where specific is the
opposite of general, and not of universal.

The most important objections to utilitarianism can be summarized
as follows: first, reason is inadequate in the assessment of the utility of
various goods and in making interpersonal comparisons of utility (or
one's inability to decide what is good for another); that is, the problem
of subjective evaluation appears insurmountable from the rational point
of view. Furthermore, there is a logical error in the principle the
greatest happiness or good for the greatest number as one cannot
maximize two functions at once, as Edgeworth made it clear in the
nineteenth century. Finally, difficulties arise, due to physical or
genetic differences, such as the differential endowment of people
achieving different results in the same circumstances, or the fact that
the utility of an object oscillates considerably even for one person in the
view of varying availability of other similar objects.

(b) The Ethics of Rights

The most recent and dominant trend in ethical thinking is the ethics
of rights or ethics of justice, represented principally by John Rawls.
Society's harmonious existence cannot be assured, in accordance with
the ethics of right, if it is based on any particular, assumed to be
arbitrary, conception of the good life (because shared belief and value
systems of the society as a community disappeared under the onslaught
of modern economic and social developments). Priority must,
therefore, be given to right a moral category placed above and
independent of the good, a category which stands alone as the supreme
judge of moral action without specifying the duties or obligations which

are the counterpart of a right. As the right is prior to the good, expressed in terms of principles of justice, it is regulative for virtues or good life, in conformity with the Kantian pronouncement that the moral law is prior to the concepts of good and evil. Neither the intensity of feelings nor the preferences expressed by a majority can have any value without being *antecedently* founded in the principles of justice. Here, Rawls becomes entangled in an ontological twilight when he pretends, on the one hand, that the self is prior to its ends and that its capacity to choose is what is crucial because, on the other hand, "the essential unity of the self is already provided by the conception of right" [Rawls 1971: 560 and 563]. This ontology is completely in error, because the human being is not born with the principles of justice, but with the awareness that it is a being-in-the-world, living therefore in solidarity with others and having an identity defined by his community. The ethics of right denies that man is living in the context of a lifeworld, because his "antecedent unity of the self," his sovereign agency, is given to him before his existence, independently of his roles, his values, his ends, and his commitments. This is untrue, as no man can have dignity without self-knowledge, without avowed identity, and without a strong sense of belonging to a community. The Rawlsian self is a theoretical construction, and an inhumane one, for that matter.

Rawls' whole theory is thus paradoxically based on the idea of "original position," in which men ought to make a choice, a choosing together, an agreement between a group of individuals. This original acceptance of certain principles, such as equality and fairness in a hypothetical situation, is the basis of justice. These principles, chosen together constitute the basic structures of society. The ethics of right based on the original position is completed by two indispensable assumptions in man's pursuit of justice. One is the assumption about the conditions under which one must act in order to satisfy the claims of justice. This is the thesis about the "veil of ignorance" which means that men must act in complete ignorance of human diversity, of biological endowments and cultural conditionings, of having a physical body with finite capabilities and being a cognitive, sentient, emotional, and transcendent human being. The veil of ignorance requires man to disregard all human diversity and deal with fellow humans as with disembodied selves, nobodies constituted exclusively by their dignity, founded on the concept of right. The intended result is to eliminate all prejudices in the choice of principles, all accounting for natural, cultural, and social contingencies in individuals' existence, and to reach a "pure" equality and fairness in moral judgements and attitudes.[5]

The second assumption is an even less intelligible one, as it concerns some sort of social goods, essential things a rational man is supposed inescapably wanting (income, wealth, liberties, rights, powers, and so on), though the rational man is ignorant of his own particular desires. This assumption constitutes some minimal motivation necessary to avoid the void without action created by the veil of ignorance, and to induce people to initiate rational action (whatever rational may mean here). It is expected that these two assumptions ensure the required conditions for rational people to act in accordance with common interests, or to establish a cooperative society reflecting social solidarity. Naturally, empirical or transcendental criticisms do not disturb Rawls, because he affirms that "moral philosophy must be free to use contingent assumptions and general facts as it pleases" [ibid. 51], hence he advocates an "anything goes" morality, the like of Feyerabend's "anything goes" philosophy.

Denying the entire meritocratic system of morality, Rawls' theory only acknowledges the entitlements he designates as legitimate expectations for services rendered to the collectivity, as these entitlements are granted by social institutions to individuals in order to elicit their efforts in the collective interest. In a way the circle of contradictions of the ethics of right is thus closed. The community or society is not prior to the principles of justice because it is itself based on them. But individual beings share final ends, values, common institutions and activities as, in Rawls' words, "only in the social union is the individual complete" [ibid. 523].

4. Ethics and Morality in Other Civilizations

(a) HINDUISM

The Ethics of Transcendence: Brahmanism

The ethical view of Hinduism is based on the illusory, transient character of the phenomenal world and, at the same time, on the unity of *Brahman* and *atman*, of the transcendent and the immanent, in a holistic perspective comprising the natural as well as the non-natural aspects of man's being. The doctrine of Four Aims (*artha, kama, dharma*, and *moksa*), classifies the various epochs and their corresponding ends in this earthly life, which must not only contribute to the development of the individual, but also to the well-being of the community.

Among the laws governing human behavior, *rta* is the law of "essential selfhood," not determined by anything external to it. The source of *rta* is the moral conscience, which, if expressed in acts of moral determination, could necessarily lead to right conduct. Although this appears to resemble the Kantian ethical approach, it is entirely different from it, due to the doctrine of identity of *Brahman* and *atman*, the Supreme Being and the human being. In consequence, *rta* is a law sustaining the entire universe and is the condition of anything determinable. The Brahmanistic ethics, as illustrated by the *Bhagavad Gita* [Chapter II, 47; Radhakrishnan and Moore eds. 1957: 110], seems somewhat similar to Protestant ethics, though Brahmanism places a very strong emphasis on the ideal of world-renunciation. According to Singh, the two trends, representing the obligation to respect one's worldly duties, on the one hand, and total renunciation of the world, on the other hand, correspond to two traditional paths of renunciation which, in the *Gita's* teaching, become the paths for the man of knowledge and action [Singh 1987: 85]. Nevertheless, it is renunciation of the illusions of this world that is the unifying factor in both, but renunciation in *karma*, which means that even for the man of action, the performance of actions must be in strict conformity with *karma*.

In fact, *karma* unites mechanical and moral causality, in the words of a contemporary Indian scholar, Daya Krishna [1991: 177-186]. His explanation of *karma* is unique, as it is not a descriptive concept but represents an effort to render intelligible the moral aspect of human action. Natural causality cannot apply to human action because its moral character is not intelligible in terms of such causality, only in terms of moral values derived from religious precepts. Krishna sees the singularly Indian character of moral intelligibility in the principle that any human being can only reap the fruits of his own actions, but cannot be affected by the results of actions of others. However, this makes moral consciousness impossible if the existence of each man's anterior lives is not logically postulated in order to link moral intelligibility only to a human being's personal destiny, without considering any exterior circumstances. In accordance with the same logic, once anterior lives are postulated, there is no reason not to postulate the coming of future lives as well.

In consequence, the dialectics of "*is*" and "ought" is an interplay between two states of consciousness as one, in which a man contemplates his actions and in which he realizes what he ought to be doing. But this does not mean that natural causality is not at work in moral actions, because the latter unavoidably are part of the realm of nature; the law of *karma* is effective only in moral respects. Non-moral consequences of anyone's actions can and do affect others. Man can only be liberated from this moral bondage, a total contradiction to the Kantian ideal of human moral freedom, by the liberating power of *moksa*, or "spiritual release." In conclusion, and with reference to Western ethical teachings, Krishna recognizes that the most fundamental problem, nevertheless, is whether any human action is possible without an "other," whether action is not always situated in an interactive framework.

The Ethics of Salvation: Jainism and Samkhya

Jainism is known as a creed of profound pessimism, where the eternal wheel of *karma* offers no solution for man living in a world of suffering. Only those capable of exceptional efforts can obtain, after long years of striving and heroic endeavors of self-negation, a release from the endless round of rebirths. This ethical posture is, of course, a consequence of the dualistic view of the world and the transmigration of souls. The proper objects of the *Jain* contemplation therefore are the *Tirthankaras*, the "Makers of the River-Crossing," who are beyond spatial and temporal existence, without action and absolutely at peace [Zimmer 1974a: 253]. This view of earthly existence was common to Brahmanism and Jainism, but the latter parted ways with the former, ascribing to *karma* a strictly mechanical necessity against the immaterial, spiritual outlook of the *Upanishads* and other *Vedic* writings. A sort of moral solipsism is a feature of *Jainism*, a personal striving for salvation (in which only the monastic community plays a role) and in which only the individual's own intentions count: he must destroy *karma* and attain the *moksa*.

The *Samkhya* ethics is different from the *Jain* in that it believes in the release of the individual from the bondage of the matter, as attainable by knowledge; therefore, the *Samkhya* doctrine is more metaphysical than ethical. It is the activity of the mind that is liberating; the bondage, passivity, and servitude to emotions is physical. The evolution of the material universe obeys necessity, but the freedom of man is possible, due to his mental powers which permit him to eliminate the misunderstanding of the real being of the self, i.e., identifying the self with body, emotions, and desires. Although the migration of the soul is maintained by the *Samkhya*, there is a naturalistic character to their belief as even the mind with its liberating powers is part of nature and, consequently, salvation takes place in a natural framework.

The Ethics of Pleasure and Good Life: Carvaka and Tantrism

The *Carvaka* is the only school in India, which unqualifiedly endorses the life of pleasure and enjoyment. In a way, their teaching corresponds to the utilitarian philosophy in the Western civilization, as they consider virtue consisting in living in such a way that maximizes pleasure and minimizes pain [Radhakrishnan and Moore eds. 1957: 229]. The life of enjoyment and pleasures is justified entirely in naturalistic terms, rejecting any metaphysical speculations, religious beliefs and values.

In *Tantrism* the theistic belief in a personal God, the Mother Goddess *Kali* replaced the abstract transcendentalism of the "Formless Brahman." Although Tantrism accepts the teachings of the *Advaita Veda*, it shifts the emphasis completely to the positive aspects of *maya*. It endorses an attitude of world-affirmation. In consequence, its ethics is fundamentally different from the transcendental renunciation of Brahmanism. Worldly activities are interpreted as representing positive approaches to everyday life which are justified by the belief in the purity and holiness of all things. The *Tantra* therefore accepts no dualism; the whole world is one in purity and holiness. All beings and things are members of a mystic family. *Tantrism* eliminates biological and social differentiation, as well as all personal peculiarities or individual distinctions. Everything is the manifestation of the absolute; differences and distinctions are part of the world, therefore no reform, no renunciation is promoted by the *Tantrists*. Instead, the world is affirmed and appreciated as it is.

The transformation of *dharma* is especially noticeable in *Tantrism*. The sacrament of the "five forbidden things": the *Tantric* ritual of wine, meat, fish, parched grain, and sexual intercourse, are not accomplished in a libertarian spirit as breaking the laws of Heaven or

Earth, but in a controlled state, under supervision, and as fulfillment of a long sequence of spiritual disciplines. There is no feeling of guilt, no need to amend one's life. Laws of the world are good and respected, as they are part of the unity of all existents. Through the all-inclusive rituals the antagonistic polarities of the existence are annihilated. This vanishing away is, for the Tantrists, *nirvana*.

(b) BUDDHISM: THE ETHICS OF SELF-DEVELOPMENT

Buddha did not deal with metaphysical questions but retained from Hinduism two ethical aspects: the teachings of *dharma* and *karma*. However, the essence of these notions changed, in accordance with Buddha's view that not substances but qualities are only real ("all things are without a self"). The *dharma*, therefore, became the particular being whose behavior shows his *dharma*; every *dharma* is dependent on others as the only point of reference is the *dharma* of others (in view of the fact that all things are inconsistent, they cancel themselves out, and nothing remains but a void).

This fundamental opposition of Buddhism to the concept of individual identity is explicable by the fact that the empty and unreal self resides in the individual persons or entities, and only through the destruction of the locus of it can the deliverance from bondage in this world be achieved. This is the truth expressed in the impermanence of all selves and things, which are mutable in their very essence. Correspondingly, the *karma* was also left without an agent, as there is no self who would be the bearer of it; it therefore stood for the law of mechanical causality. The true perspective, called *dhamma* by the Buddha, is only acquired through understanding the process of causation; this is the path of *dharma* that leads, if properly followed, to the disappearance of the non-self, the *nirvana*. The Buddhist view is deterministic, in confessing the strict necessity of causal laws annihilating human freedom and responsibility. Such an interpretation of Buddhism is, however, not intelligible in Buddhist terms. For the Buddhists, causality governs the process of liberation, a process aiming at the Final Deliverance from the bondage of empirical existence. It is then normal that all events and activities of everyday life should be subjected to strict necessity. The necessary causal mechanism leads to a necessary finality: *nirvana*. On the other hand, man is free to will one or another thing in life, because the self is changeable and its power to change itself is posited. Strong volition can be either virtuous or evil, followed by reward or punishment by the law of karma (this excludes the effect of former deeds which are quasi-automatic and cannot be counted as results of a free decision). Thus, the law of *karma* and deeds resulting from a strong will are both special cases of causality. In this sense, many Buddhists consider that their ethic is an ethic of intention as it concerns only volitional and motivational acts, or, one might conclude, that Buddhist ethic relates not to individual acts but the whole attitude of a person.

The Buddhist ethic appears to us as one full of paradoxes. The later Buddhist schools, for example, debated on the possibility that the world is nothing but suffering. The greatest paradox of the Buddhist ethic, nevertheless, is that all the efforts of human beings to strive toward deliverance from the world of illusion are, and must be, without consequence, a result of the "iron law" of *karma*, the inexorable causality at work in the universe. This paradox engenders a tolerant attitude toward human weaknesses, toward those who are not able to follow the path of the Five Precepts, and reflects the basic tension between the ethics of *nirvana* and the ethics of karmic rebirth: between the world of the indescribable and unpronounceable and between the world of the space-time order and the ethics of looking forward to the *nirvana* and the ethics of equanimity in immanent existence.

(c) ETHICS IN THE CHINESE CIVILIZATION

Confucianism: The Ethics of the Mean

The Confucian ethics is an earthly ethics, an ethics of the lifeworld, as summarized in the *Doctrine of the Mean*, one of the most famous documents of the post-Confucian era. This ethical teaching was not based on a dualistic view of the universe, but on the consideration of the joint permanence of the immanent and the transcendent in human nature, the latter being designated as the Way of Heaven (transcending time, space, substance and motion). Man and nature form a unity. In *Confucius' Analects*, the expression *chung-yung*, which later stood for the words "mean," "moderation," or "equilibrium," was used in the sense that *chung* stood for human nature and *yung* for the universal and harmonious. But precisely this effort of Confucius to bring into harmony the "condition of the world" and the "universal path" led him to describe his ethics as the doctrine of the mean. His ethical teaching was thus based on the conviction of man's perfectibility and the possibility of a morally superior man.

Two further concepts of have to be noted here, as they are also fundamental to the Confucian ethics: the rectification of names, and the concept of *jen*. The first was important not only in the social domain of the proper regulation of names and ranks, but especially in the moral sphere, the correspondence between words and action, between signifier and signified, or designation and actuality. The *jen*, in contradiction to the preceding custom, which used it to designate a particular virtue, became for Confucius the designation of virtue in general; Confucius said that "Do not do to others what you do not like yourself" [*Lun-yu*, XV, 23; Fung Yu-lan 1983, Vol. I: 71], almost in today's fashion of universalizability. The man of *jen* is the perfect man, the *chun-tzu*, the morally superior man; *jen* encompasses the qualities of conscientiousness and altruism through which the unity of human being and nature and the integration of society are realized.

Finally, *Confucius* emphasized the character trait he called uprightness or *chih*, though he also preserved the concept of *li* inherited from the Chou culture. *Chih* stood for the fundamental correctness in man's attitude [*Analects*, VI, 16], whereas *li* represented the rules of propriety, the sense of restraint in all situations, regulating without regard to one's own interest or to utilitarian motives. In the perspective of *chih* and *li*, education, self-cultivation, and self-development were emphasized. The Great Learning consisted of knowing the proper distinctions between different classes of subjects, and thus reaching a comprehensive knowledge on which one could stand firm and undertake the education of others, changing people's customs. To be a Sage meant to know one's place in the universe, to fulfil one's natural duties, to have a definite goal toward which one strives. In this way a Sage would be tranquil, settled, and unperturbed.

Mo Tzu, who preached frugality, universal love, and the condemnation of war, turned the Confucian doctrine of the Mean into a kind of utilitarianism. His followers, the *Mohists*, laid strong emphasis on result, material return, profitableness (*li*) and accomplishment (*kung*). For Mo Tzu, the usefulness of an action could be established following a threefold test concerning its basis, its verifiability, and its applicability. It is, however, clear that Mo Tzu's utilitarianism was very different from the one reigning today, because it was not directed to the individual's benefit but toward "benefit to the country and to the people" [ibid. 86]. In a very modern vein, he opposed heavy taxes or the use of music (and big ceremonies) when people were lacking food, clothing and shelter [ibid. 90].

Mo Tzu's insistence on the necessity to eliminate partiality is almost identical with the universabilization thesis of Hare. Partiality is antagonizing people against one another and causes major calamities in the world; it is therefore wrong and should be replaced by universality [ibid. 92]. Mo Tzu's opposition to war was also constructed on the basis of profitableness (not like Mencius, who opposed war because he did not think it to be righteous); he believed in the necessity of universal love, though knowing that man's original nature does not favor this condition. On the other hand, he was against plurality, difference, the divergence of standards and opinions, and defended the rule of absolute uniformity. He was, consequently, criticized quite early in the history of Chinese thought, for example, by Hsun Tzu, who wrote: "Mo Tzu had vision regarding uniformity, but no vision regarding individuality," and later, "Mo Tzu was blinded by utility and did not know the value of culture" [ibid. 102-103].

Mencius, the great Confucian scholar who summarized the Master's teachings giving them a mystical turn, also insisted on the virtues of human-heartedness (*jen*), conscientiousness to others (*chung*), and altruism (*shu*). But while Confucius applied them only to the individual's self-development, Mencius emphasized the necessity of their application to government and society. He believed in the original though limited goodness of man, that all men possess the "four beginnings" [ibid. 120-121] which they can develop over the course of their life. Good acts conform to man's natural constitution, but an evil act is of his own initiative; it is a moral defect. Man's main distinction from all other creatures is that he has a mind; this is the nobler part of his constitution which enables him to think and to have recourse to the principle of reason in his action (*li*) and to recognize righteousness (*i*) as a guide. "We must try our best to do good, and that is all" [ibid. 128], said he.

Hsun Tzu was a convinced naturalistic thinker who denied that there are ethical rules imposed on man by religion. His view of man's nature is at the opposite the view of Mencius because Hsun Tzu taught that man is born evil, and only education (*wen*) leads him to do good. Man's metamorphosis is brought about through the intermediary of mind, the influences of teachers and laws, and, especially, the guidance of standards of justice (*i*) and the rules of proper conduct (*li*).

Taoism: The Ethics of Quiescence

"Tao never does, yet through it all things are done" says the Lao-tzu. In accordance with this description of the inactivity of Tao (the Non-being, the Mystery of Mysteries), Taoist ethics is an ethics of quiescence, of withdrawal from the world, an evident negation of Confucian morals. "The world is invariably possessed by him who does nothing" [ibid. 181] because the aim of life is to return to one's root, the quiescence (*ching*) or submission to fate (*ming*). The Taoist enlightenment consists in this quiescence, in this submission to fate. Therefore, one must not follow one's own impulsion, one's prejudices, but to follow the all-pervading Tao; this is also called "practicing enlightenment" [ibid. 162]. Here, a strange dialectic intervenes. Tao's law is the law of "reversion," or "return;" the enlightened man must start to live in an opposite way to what seems appropriate for him. It appears strange that this Taoist dialectical turn in ethics shows that Tao did not believe in a fundamental negation of human life, like Buddhism, but admitted that human beings are not emotionless and desireless. It therefore aimed at eliminating "the excessive, the extravagant, the extreme' [ibid. 188].

The Ethics of Reason: Wang Fu-chih

In opposition to most of the Neo-Confucian dualist ethical teachings, *Wang Fu-chih* was the advocate of rational ethics. Reason and desire are manifestations of indeterminate substance, but reason is much more refined than desire. Desire is part of natural life, and as such, constitutes life's pattern and order, thus forming the existential structure of reason. Each can be transformed into the other because "reason is desire universalized or universalizable to all men, but desire is more or less localized in a person" [Chung-Ying Cheng 1979: 487]. Consequently, in Wang's view, the only way to realize reason worldwide is to fulfil the desires of each individual. Desire embodies reason, but reason also represents the potentiality of natural perfection. It is therefore the conclusion of Wang's ethics, in a complete reversal of Neo-Confucian ontological dualism, that the unity between desire and reason reflects the unity of nature (*hsing*); morality is part of nature, or, perhaps, it is a better nature.

Neo-Confucian, Pragmatic Ethics

Neo-Confucian thinkers all had a more pronounced moral and practical approach than the great scholar *Chu Hsi*, the systematizer of the Confucian doctrine. For example, *Wang Yang-ming* interpreted the term *ko-wu*, the investigation of things, not as a rational and objective investigation like Chu Hsi, but as the process to eliminate "what is incorrect in the mind so as to preserve the correctness of its original substance" [Wing-Tsit Chan 1969: 655]. In fact, his version of the thesis of the investigation of things became "the extension of the innate knowledge of the goodness (*liang-chih*)." In this sense, "knowledge is the beginning of action and action is the completion of knowledge" [ibid. 656]. This thesis became known as the "unity of knowledge and action" closely linking, as Chung-Ying Cheng has shown, the intentionality of knowing and practicing, the dialectical inter-twining of these components of mental operations. In this sense, Wang's practicality is more profound than the *shih-shueh* of his successors because it is the "unifying force" of all practicalities [Chung-Ying Cheng 1979: 58]. As a consequence he objected to all kinds of utilitarian and not moral practicalities.

Continuing the reasoning of Wang Yang-ming's "unity of knowledge and action," *Yen Yuan* expressed a pragmatic approach to morality in affirming that the investigation of things is, in reality, learning from actual experience and solving practical problems. His *shih-shueh* or "practical learning" is based on the concept of *shih*, which represents, on the one hand, moral accomplishments and, on the other hand, a principle of the universe, namely, the reality manifest in the activities of all things. He linked, through his thesis of learning from actual experience, the cultivation of the self to the will in order to transform the world; one keeps one's identity without being transformed by the world, but changes the world through firm intention and conviction. This was clearly a social and cultural dimension introduced in Neo-Confucian ethical reflection, as it aimed at a tangible contribution by everyone to the environment one lives in and offers an exemplar of moral behavior to one's fellow humans.

(d) JAPANESE ETHICS AND MORALS: JITSUGAKU

The unity of man and nature is the fundamental tenet of Japanese ethics; man lives in the unity of nature, and he interacts with everything natural. This meant that the ancient Japanese religion, *Shinto*, never knew of absolute gods, and that the Japanese did not develop absolute concepts such as good or evil. Such an interactive relativism (the expression is from Takie S. Lebra) obviously had a strong influence on ethics and morals, as well as on the development of society. As a result of this orientation, and following the reception of Confucianism in Japan, the virtue of human-heartedness (*jen*) was transformed into the complete recognition of other selves and the acceptance of the equality of others.

Japanese ethical thought developed in the Neo-Confucian framework during the last centuries, particularly in the framework of *jitsugaku*, or "real learning." For this reason, *Minamoto Ryoen* could write of *jitsugaku* as "empirical rationalism," i.e., a type of thinking which does not oppose rational principle to actualities and realities [Ryoen 1979: 376]. The meaning of *jitsugaku* is contextual; one could say that it corresponds to Popper's "situational logic," and stands for efforts improving actual thinking and learning in order to find new or alternate forms for them.

Ryoen suggests that there are two forms of *jitsugaku*: the moral-practical, concerning value judgements, and the empirical, remaining in the field of objective, non-partial thinking. The moral-practical *jitsugaku* is also called "*jitsugaku* in pursuit of human truth" [ibid. 379], a truth embracing individuals and communities alike.

In this all-encompassing perspective of *jitsugaku* a great variety of views flourished. *Toju* believed that the "illumination of virtue" [ibid. 394] makes man naturally able to act according to time, place and rank. Moral is adaptation to the circumstances of the moment. *Kumazawa Banzan* saw *jitsugaku* in accordance with the Confucian teaching on equilibrium and harmony ("action and non-action penetrating to the source of the world" [ibid. 401]), and was certainly holistic and vitalistic in his moral conception. *Kaibara Ekken* enriched Japanese moral thinking by considering not only learning, as those reviewed above, but "useful learning" [ibid. 410] in the sense of useful and practical morality. He was the creator of *shushigaku* thinking, which denied Hsu Chi's dualism and affirmed the unity of principle and material force. Ekken concluded that natural laws and ethical principles were the same. *Yamaga Soko* refused the unitary tendencies of the age, because he thought that they reduced life's complexities. For him, *jitsugaku,* embracing everyday life and humaneness, meant acceptance of everything human. Self-cultivation was responsiveness to the requirements of everyday life, to the challenge of everyday things. Similarly to Heidegger's and Dewey's ontological conceptions, *Ito Jinsai's* affirmed that nothing real could be outside experience. The living and active cosmos can be known through the living and active beings which constitute it. Reality is the world of commonplace, ordinary and familiar things in which man acts as moral agent. Humanenness is love and morality, the highest manifestation of life. Therefore, for him, *jitsugaku* as practical morality was correlated with *jitsugaku* as the search for objective facts.

Finally, *Ogyu Sorai* advocated a concrete social morality, not based on a belief in the fundamental goodness of every man, but on government through institutions. But he did not project the idea of institutions as simply the loci of power but as culturally motivated organisms, organisms installing social morality through the objective learning of empirical realities and not of speculative phantasms. He gave to *jitsugaku* its determinate positivistic meaning in a Western scientific manner by emphasizing the search for facts free from any prejudices or values. He, in fact, affirmed that only in the natural world can one learn what is, and in the ethical domain only what ought to be. Morality therefore was an empirically determined sphere and, consequently, fell into the domain of the subjective. Sorai was therefore an ethical relativist.

(e) Ethics and Legalism in Islam

It is well known that in Islam the legal order is as much a system of religion-based ethics as it is law. In Islam, any human activity or any social institution has, in final analysis, religious significance. According to the *Quranic* doctrine, what man ought or ought not do is revealed by God through his Prophet Muhammad; consequently, to violate the law is to violate God's commandment, and this induces not only legal but divine sanctions. It is, however, important to note that among the sources of law (in addition to the *Quran*, the *Sunnah*, and analogical reasoning), the consensual agreement (*ijma*) of the Muslim community is also included; the Prophet said that "my community will never agree upon an error," thus granting Muslims the freedom to formulate a social ethic. But *ijma* had to be based on *ijtihad*, reflective adaptation of stipulations of the law to an actual situation. The development of Islamic jurisprudence shows, as Coulson pointed out [Coulson 1969: 81-84], that in legal practice, religious duties and social duties were separated, reflecting the divergence between legally-enforceable and morally-desirable rules, or rules observed in practice and those which are not. As in other societies, the morally desirable rules constituted sometimes more important ethical standards for the Islamic community than did those enforced by juridical authority.

This distinction was made by the reformist Grand Mufti of Egypt, *Muhammad Abduh*, in the form of *usul* (roots) and *furu* (branches), of which the first related to matters of doctrine, worship rituals and fundamental ethical questions, whereas the latter concerned human transactions and social relations [Abduh 1966: 73]. Abduh, as well as the *al-Manar school*, recognized, taking into account the classical legal principle of *maslaha* (the public interest), that the *usul* cannot be changed but the *furu* can be modified in accordance with evolving circumstances in the lifeworld. All these legal distinctions are only applicable in the unity of the *ummah*, within the Prophet's community created by the bond of religious conviction.

Social ethics in the Islamic community is contractual, as it is based on the "covenant" between God and his people. Justice is based on positive law and virtue, which are completely interdependent. The *dar al-Islam* (the Land of Islam) is also designated as *dar al-adl* (the Land of Justice) if the Muslims follow the *Quranic* prescriptions and if there is a legitimate government that promotes the good and prohibits evil. Promoting the good is, in Islam, not only the responsibility of the chief of the community but of all Muslims; it is a public duty. In respecting his commitments and in acting virtuously, the Muslim's intention, veracity, and sincerity are most important, because virtue, derived from justice, links the believer to God in the framework of the covenant's contractual obligations. Contractual justice is also the basis of international relations; the only exception is the deviation in virtue of necessity.

(f) COMMUNITY ETHICS IN AFRICA

The ethical order and practical morality in Africa often corresponded to community structures. Particularly within the kinship system, where everybody was related to everybody else, a damage caused to one person affected the entire community. Some laws, rules, customs, or observances were considered sacred, as given by God; therefore, breaking them was an attack on, or destruction of, the accepted social order and had to be sanctioned by the whole community, including the living and the departed. It was also believed that God would punish the delinquent and bring about justice when necessary.

From this community-oriented ethical point of view, any form of evil, moral or natural, was caused by members of the community through magic, sorcery, witchcraft, and such other practices. Moral evils meant any breach of conduct in contradiction to prevailing moral and social rules, while natural evils such as sufferings, pain, calamities, and misfortune, though explainable in natural terms, were believed to have originated by an agent, human or spiritual. This moral conception led to the attitude that no natural evil could befall a community unless immoral individuals in its midst were performing evil deeds. This view reflects a sort of unity between nature and man, in which the universe was conceived in anthropological terms [Mbiti 1969: 214-215].

5. *Universalism and Relativism in Ethics and Morality*

The preceding review of ethical and moral conceptions and their consequences for human actions clearly demonstrates that ethical universalism is only possible if ethics and morals are conceived on an exclusively formalistic basis such as Kant's rationalistic ethics founded on *a priori* convictions and not on experience, or Rawls' theory of justice, a typically Western product. However, if ethics and morals are placed in a concrete human context, all-encompassing relativism as a limited core of fundamental ethical and moral concepts endorsed by all cultures and civilizations, may be found.

The incompatibility of intentions, beliefs, and actions of various human groups must be accepted as a feature of morality, and this acceptance would not exclude remaining steadfast in one's own ethical tradition and way of life; this could not be considered as an incoherence or error, but as an understanding of the reality of man's existence. The Ancients recognized that certain ethical requirements are grounded in human nature, whereas others are derived from particular customs and conventions. They acknowledged that moral principles rooted in a particular way of life are as legitimate as those inscribed in every man's being.

In regard to situations of moral conflict, Charles Larmore emphasized that a moral judgement is not a simple application of internalized rules but a transcending of them, an application of such rules to particular situations implying different and divergent alternatives. Virtue, therefore, is the exercise of correct moral judgement as opposed to duty in which the moral imperative excludes an exercise of man's judgement [Larmore 1987: 15-16]. The emergent reality in experience is all the more decisive in that there is no absolute ranking of high-order principles (such as utility or universalizability) which may impose divergent solutions; moral judgement therefore has to be formulated with reference to the particular context. Morality is an autonomous, *sui generis* domain of value; moral commitments make a moral agent of a person, and these commitments lead to creative acts.

Ethical or moral freedom, or the possibility of personal choice, may, of course, lead to terrifying conflicts in man, as one can witness in Sophocles' tragedies. It is not in choosing between good and evil or between right and wrong that these conflicts appear but, as MacIntyre noted, "when different virtues make rival and incompatible claims on us" [MacIntyre 1984: 143]. The tragedy is that the authority of both claims has to be recognized; it is always in a given framework that one has to choose. The framework cannot be chosen.

Divergences between contemporary civilizations in the ethical domain show that there definitely are "core" ethical convictions common to all human cultures, and that extremes like "world renunciation" appear in different culture areas as well. The disjunction is not civilizational in ethical matters, it is, between modern and pre-modern moralities (as it is usually called today). The resistance of people in other civilizational orbits is against what we consider modern ethics and morality such as, for example, the totally divergent interpretations of moral freedoms and of moral conduct of life.

CHAPTER FIVE

INTERACTIVE SOCIAL ORDER AND CONTEMPORARY SOCIETY

The central focus of this chapter will be the main features of the structural build-up of society, and a definition and analysis of the social phenomenon. This analysis emphasizes the characteristics of the evolution of Western society, based on selected ideas of Parsons, Luhmann, and Giddens within the framework of interactive ordering, in order to show the overwhelming *differences* in societal organization and development between Western and non-Western civilizations. For this purpose, review of three elements is essential: first, the impact of culture patterns on social interaction; second, structural and institutional features (including Parsonian factors like pattern-maintenance as well as functional differentiation and social roles in the Luhmannian perspective); and, finally, pinpointing the major disjunction between different social organizations in Western and other civilizations, maintaining that "social reality is neither incoherent nor total, it consists of a multiplicity partially ordered, though does not evidence a globally valid order" [Aron 1962: 27; my translation].

1. Culture Patterns and Social Ordering

The most convenient way to distinguish between culture and society is to consider the first as an ordered system of meanings and symbols, and the second as the framework of social interaction patterned in terms of the cultural world. The relation of the two can then be viewed, following Parsons and Shils, as culture offering normative and motivational standards for the selective, interactive ordering of society. This view recognizes that for culture as much as for society, individuals and groups are simultaneously bearers and actors, culture as well as society, do not exist independently of human beings and their more-or-less stable groups. It must be so in respect to culture (as the channel of socialization of individuals) because meanings and symbols are brought to life by individuals but are transmitted from generation to generation through cultural heritage; this heritage, in its turn, contributes to the reformulation, renovation, or remission of certain meanings and of gradually irrelevant symbols. In social interaction, agents are individuals as much as institutions, communities, or any kind of social groups that are constitutive of the society. If such a view of the relationship of culture and society is right, then the Durkheimian thesis about traditional societies, in which integration was secured by a normative consensus, and modern societies, in which it is achieved through the systematic interconnection of functionally differentiated domains of action, cannot be held valid. Integration is a result of the congruence of cultural order and of social reality, revealing a normative consensus, which assures the fullest possible harmonization of action orientations of individuals, and of society's constituent subgroups.

One of the main reasons for cultural and social change is that at certain moments of history, in Geertz' words, "an incongruity of the cultural framework of meaning and the patterning of social action" [Geertz 1973: 169] is produced (sometimes as a result of the evolutionary process); the result is a delegitimation of either the cultural or of the social worlds. The principal problem of today's Western and other modernizing societies is exactly such an incongruity or delegitimation, though in the case of modernization there is a double incongruity: first, the incongruity between cultural framework and social development; another, added by the imposition of foreign cultural meanings and symbols, an incongruity between concurrent cultural worlds in the same space and time.

The *ethos* of a culture is the strongest factor in integrating a human group, as recognized by most contemporary thinkers. In this respect, it is worthwhile to go back to Hegel, who strongly emphasized the role of *Sittlichkeit*. He expressed, in this concept, one of the essential aspects of the interdependence between culture and society, namely, the fact that a member of a social group reinforces it by respecting its inherited values and beliefs, in fact, reproducing the cultural and moral cohesion of his community without creating it - because he is educated or internalized in it. Man has to find his place in his community through mutual recognition with others, and this mutual recognition constitutes the community's rational structure [Kolb 1986: 100-101]. Language and conceptual schemes, existential distinctions, and moral rules are all part of a culture's *ethos* and as such, underlay our experiences and interpretations. For this reason, Hegel emphasizes that a human being can only be a human being in a community. That vision is perfectly concordant with culture's role in the evolutionary perspective as an action-oriented information system.

Hegel's well-known expression for disruption between culture patterns and social structures is alienation (popularized by Marx). The alienation of the individual occurs when shared values and norms are felt irrelevant to, or clearly contradict the new and emerging way of life of people. Hegelian alienation is the gradual evanescence of the identification of people with some of their culture's beliefs and norms, which led, in modern times, to a more individualistic conception of existence. The revolution of modern subjectivity rejects the structures of mutual recognition, which were hitherto dominant, and this is the reason why people lost their identification with their society. For many, this results in an introverted life where meaningfulness is reached in inner or private experience. For others it resulted in a violent reaction against the apparently obsolete tenets of cultural and societal existence. Concurrently, an individualist ethics is born (what Hegel calls morality as against *Sittlichkeit*).

It cannot be ignored that at their origin, every culture had, and most of them still have, a religious belief system as a focal point. The central role of religions in the formation of particular cultures involves the acceptance of a transcendental authority which transforms everyday experience.[1] It also gives meaning to earthly experience, especially to inexplicable suffering or other similar occurrences as well as to genuine moral paradoxes. Religion frames man's frail existence within a global, holistic framework thereby giving him a transcendental sense of earthly life ("a unified view of the world derived from a consciously integrated meaningful attitude toward life" [Weber 1978, Vol. I: 450]). Religion is not a retreat from reality but represents a pervasive commitment to the principles and attitudes it approves and an encounter with nature and other human beings in such a committed, 'ethical' way. It shapes culture and society.

Closely related to the central role of religious beliefs is the universalistic versus particularistic configuration in different cultures. There is not one culture that could be characterized as universalistic or particularistic as such, it is not even certain in what proportion one or the other type characterizes a given society [Bendix 1977: 391]. The integration of universalistic and particularistic elements of a culture is important, as there is a need to mediate between them through a meta-level or transcendental entity; this is crucial for the relations between individuals and society, from the point of view of what Geertz called the culture's *ethos*.

The importance of mediation between universalistic and particularistic elements of a culture varies with the type of society bearer of that specific culture. If society is an organically coherent community, then such a mediation is quasi-automatic; but if individuals live in an "atomized" society, practically on their own, then mediation is thoroughly needed. Charles Taylor considers that being in society is a "constitutive element of seeking the human good" and is "essentially bound up with human dignity" [Taylor 1985: 292]. Seligman is therefore right in pointing out that in modern society, the dominant type of universalism is a derivative one, derivative of the individual[2] or, in other words, the particular is invested with the characteristics of the universal [Etzioni 1968: 123-124]. This means that the individual was divested of personality and became an empty concept, represented by the common denominator of every individual; the fact that he is an individual representing the ultimate standard, as no other universal criteria exist, no meta-level survived which would transcend the individualistic ethics' requirements. The concept of the individual as ultimate standard has been completely emptied, became abstracted from the living human being and invested by theoretically formulated "preferences" or "interests" [Bowles-Gintis 1986: 123].

Modern universalism based on abstract individuals exists parallel with particularism of universalist pretensions at sub-societal levels, as well as with intersubjective and general types of action such as communicative interfacing so much cherished by Habermas. Categories of the universal and the particular are confused, not distinct and separate. This modified cultural patterning of social interaction then leads to the notion of society as an amalgam of individuals mutually recognizing each other, society as "a *metaphor* for the universal," instead of a society which "*is* the universal" [Seligman 1990: 126; italics in original]. In the first case, the standard of *ethos* is represented by the individual and reflected by the universalism of utilitarianism; in the second case, it transcends the individual in the form of shared norms of the community, validated by social interaction (of which communication is one manifestation). The reign of instrumental reason corresponds to this modern development of individualistic and particularistic *ethos*, a truly self-referential system.

Modern developments of society led Alain Touraine to affirm that "the idea of society is to a large extent a myth," or that the decline of the society is due to the "decomposition of collective action" and lack of unity [Touraine 1992: 58 and 63]. It is on this paradox of modern society founded on the universalized individual that most theories and concepts of the state and society have been based since the 18th century. These tentatives include theories of social contract, expressing the general will of individual citizens as contracts of association where a hypothetical will of the majority replaces the preceding social system's hierarchical ordering of classes, strata, and collectivities. However, even a contractual association between individuals may cause fears that individuality will be completely suppressed by the elimination of differences realizing the dream of uniformity, a "community so undifferentiated that no member of it could possibly seek anything that might possibly distinguish him from the rest" [Kolakowski 1989: 100].

It is interesting to recall at this point Riesman's classification of social characters in his famous study *The Lonely Crowd*, corresponding to various types of societies. Here, the tradition-directed character is linked to societies with high growth potential, the inner-directed character denotes societies in a phase of transitional growth, whereas the other-directed social character is dominant in societies of incipient population decline [Riesman 1950: 8]. This much-criticized typology gains a particular significance today, when the societies of the West and of other civilizations are competing in the world arena, and when societies of those other civilizations clearly witness tradition-directedness, compared to our society. Riesman's description of other-directedness and its characteristic bearers [ibid. 21] and the emphasis he placed on the mediating role of mass communications between the individual and the outer world appear even today, strikingly true almost

a half a century later. It relates well to the description given by
Gouldner of the effects of utilitarianism leading to a double alienation:
alienation of the self from itself and from society [Gouldner 1970:
103]. This alienation corresponds to the other-directedness described by
Riesman.

2. Interactive Ordering: Growing Differentiation and Structural Complexity

Social interaction is understood here in the Parsonsian framework,
as modified by Jonathan Turner [1988]; it is far from being identical
or coextensive with the Aristotelian *praxis*. It definitely has nothing to
do with the so-called postmodernist description of the social as evoked
by Lyotard, who defines it in linguistic terms and narrative myths
[Lyotard 1988: 139]. Social action is, as Hannah Arendt remarked, the
only activity "that goes on directly between men without the
intermediary of things or matter;" from the perspective of the plurality
of "human condition," she saw such action as a requisite of existence,
not a contingent phenomenon [Arendt 1959: 9-10, 119, and 156-160].
Gadamer's definition of practice represents a real interactive mode:
"Practice is conducting oneself and acting in solidarity. Solidarity,
however, is the decisive condition and basis of all social reason"
[Gadamer 1986: 87]. This conception of practical action, understood
as social interaction, is closely related to the concept of ontological
interdependence of the individual and the community. It also
emphasizes that action, "guided by consciousness and the actor's
values," has a value in itself, as Amitai Etzioni affirmed, because a
value commitment which does not lead to an action with practical
consequences, is no commitment at all [Etzioni 1968: 12].

The evolution of the human lifeworld is a successive series of
differentiation and the consecutive appearance of higher and higher
structural complexities, or so it seems. Instead of such a systemic
approach, some selected elements of system-constructs like
functionalism or differentiation will be used in this study, emphasizing,
first, *interaction* as the basic phenomenon. This implies that there are
several actors, individual or collective, in an interplay involving
physical, mental, and cultural elements, *and* thereby excludes the
interpretation of interaction in the sense of an exclusively purposive-

instrumental action corresponding to the supposition that an individual could act without any reference to the situational context.

Social interaction is, from this perspective, constitutive of individual as well as collective action, as it shapes the ends and values guiding and conditioning it. Ontologically, social interaction partakes simultaneously in being and becoming through the freedom of choice, eliminating the problems of the juxtaposed *is* and *ought*. Furthermore, the concept of interaction does not imply any teleology, nor does it highlight any one specific element in the life of social groups in a given environment; interaction stands for the occurrence of an event, the performance of an evolutionary phase, the appearance of a new cultural pattern, or the realization of an innovative and creative modification in the action of human beings or collectivities.

Finally, the concept of social interaction is taken as an *interactive ordering* of men's life, in which ordering is conceived in its simplest and most common sense, having nothing to do with Weber's "life orders," but standing as a global, neutral term for structural changes, functional differentiation or time-space distancing. At the same time, the concept of interactive ordering does not exclude that the interaction process which reached such a complexity in human life as demonstrated by the contemporary social world, would or could take a modified direction or be channeled, through individual or collective creative efforts, toward some completely different lifeworld with unimaginable cultural, structural, functional, or time-space patterns.

In this sense, social interaction is, as Giddens pointed out, production or reproduction, at the same time, of social practices. Such dual social structures are constituted through the medium of human agency and through the reflexivity of human beings themselves. This duality explains how individual actors can reproduce the structural properties of large groups: collectivities and societies. Individuals and collectivities or other subgroups are dispersed in the social space; their action as situated agents is carried out in an atomistic way, but precisely constitutes an interaction because whatever the act, it has an impact on the integration or disintegration of society's great ensembles.

Structuration of social interaction does not imply reification (or dehumanization, using the expression of Berger and Luckmann) or ontological stratification, but a sort of objectification through distanciation, a distinction involving the reflexive acknowledgement by actors that structures are products of their interaction that enable them to envisage control of these structures. Here, the transcendence of human beings evidently plays an important role. The lack of temporal perspective separates structures from functions that, by definition, imply reference to temporality. Therefore, functional interdependence means only functional equivalence, whereas interdependence in structured social interaction is a matter of character and degree, as it always reflects relations of power.

Culture patterns, called by Giddens structures of significance [Giddens 1976: 123], include symbols and symbolic orders. Symbols belong to the institutional order as they are based on accumulated ensembles of meaning and form the symbolic order. Symbolic orders are of different sorts. For example, *ideological* orders serve interests of legitimation or domination. They can also express the *moral* order, itself constitutive of the social order, as there are always and everywhere rights to be respected and actualized and obligations to be enacted and satisfied in the course of interaction. The validity of a symbolic order depends on whether norms and values are shared, whether the participants' worldviews are compatible, or whether they clash because of non-identical normative judgements.

To take a concrete example of the difference between the interactive ordering and current views of the functioning of society, one might compare it with Weber's rationalization of the orders of life. Rationalization means, for Weber, the adaptation of "life orders" to the requirements of reason, a process which goes in the direction of realizing the objectives of purposive-instrumental rationality, of secularizing the lifeworld through the differentiation of various spheres and consequent reduction of the role of the normative sphere in favor of the purposive-instrumental. However, the process of rationalization as the road to progress and modernity is not at all obvious; it is based on two underlying assumptions: the belief in the universality of rationality as conceived in the Western culture, namely the rationality of science; and the Weberian belief in the inevitability of the process toward the "iron cage" of the disenchanted world, a *post facto* justification of the development of the modern world.

The dogma of the Weberian religious rationalization is a fallacy, because there is an incompatibility and incommensurability between faith, the center of any religious belief, and reason, an autonomous faculty of the human mind. Faith is faith and reason is reason; there is no intervention of the latter into the domain of the former, and vice versa. Kant simply settled this question by establishing the validity of human reflection within the boundaries of reason, placing all religious beliefs inside the boundaries of faith. What is, then, rationalization but a gradual transition toward uniformity between two incompatible and incommensurable domains, a prerequisite assumption of the Enlightenment's ideology of progress and secularization, a retrojection in history and a projection into the future of the outlook of a certain age? Thus, rationalization as a historical process is presented in a teleological perspective, as something inevitable (therefore implying a value judgement), but which, in fact, is a simple justification of the existing and seemingly inexorable, course of history in accordance with the comprehension of the "situational logic" of the age by one, however brilliant, thinker. Presuppositions and assumptions always underlie the concept of rationalization, a directionality of the action process in history which, in Parsons' crude formulation, means striving for the "optimization of gratification" [Parsons 1951: 352].

In contrast, the interactive ordering concept of social evolution and related cultural patterning analyzes the same events as Weber, describing the course of history without trying to give them the appearance that they had to be in unison with the requirements of rationality, which are merely the products of a particular period of man's temporal and cultural existence. It does not pretend that it was historically necessary for modernity to dawn upon us in a march forward on the road traced by the Enlightenment ideology, nor that it is to be assumed that there is no other way in which humanity's future could be shaped by men and their collectivities. Interactive ordering is, however, not a relativistic concept, though it recognizes relativism as an inter-cultural fact, because it does have a non-relativistic basis. First, the interactive perspective reveals certain similar features of social interaction as they appeared in the course of history and are detected in various civilizations today. Second, it recognizes that the "situational logic" of our age dictates a complete re-evaluation of the prevailing and future conditions of man's existence in view of the dramatic upheavals humanity witnessed during the last century and, especially, in view of the inevitable interaction of various, seemingly incommensurable, civilizations. Recourse to the concept of interactive ordering also means that legitimation through force or power rule is also taken into account, because consensual agreement can break down or be pushed aside by popular movements or autocrats put into power by such movements. The interactive ordering concept does not presuppose universal human reason, but takes as an empirical fact that various cultures show similarities in their reasoning, similarities on which their commonly shared norms and values are based. In this perspective, social interaction can be explicated in various civilizations with reference to comparable reasoning patterns, or it can refer to completely divergent normative positions, opposite or incommensurable reasoning in the interaction process.

(a) Interactive Ordering: Cultural Differentiation and Re-structuring

In view of the overwhelming importance of cultural differentiation, which completely modified the social order in the centuries since modernity was born, it is necessary to start the review of interactive ordering processes by analyzing two forms of fundamental mental differentiation and re-structuring emphasized by Giddens: "time-space distanciation" and the increased reflexivity of human interaction. It is indisputable that "all social interaction is situated within time-space boundaries of co-presence" [Giddens 1984: 332], though the existence of human groups and the institutional orders of society embrace whole historical periods. It was a crucial change, in comparison to the life in former societies, that in modernity, concepts of time and space were transformed in order to link events distanced temporally and spatially, by giving a new sense to human presence or absence. This factor of cultural differentiation was closely followed by the phenomenon of the "disembedding" of social structures and the continuous "reflexive ordering and reordering" of social relations. "Time-space distanciation" means, first, the transformation of local time, bounded by natural rhythms, into universal time which now embraces the whole world through the invention of more and more perfect instruments of measurement and ever-larger coordination efforts [Giddens 1990: 17-20]. Both phenomena are due to new cultural patterning. Temporal distanciation became possible through continuously advancing scientific inventions and their technological applications in transportation, travel, communication, and mass media. Today this is one of the real hallmarks of modern civilization.

Spatial distanciation (linked to temporal distanciation) was a consequence of the differentiation of space from the *place*, which referred, through history, to the limited geographical and historical setting of social interaction. *Place* was characterized by "presence" [ibid. 18], that is, a framework of action known and understood by everybody in the limited lifeworld it designated (if it was not a face-to-face interaction); on the contrary, space in modern times is vast though within the reach of most people through communication systems and mass media, which eliminate spatial distance as well as the phenomenon of absence even if what they create is not a real but only a quasi-presence.

The separation of local and universal time and of space from place allows for substitutability and recombination in relation to social events. This process made globalization possible, that is, a generalized insertion in globalized cultural and informational worlds through the quasi-presence created by communications networks and mass media. To local involvement ("circumstances of co-presence") is juxtaposed the interaction across distance ("the connections of presence and absence") [ibid. 64], part of a process of time-space distanciation. Giddens does not state whether this "displacing" effect of modernity leads to a loss of community, to an estrangement in an alienated world, or to an integration within "globalized 'communities' of shared experience" [Giddens 1990: 141].

The development of mass communications (the Thompsonian "mediazation" of modern culture) was accompanied by the spread of the ideologies for which they became an appropriate medium. Ideology was aptly defined by Thompson as "the thought of someone other than oneself" [Thompson 1990: 5], who explained it as the mobilization of meaning in the service of power. For Thompson, power represents "relations of domination" [ibid. 7] through maintenance, support, and enhancement of regularly asymmetrical power relations, as well as through ideologically conceived symbolic forms in socially structured contexts. Dialogical communication disappears; a fundamental break is produced in the relationship between the two sides of a communication process. The receivers-respondents cannot redirect the flow or reshape the character of information. Therefore, mass media became the preferred tool of intervention in the context of power relations [ibid. 15-17].

The concept of "disembedded"' institutions involving the "lifting out" of interactions from local contexts [Giddens 1990: 21], as well as the restructuring human relations across indefinite spans of time and space [Giddens 1990: 21], is a consequence of the time-space distanciation. It means that dis-embedded institutions are not tied to any definite temporal or spatial framework but necessitate an enormously extended coordination. Thus, they also provide the justification for the huge contemporary bureaucracies. The most important social consequence of time-space distanciation is, however, the opening up of wide possibilities in breaking away from the restraints of local habits and customs, from all communal traditions. This results in unexpected "insertions" and recombinations unavailable in other cultures and societies.

Giddens gives two examples of disembedding institutions: symbolic tokens such as money, and expert systems [ibid. 21-29]. Money, it is true, is the predominant means of time-space distanciation, and is the truly universal mode of temporal deferral. "Expert systems" include the professional expertise of technical competence in shaping material and social environments in which one lives; they remove activities from the immediate context, but are never able to properly handle problems because they do not have the local knowledge [Geertz 1983] required to find solutions for them. Therefore, *trust* in disembedded institutions is crucially important enabling them to fulfil their objectives; today, however, it seems that distrust in expert systems is growing more important as loss of confidence in such disembedded institutions is becoming more widespread [Giddens 1990: 83-84].

Reflexivity is fundamental in modern social life; it is closely linked to the time-space dimension of human experience. In interactive ordering, reflexivity stands for the "reflexive monitoring of action" [ibid. 36]. Such reflexive monitoring is pursued in all cultures; in non-Western civilizations, tradition assumed this task. Although tradition continues to play a certain role in modern society, reflexivity became a basic element of the collectivities' lives, "thought and action are constantly refracted back upon one another" [ibid. 38]. One of the many paradoxes of the modern predicament is that this wholesale reflexivity goes against the rationalism of the age, and does not secure epistemological certainty [ibid. 38-39], because in modernity, knowledge is doubly circular in the social domain. All knowledge is, in principle revisable, and through reflexivity, it is effectively "revised" as it seeps into public conscience and hence becomes constitutive of it.

The most recent phenomenon which entered human consciousness and which belongs to the theme of reflexivity at a societal level, is the transformation of modern society into *risk* society through the development and employment of newer technologies as well as through the aggravation of social problems due to economic hardship and the exclusive validity of the instrumental-purposive rationality. This concerns environmental damage, the growing urban pauperization, or the appearance of large-scale terrorism linked to religious, social or political transformations of society. Civilizational risks are ascribed and universal, based on race, skin color, ethnicity, gender, or age.

Though these risks should be a matter for the reflexive monitoring of all members of society, it is escaping their attention and competence because in most cases evaluating such risks involves specialized professional knowledge. In addition, people realize only gradually that the present form of interactive social ordering, based on the reign of the individual, is not satisfactory anymore. This means, in our perspective, that modernity's culture patterns exhausted their possibilities and that a new cultural framework of social ordering must be elaborated in view of rendering life better for the coming generations. This, of course, cannot be admitted by scientific and bureaucratic mentality, because to evaluate risks from the point of view of society, one has to refer to ethical principles and moral practice and assume the meta-level of meaningful rationality. Generally, excuses refer to the system which is as it is, which cannot be totally changed, and which authorizes an irresponsible attitude toward everyone.

The most threatening aspect of this situation is that the majority of people do not realize the dangers of risk society, or are only slowly awakening to what these dangers signify. The ultimate menace in a risk society is, in the words of Ulrich Beck, that such civilizational risks encompass even the natural environment of our lifeworld. Thus, the antithesis of nature and society disappears: "At the end of the twentieth century nature *is* society and society is also *'nature'*" [Beck 1992a: 80].

(b) INTERACTIVE ORDERING: STRATIFICATION AND HIERARCHY

Every human group and society is structured in accordance with its particular cultural patterning and through various modes of division or subgroupings, such as tribal organization or a kinship system. With the growing complexity of the group's lifeworld and of its activities linked to environmental changes, including more developed techniques of land cultivation, craft, or industrial production, the divisions and subdivisions of the group are increasingly stratified. According to Weber, stratification is based on *social status*, which reflects a style of life or an occupation pursued; a "hereditary charisma," a position of prestige obtained by virtue of birth, or "the transformation into monopoly of political and hierocratic authority by certain groups in the society" [Weber 1947: 428-429].[3]

The most important case of social stratification is the Indian caste system, which applies an invariant principle in the mode of social structuring. Its religious origins are well known, as it is derived from the divine moral order (*dharma*) and, therefore, it is an innate part of the personality of a Hindu. In principle, it is based on aptitude (*guna*) and function (*karma*), but not on birth (*jati*), though the existence of the *jati* caste (due to mixed marriages of members of the original four castes) voided, from the beginning, the immutable and preordained order of the caste system. The particular stages of life (*asrama*) introduce, in this combination, the temporal perspective of human life. The individual disappears behind the divinely-established structure and effaces himself in the vast, impersonal cosmic law and movement. It is important, however, to insist on the fact that the soteriological value of the mundane world for the individual does not become effective through caste and hierarchy, but through *dharma*, the dutiful performance of prescribed rites and duties.

Stratified societies are in general *hierarchically* ordered, and this presupposes a coherent worldview regulating such hierarchical ordering. Following Dumont, the definition of hierarchical ordering consists in ranking the elements of a whole (defined by the worldview) in relation to the whole [Dumont 1980: 66]. He conceives of hierarchy dialectically as a bidimensional ordering and, contrary to the contemporary condemnation of it as instituting inequality, affirms that a hierarchy can be ordered in a symmetrical or equi-statutory as well as in an asymmetrical way. Hierarchy as ordering principle of interactive social action is widely condemned today, because it contradicts the individualistic egalitarianism of democratic Western societies. It is all the more striking that hierarchy was recently defended by Niklas Luhmann, who called it a "discovery of genius", because it means a unity represented in diversity [Luhmann 1987: 105].

(c) INTERACTIVE ORDERING: FUNCTIONAL DIFFERENTIATION

Recent theories of society examine its complex nature due to functional differentiation. These theories are generally combined with some version of structuralist views, therefore frequently the structuralist-cum-functionalist designation is used. Robert Merton, for whom function signifies adaptation or adjustment, considers the postulate of functional unity as an empirical matter; one cannot assume that functionalism evidences full integration in a society (integration being for Merton a formalistic concept). Against those holding the thesis of *functional universalism*, he considered that persisting forms of culture are inevitably functional [Merton 1957: 55-60]; in fact, social structure and function determine and affect each other in every society, though structure limits functional possibilities [ibid. 52-53]. Social forms contain functional as well as dysfunctional phenomena. In regard to the postulate of functional indispensability, he noted that this either means indispensability of certain functions (functional necessity or functional prerequisites), or indispensability of certain cultural patterns or social institutions [ibid. 32-37].

Differentiation in Parsons' System

A social action system is defined by Talcott Parsons as "an integrated structure of action elements in relation to a situation" [Parsons 1951: 36] or, in a second formulation elaborated with Shils, as "modes of organization of motivated action" [Parsons-Shils 1951: 55]. Distinguished from social action systems, are cultural systems which consist of symbolic patterns; the interrelated parts of such cultural patterns are, first, value and belief systems and, second, systems of expressive symbols.

According to Parsons' theory, *the structurally significant components of the action system are differentiated.* In the first place, there is the paradigmatic case of instrumental and purposeful action based on the reciprocity of goal orientations of the participants in social interaction which, therefore, is *universalistically* determined. Such an action is entirely linked to the individual's egotistic goals, though it might happen that a plurality of individual actors act in common, and the result of their cooperation is something which enters as a unit into the exchange process. The second type of action, obeying a *particularistic* orientation, is the expressive or emotional one in which the goal attainment is expected within the boundaries of the immediate action though it may include as desired entities, or as possible symbols, an infinite range of environmental objects. In the cathectic and expressive domain, solidarity or loyalty corresponds to cooperation in the instrumental-purposive domain. Parsons links, through the expressive symbolism of solidarity or loyalty, the individual actor to the collectivity of which he is a part and in which he obtains a status without eliminating the pre-dominance of the actor's purposive-instrumental behavior.

When an actor must choose between relevant alternatives, he acts in accordance with value-patterns to which he is committed. Value-patterns, goal-attainment, adaptation, integration, latent tension management, and pattern maintenance represent certain norms, standards, or criteria of selection and are integrated in a whole within the personality of the actor and the culture he belongs to. Such integrated value-patterns allow participants in interaction to have reciprocal or complementary expectations through communication in a common system of symbols.

As value norms are institutionalized in interaction contexts, they appear for the actors as: role-expectations for the behavior of the actor, and as sanctions, positive or negative, which are also expectations but relative to the contingently probable reactions of others. Role is defined by Parsons as [the] "sector of the total orientation system of an individual actor" [Parsons 1951: 38]. *Role types are differentiated in accordance with the differentiated cultural patterns institutionalized in roles.* The three types of role-orientations, cognitive, expressive and evaluative, can be combined but each has primacy in specific types of roles. The differentiated roles or role-clusters are integrated in a functioning system. The totality of differentiated roles constitutes the social structure because it is a mode of integration of social interaction. Collectivities or role-clusters also contribute to integration through role-orientations which overlap or are connected on the edges.

Institutionalized role-expectations governed by value patterns relate directly to the moral order and social solidarity. The *integration of value-orientation patterns* imposes imperatives on the social system, as these patterns have to be articulated in accordance with motivational and situational constraints pertaining to the situation of the human species or to other elements within the same social system. Such coordination is indispensable in ensuring the stability of mutual expectations based on shared acceptance of value-orientations, and can only be achieved if culture patterns are internalized by individuals and thus become constitutive of the interaction processes. In his first conceptualization of pattern-variables (of which the first and the fifth were later abandoned), Parsons enumerates five such variables in respect of role definition. He then proceeds, through binary associations, to elaborate four main pattern-combinations that characterize all social interaction. These four are: the universalistic-achievement pattern (an ideal conceptualization of post-War America); the universalistic-ascription pattern; the particularistic-achievement pattern (represented by traditional Chinese society), and the particularistic-ascriptive pattern (which would certainly fit a number of African societies).

It is clear from the preceding pages that the main elements of the Parsonsian system are the individual actors, the interactive action process, and the cultural patterning of the latter (the natural world as non-active environment being presupposed as the framework). Each can vary only to the extent determined by the others in the sense that the minimum conditions of functioning of the others should be maintained. There are three aspects to the operations of the social system's units: the act as part of a process of interaction between an actor and others; the status-role reflecting the structure of relationships between different actors involved in the interactive process; and, finally, the participation of an actor in a plurality of patterned, interactive relationships. In Parsons' conceptualization, an actor represents more complexity than a bearer of one status-role because he is a *bundle* of statuses and roles. Collectivities, simultaneously actors and objects, represent composite units of parts of the individual actors' interactions detached from their other status-roles.

Institutions, relational, regulative and cultural, are complexes of integrated role clusters of strategic structural significance for a social system. In consequence, they are of a higher order than roles that are composed of a plurality of role-patterns; institutions always involve common values and morality. The distinction between a collectivity, a system of concretely interactive specific roles, and an institution is that the latter represents a patterned complex of role-expectations. It can apply to any number of collectivities, but the same collectivity may also be encompassed by several institutions. The antithesis of full institutionalization is the Durkheimian *anomie*, the breakdown of the normative order and the absence of structured complementarity between interactive individuals or collectivities.

Power, economic or political, is not as pervasive in Parsons' social system concept as in Giddens' structuration of society because Parsons' conceptualization is reductive in the sense that he links the problem of power to the relational context of instrumental action in the form of a network of exchange relationships of functionally specific institutions. Power is the totality of facilitating-rewarding instruments available for use when the totality of differentiated roles has to be adapted to the capacities and requirements of incumbents. This conceptualization justifies the linkage of power to universalistic orientations and the breakdown of particularistic ties, though instability or reversal to particularistic orientations occurs if universalistic norms are not institutionalized.

Power, for Parsons as for Giddens, stands for a generalized capability to act, a potency or disposition, having the means to act with results; it does not characterize specific types of action, but is a property of interaction where the outcome of the interaction depends on others as well.   Power, in most cases, is asymmetrical but the reciprocity of influence is never entirely eliminated in any social relation.   Frequently, though, power relations are hierarchical, overshadowing the residual reciprocity that still exists. It is in this case that occurs what Bowles and Gintis call "socially consequential exercises" of power, implying not only power of coercion, but also substantially affecting the lives of others in the actor's own interest [Bowles-Gintis 1986: 79]. It is power which draws upon resources enabling agents to reproduce them in the course of their action, because power and, in consequence, domination are also constitutive of social interaction.

Niklas Luhmann: Differentiation in World Perspective

Luhmann's definition of a social system is much more complex and all-embracing than the system concept of other representatives of the systemic approach, and, without doubt, is a non-ontological and constructivist frame of reference. His definition conceives of society as constituted by meaningfully interrelated communicative interactions which, through their intervoweness, are differentiated from the environment.   A meaningful, communicative interaction reflects a single set of interrelated choices.   Consequently, the social system produced is only one actualized out of a large array of possibilities inherent in the environment. Thus, environment, for Luhmann, has a wider scope than a specific social system and it is of much higher complexity [Luhmann 1982: 230]. The decisive factor as a "single set of interrelated choices" means that societies, like any other organisms, proceed by self-selection, that is, they constitute themselves through an inner development.

Communicative actions as selective processes can be constitutive of a plurality of subsystems like interaction, organization, and social groups, but their ordered and patterned environment is the global social system.   In addition, social systems and their subsystems are not mutually exclusive, and their degree of compatibility is more or less co-variant with the degree of complexity of their internal environment. This interplay between various systems-configurations makes it possible to have a certain freedom in system development. Acts of communication set in motion reciprocal selection processes representing conditions of future communicative interactions. Such a concept serves Luhmann to develop his views of societies as carriers of evolutionary processes. In a pronounced dialectical manner, he considers that evolution builds on pre-existing circumstances and events, dispensing society, at the same time, from being conditioned by what contributed to its genesis.

The formulation of the concept of social system in terms of communicative interaction leads Luhmann to the idea of horizon-formation based on meaning. Meaning is understood in a very peculiar way, as an ensemble of meaning-horizons offering a range of possibilities for selection; it thus becomes a manipulative tool in the management of communicative interaction based on expectations shared by participants through reducing a plurality of uncoordinated but available choices to one which satisfies the mutually expected, possible behavior of actors.

Interaction is simultaneously meaning generating and meaning using, it marks off expectations as well limits to action. Meaning generating and meaning using are rational expressions of reflexivity and constitute the ground for self-thematization. Meaning becomes reality, the world a meaningfully constituted world, but not in the sense according to which culture, society and person commonly share a unique lifeworld. The role of meaning is to facilitate the generalization of communicative practices. It can be compatible with several heterogeneous states of the system or of the environment. The temporal dimension, finally, signifies that society is primarily thematized either with a view to its past or to its future, with the present always staying as the focal, directive point of communication. The co-variation of temporal structures with forms of social differentiation is evident or, in other terms, time mediates interdependencies in a functionally differentiated society.

Luhmann presents his concepts describing *system differentiation* in a logical sequence. First of all, system differentiation is system building, a reflexive and recursive form of replication resulting in the creation of two environments: one external, common to all sub-systems, and one internal, in which subsystems represent an environment for each other. In this sense, differentiation is a reproduction of a system by internal disjunction. Therefore, the function of differentiation is increased internal selectivity, or increase "in available possibilities for variation or choice" [ibid. 231-232]. In this process, different degrees of differentiation and complexity are reached, reflected in various forms of systemic setup. Only three forms: segmentation, stratification-differentiation and functional differentiation were selected in the course of evolution, according to Luhmann. These represented combinations of two asymmetrical dichotomies: system and environment, equality and inequality.

Functional differentiation displaces the emphasis to the level of subsystems; through integrating specific functions in a new combination of system and environment, it creates new problems with new solutions which did not exist in preceding societies. Equality and inequality, for example, are distributed very differently: functions are by their nature unequal, but access to them has to be equal, that is, independent of any relations to other functions. Society thus simultaneously increases and decreases internal dependencies and interdependencies of its subsystems. An increase is the result of specialization and institutionalization of functions, a decrease is engendered by loosening complementary structures between sub-systems and environments.

Socio-cultural evolution thus consists in the increasing separation or differentiation of interactive systems, organization systems, and societal systems, though their total disjunction is not possible. However, as differentiation advances and the three sub-systems become increasingly segregated, the interconnection and coordination of dissociated levels becomes more and more difficult and urgent. Various stages of societal evolution coexist simultaneously, but at the age of functional differentiation stratification appears no longer legitimate. Luhmann, consequently, treats historical development teleologically. Socio-cultural evolution is viewed as a gradual differentiation process from primitive societies to world society, passing through a sequence of regionally limited high cultures — as was ours before the modern age and as are, at present, the other great civilizations of the world. This view justifies the absolute priority of the modern Western culture, the only one in which system formation took place in Luhmannian terms, terms that definitely ignore the dramatic drawbacks and other inconveniences manifested at this level of systemic evolution.

Change depends on chance ("the contingent coincidence of contingencies") if the conditions required by evolutionary imperatives are present. However, functional differentiation in the Luhmannian framework can promote social change by increasing and diversifying the horizon of possibilities necessary for selective adaptation of each social system and subsystem. This scenario is particularly evident in cases when functional differentiation reaches an extreme intensity and, in consequence, structural modifications "outrun each other," not capable of keeping up with the required pace of change. Social change from more simple toward more complex, horizontal differentiation is fundamentally linked to the direction taken in the evolutionary, temporal dimension. Therefore, in functionally differentiated societies, as Bernard Giesen demonstrated it, "order is always a process-generated, provisional and transitory structure that has its continuity solely in the infinite nature of the process itself and in the lack of simultaneity among different spheres."[4] It implies a reconstruction of temporal concepts and perspectives, as well as the transformation of the lifeworld into several, impersonal, abstract entities of "collective singulars" such as the nation or the state.   The process of change becomes an empty frame of reference, because social reality is severed from human intentionality and agency.

3. *Interactive Social Ordering and Other Civilizations*

In cross-cultural comparisons, especially in regard to social structures and social change, it is good to keep in mind that social reality is built on differential systems and positions. Herskovits wrote on the respect of difference in social life,

> The very core of cultural relativism is the social discipline that comes of respect of differences -- mutual respect. Emphasis on the worth of many ways of life, not one, is an affirmation of the values in each culture. Such emphasis seeks to understand and to harmonize goals, not to judge and destroy those that do not dovetail with our own [Herskovits 1948: 77].

The total destruction of traditional elements and of conventional features of social systems in different cultural areas of the world is, however, seen by many as a necessary condition to modernize countries with non-Western civilizations. Modernization includes industrialization, social mobilization following the Western pattern, purposive-instrumental rationality, and commercial or gratification-oriented mentalities, which would (or is so imagined) automatically be accompanied by secularized and universal norms: progress, democracy, and freedom. This view is essentially based on two assumptions: first, that the transitional phase of transformation toward a Western-type society has to follow comparable and similar patterns whatever the cultural environment should be, forgetting that social reality is culturally defined; and, second, that once some important institutional frameworks are established, irreversible structural and organizational developments will follow and a sustained growth in all social spheres will be initiated in accordance with a common evolutionary orientation, *even if cultural and social-psychological foundations are not adapted.*

In addition to these characterizations of developmental and modernization processes, many others have been discussed in the various social sciences, such as the important difference emphasized by Mead between "primitive" and "civilized" societies, concerning the position of the individual. He refers to the fact that traditional societies offer much less scope to the individual and to his creative and innovative capabilities. On contrast, modern societies, in his view, developed as a result of the "progressive social liberation of the individual self" [Mead 1934-1938, Vol. 1: 221] leading to general human progress. The individual in traditional societies had to perfectly copy a definite social type, given and exemplified in the reigning worldview and lifeworld; that is, he had to conform to the social conduct prescribed for particular situations. In modern society, on the contrary, the individual can mould his personality and behavior more freely, and modify stereotypes generally applied by society. But, in accordance with Mead's whole "social self" theory, even in highly evolved human societies, the individual is never freed from its concrete relations to the social collectivity it belongs to; he reflects in his self or personality the overall pattern of experience and the features of the organized behavior of the social whole of which he is "a creative expression or embodiment" [ibid. 222].

All descriptions of social evolution are based on a simplistic evolutionary model of unilinear development, excluding pluralistic choices. An attempt to conceptualize this trend was made by Talcott Parsons in his theory of "evolutionary universals." He also calls them "structural innovations" that substantially increase generalized adaptive capacities and put those species not inventing them at a definite disadvantage, from the point of view not of survival, but of further developmental opportunities.

The evolutionary universals whose appearance Parsons cannot explain but by random mutation include, first of all, an explicit cultural legitimation of differentiated social functions and a well-developed system of social stratification. Parsons designates these two as the most important in the fundamental change from primitive to modern societies. Others include markets and the invention of money, bureaucracy, a universal legal system, and democratic political organization. The six evolutionary universals are complemented by four pre-requisites of socio-cultural development: religion, communication through language, kinship organization, and technology. The ten enumerated features of evolution are expected to facilitate the diffusion of the Western model to other civilizational areas.[5]

In the same vein, Habermas tried to apply Piaget's stages of cognitive development characterized not as modifications of content, but of structural levels of learning ability. He distinguishes between mythical, religious-metaphysical, and modern modes of thought, and suggests that the transition between them implies the categorical devaluation of the former stage ("devaluation shifts") [Habermas 1984-1989, Vol. 1: 68].

In opposition to the Parsonsian conceptualization of the evolution of society, Etzioni refers to a neo-evolutionist model. This assumes that there is certain directionality in social change, and that genetic processes select one of a limited number of theoretically-determined available options; he calls this model the sequential-option model [Etzioni 1968: 572]. Such a sequential-option model of socio-cultural evolution appears to be much closer to reality, as selection among the options available is made, in addition to genetic processes, by cultural orientations and related information systems.

Among the opponents of undue generalization of the limited historical experience of the modern West were Freud [Freud 1961: 36 and 88-89] as well as Max Weber. The latter cautioned against the use of ideal-types [Weber 1949: 101] which, through exaggeration and simplification, could lead to an underestimation of the role played in European evolution by kinship ties and communities. Weber also thought that kinship and community allegiance may be compatible with modernization in other areas of the world, and, most importantly, he pointed out that it is not necessary that all people should reach modernization in the same way, or be modernized or "developed" at all [Bendix 1977: 394-395].

Weber's presentation of the problems related to modernization acquired a special importance today, after thirty five years of developmental efforts which tried to ignore the influence of traditions, and people's inherent, culturally conditioned desire not to abandon their lifeworld and community for an atomized, individualist society. Jacques Ellul complemented his scathing attack against the modern civilization of technocratic society and gave a particular insight into problems of modernization. He was convinced that technique already eliminated humanism from Western civilization in which it completely dominates man's destiny, and that technological development will completely transform all countries on the earth's surface by annihilating their culture, their particular features, and their specific social structures. This seemed all the more ineluctable, as every culture is a whole; technique imposes changes in some of the spheres of a particular culture, the whole structure will crumble. Referring to the experience of the West, Ellul insists on the evident truth that technical advance does not bring mental equilibrium, therefore, civilizations encountering external impulses to follow the path of technical progress and atomization of society may escape from a complete disequilibrium through preserving their traditional values for as long as possible [Ellul 1964: 122 and 126].

If we compare descriptions of interactive social ordering in the West through the phases of segmentation and stratification to the immense complexity of a functionally differentiated society, the principal question to be answered is whether all such analyses have any practical relevance for non-Western societies. What are the pre-requisites of social change? What are the characteristics of the manifold ways in which change occurs? It is certain that change in a society must simultaneously be spatial and temporal; it means a spatial juxtaposition of varying patterns and structures, on the one hand, and, on the other hand, a movement, a sequence of events marking off turning-points or occurrences in a transition toward a more stable position. The most important characteristic of change is independent from the spatio-temporal modifications and denotes a clear difference as between patterns and structures, or put differently, change takes place when a novel cultural pattern is created or a previous pattern appears in a completely new relational context.

It seems the most appropriate method in dealing with inter-civilizational differences, whether they consist of converging tendencies or conflicts, is the *pattern analysis* set forth by adherents of the institutional school and, in particular, by Kaplan, Diesing, Wilber, and Harrison. The justification of such an opinion is the great number of factors to be considered as well as their relational nature, which influences their evolution toward functional differentiation [Wilber-Harrison 1978: 85]. As Diesing [1971: 137] pointed out "the holist standpoint includes the belief that human systems tend to develop a characteristic wholeness or integrity." In opposition to the covering law model of the natural sciences, pattern analysis is uniquely suited to the study of social phenomena. A process of change is always inherent in social interaction, a process not mechanical (as believed following the Newtonian paradigm in physics), but shaped by human intentionality and by the cultural conditioning of society. Therefore a holistic and evolutionary analysis of pattern relations is only able to resolve problems inherent in sociocultural changes [Kaplan 1964: 71] through the inclusion of "validated hypotheses or themes" into a pattern or network reflecting the multiple interconnections of parts and of the whole. Pattern analysis leaves open a range of possibilities of occurrences; this is crucial in view of the fact that only *ex post facto* can be established which possibility has actualized.

It is essential to remember here Giddens' insistence that structural properties (or institutionalized features of social systems) are simultaneously enabling and constraining because the dualistic nature of human agency is related to time-space distanciation. Human societies would not exist without human agency which, in a continuous praxis, produces and transforms them through interaction with other members of society. In addition to structural constraints, there are internal structural contradictions (distinguished from conflicts which denote struggle between individuals and collectivities); these contradictions are due to constitutive factors. Primary contradictions involve social totalities centered on the state; secondary contradictions follow from the effects of the primary ones.

Giddens describes tribal societies as not only consisting in an order of co-presence following the rhythms of nature, but also as cognitively integrating the natural world in their lifeworld. He considers, following Lévi-Strauss, that mythic worldviews establish "homologies" between natural and social conditions, or an equivalence between fundamental contrasts or disruptions in the natural and human worlds, and concludes therefore that "myths mediate existential contradiction cognitively" [Giddens 1984: 194]. It is consequential to this conceptualization that in tribal societies, the reason for their resistance to change is not their lack of adaptation to nature, but exactly the opposite, their direct proximity, their all-embracing and immediate cognitive identification with it. Existential contradictions are lived through the kinship system and resolved in accordance with tradition which inserts the finitude of human existence into the perspective of moral timelessness. The segmentation of the social system, which is at the same time a de-centering into multiple entities, excludes, by its nature, structural contradictions.

The appearance of cities, and of the corollary phenomenon of the state, signals the corresponding appearance of structural contradictions. Existential and structural contradictions co-evolve; the lifeworld of the city is alienated from nature with attitudes and symbolic systems detached from natural elements and events. At first, the power of the state is based on the symbiotic-antagonistic relation of the city and the countryside (a thesis not yet convincingly established); the state prefers the ahistorical character of the culture of tribal societies and maintains a continuously ambivalent relationship with tradition, despite the consolidation of its power. At this moment of social evolution no secondary structural contradictions yet exist. These only appear when, using Giddens' expression, the era of "state-based" societies greatly modifies social relationships across a wide space and time spectrum [ibid. 196]. The era of nation-states is characterized by an even more pronounced opposition between urban centers and the countryside, given the artificial nature ("created environments") of urban conglomerations.

The most important consequence of the domination of society by nation-states is that existential and structural contradictions are completely separated, and one could say that the total disjunction of society's organized life (though not of the lifeworld) from nature results in a sort of collective schizophrenic state in the collective psyche. Nature becomes a means of production and a subject of exploitation for the satisfaction of man's needs. Existential contradictions continue to exist in the lifeworld underlying the structural conditions that appeared in modernity. Therefore, the most fundamental juxtaposition and opposition develop between the existential and structural contradictions, between lifeworld and "created" reality and environment. The secondary contradiction of the contemporary evolution of society is the internationalization of economic activities much beyond the boundaries of sovereign states, though the development of the economic sphere was conditioned by the power of the nation-state.

In contrast to Giddens's notion of contradictions, structural and existential, the concepts of crisis proposed by Claus Offe which apply to the modernization crises in other civilizations [Offe 1984: 131-134]. Offe calls crises processes in which structures of a social system are called into question, or in which the identity of the system is jeopardized or even destroyed. He then distinguishes between three types of crisis-concepts. First, sporadic crises are caused by events outside the boundaries of the system, unforeseeable, acute and eventually catastrophic, but confined to a certain period of time. They cannot be structurally explained because not engendered by internal weaknesses of the system. Second, the concept of crisis refers to mechanisms producing successive events; they are abnormalities appearing in social processes that develop inside the system. They are therefore not contingent, but linked to structural configurations or malfunctions. The system initiates in itself counteracting tendencies and, consequently, the outcome of such a crisis is unpredictable. Third, the system-crisis describes crisis-prone developments in societal totalities, designated here as civilizational crisis.

Culture patterns, such as ordered clusters of significant symbols, traditions, institutions, and shared values, are very different in other civilizations; through them men make sense of their lifeworld and, indeed are the elements constitutive of it. As Melville Herskovits noted, there are no "objective criteria of permanence and change." Simultaneously present features of culture, like universal patterns in locally manifested forms, motivated, make the analysis of contradictions of cultural and social forms all the more difficult [Herskovits 1948: 15-20]. However, as culture is an action-oriented information system from the evolutionary perspective, it is natural that certain patterns and certain relationships among patterns may recur in different civilizations, that is, that they are common or represent similar configurations in various groups of the species, though frequently with different content [Benedict 1959: 207].

In exploring the possibility of a dialogue between civilizations, it is not indispensable to identify these common or similar cultural patterns existing in different cultural worlds. It is rather crucial to pin down the major disjunctive factors between them, in order to understand the fundamental divergence between their respective social evolution and orientations toward change. It is not enough to refer to the inquiring nature of modern man regarding choices and his basic allegiance to rationality (defined in a rather autonomous way by each group or individual), but one has to find the essential points of differentiation in their historical path. The opposition is neither of Apollonian (classical) or the Faustian (modern and rational) types, nor of Dionysian (frenzied illumination) to the Apollonian (classically measured and conscious), as Spengler defined them [Spengler 1986, Vol. 1: 183-216], because the contradiction and incommensurability between Western culture and other contemporary civilizations are of a completely different nature. It is neither a question of acculturation, cultural innovation, or drift, nor of socialization for those of other civilizations to grow into the modern cultural framework; it is a displacement or rebirth, mentally and culturally, because of the gulf created by the advent of Western modernity, as Ellul's example of technical domination or Gellner's example of generalized education clearly indicate.

Thus, the phenomenon of cultural diversity studied is, in Herskovits' terms, a *culture-change*, the total disappearance of an old and the acceptance of a completely new cultural world. It has nothing to do with selective borrowing from the West. It is all or nothing, or, at least, it appears to be an uncompromising deal. Borrowing in whatever sense does not represent a solution for the people of non-Western civilizations. A good example of this is given by Dumont, who refers to the replacement of hierarchy in traditional societies, by modern ideals of democracy and equality. If hierarchical ranking disappears and if equality and identity are fused into the concept of the individual, the natural difference of human groups and their status may be reasserted by somatic or religious characteristics, by racism or communalism [Dumont 1980: 16]. In fact, such borrowings ignore the dialectical interplay of patterns of meaning and of the forces and events of the lifeworld. They also ignore that, in the Giddensian sense, these patterns of meaning which lead to societal changes are themselves the product of changes and upheavals.

Instead of problems of borrowing, it is more useful to speak in terms of secondary socialization. Primary socialization is, of course, important, as childhood rearing gives the fundamentals for a man's whole life. Secondary socialization conceived of as either the internalization of the institutional order or "institution-based 'sub-worlds'" [Berger-Luckmann 1966: 127], or the acquisition of role-specific knowledge and vocabularies in a modern, differentiated world is of the utmost importance for the problem of development and modernization. If people went through a secondary socialization process different from the one necessary in modern society, they have to make severe adjustments to it, or to go through still another socialization in a new institutional sub-world, a very difficult enterprise with ineffective, unpredictable results. For the younger generations, even if their secondary socialization process adapted them to the new institutional order, they would still at risk not to be adapted to it because their primary socialization gave them a worldview that is incompatible with the modern institutional sub-world. Discrepancies between primary and secondary socialization processes, on the one hand, and between the secondary socialization process and the inevitable social changes toward a more complex and differentiated society, on the other, may lead to situations where individuals "internalized different realities *without* identifying with them" [ibid. 158]. The reality internalized does not become their reality, but a reality useful in specific life-situations, or to be used for specific purposes in roles from which they remain distant and detached.

As a final result, the social institutional order will not be but a system of reciprocal manipulations behind which another more real order looms. Incommensurable socialization requirements and processes are also frequently the sources of incomprehension and hostility between people raised in the orbits of non-Western civilizations and people in technical assistance programs who were socialized in the West but who want to help, through furthering social and economic modernization, in terms of their own secondary socialization.

The above analysis of interactive ordering of society and, especially, of functional differentiation shows that in the West, a functionally highly differentiated and extremely complex society did develop in the last three centuries. In other cultures, societies are segmented and in many of them, though they are stratified, no real functional, but only structural differentiation took place, Japan being the only exception to this statement. In some societies of the Far East such as China, Korea, Taiwan, or Singapore, the transition to a completely functionally-differentiated society appears not yet complete. If one wants to apply Parsons' value-pattern combinations to non-Western societies, all of the above can be used for classificatory purposes in characterizing these societies *except* the first, the universal-achievement pattern which prevails in the West. The universalistic-ascriptive pattern is close to the organization of Indian society, the particularistic-achievement pattern can be taken as describing the ancient Chinese society (as Parsons himself qualified it), and, finally, the particularistic-ascriptive pattern reflects well the situation on the African continent. However, one should not consider all these cases corresponding to different Parsonsian patterns as clear-cut, but as representing different shades of transition between different patterns, and that one should look at social development in different parts of the world as a *sui generis* evolution which *must* respect the congruence of given cultural and evolving social patterns.

As far as Western civilization is concerned, structural and functional differentiation is generally considered today as the inevitable outcome of the society's evolution, as if condemned to the "eternal recurrence of the same" or further functional differentiation, although the disastrous results, in the shape of an atomistic society, are already undeniable.   It can only be hoped that through dialogue with other civilizations, the Western path can deviate from the present ever-increasing differentiation (if this is still possible), in order to re-discover an integrative force which can save it from total disintegration. Other civilizations will, at the same time, hopefully realize to what extent their supposedly inevitable social differentiation is possible and necessary in congruence with their own cultural background, thus permitting them to adopt the West's technological innovations and, consequently, to achieve its economic and material successes.

CHAPTER SIX

ETHNICITY AND THE NATION-STATE

Ethnicity as related to the nation-state represent one of the most serious problems at the end of the second millenium. This is certainly not an accident; as Patricia Mayo noted: "To be happy and balanced, man must have its roots in a living social group."[1] Octavio Paz also recently pointed out the error of modernity ignoring the motivating force of national consciousness:

> The history of the twentieth century has confirmed something well known to all the historians of the past; something our ideologies have stubbornly ignored: the strongest, fiercest, most enduring political passions are nationalism and religion [Paz 1985: 9].

The rise of nationalism in the modern era is explained by Bernard Lewis as a product of secularization, of the Weberian "disenchantment" of the Western world, replacing religion as the source of ultimate identity, loyalty, and authority in social life.[2] Nationalism and its product the nation-state became not only the foundation of collective existence and of supreme authority, but also an object of worship in place of a transcendental God. The increasing domination of social and political life by nationalism and the nation-state from the end of the eighteenth century led to an inner contradiction in Western civilization, namely, the paradox of its fractured political reality against the expectation of a triumphant march toward the destiny of universal man and his universal history. Paul Ricoeur considered that, until very recently, history was always spoken of in the singular sense, but men were always dealt with in the plural sense. The existence of nation-states reflects reality in the plural against the idealistic belief in a unique (singular) history of mankind [Ricoeur 1965: 38].

1. *The Basic Tenets of Discourse on Ethnicity and Nationalism*

Ethnicity is based upon cultural distinctiveness and not on race or any other physically distinguishable quality, although there is a belief in each ethnic group of the common descent of its members.   The ethnic community *is* a community of culture, with shared beliefs, values, symbols, and ways of life that differentiates its members from other groups.   Ethnicity, understood as a racial difference, is not demonstrable; even where it has been fused with a state tradition in such ethnically more or less homogeneous states as Japan or Korea. In the sense of cultural community, ethnicity certainly represents the oldest distinction among human groups, whether centered on religious beliefs or a "myths of the origins" or common historical experiences [Weber 1978, Vol. 1: 388].

Ethnic groups generally strive to achieve autonomy, as in the time of the old empires, when the rulers lived at a distance of thousands of miles from them, or in modern times, when they strive to achieve political independence in the form of nation-states so as to be able to live in accordance with their own community's way of life.   The political origins of ethnicity, as suggested by Weber, are not probable at all; it is more plausible, as Arnason pointed out, that religion played a significant role in ethnic survival, especially when the ethnic community identified itself with a salvation religion [Arnason 1990: 217].   As a result, the particularistic closure of the group and the universalistic potential of the religion created a tension which, in retrospect, must have been beneficial, as in the case of the Arab tribal *ethnies* proves during centuries after the *Hidjra*. According to Anthony Smith, four features distinguish an ethnic group: the knowledge of unique group origins, such as myths of origin or of liberation; the knowledge of the group's unique history related to its destiny; the differentiation of cultural dimensions of collective individuality; and a sense of unique solidarity of the community [Smith 1981: 66].

Connor calls *nations* "self-differentiating ethnic groups" and nationalism loyalty to such groups; the "popularly held awareness or belief that one's own group is unique in a most vital sense" is a pre-requisite of nationhood [Connor 1972: 334]. He gives another important element for the definition of the nation as "an ethnic group may, therefore, be other-defined, the nation must be self-defined" [Connor 1978: 388]. Smith's definition of the political nation, in contrast to the ethnic group, though emphasizing the unmediated nature of national community, shows that the latter is a product of socio-economic and intellectual development at a certain specific moment of history:

> Nations are *ethnie* which are economically integrated around a common system of labour with complementarity of roles, and whose members possess equal rights as citizens of the unmediated political community [Smith 1983: 167].

He correctly points to the fundamental distinction between ethnicity and nationalism by saying that the former is a phenomenon in people's consciousness, whereas the latter is inspired from above, that is, by intellectuals, politicians, or idealistic group leaders. Ethnicity is, nevertheless, the main component of a nation as a community of culture, a "cultural self-determination" in Sir Isaiah Berlin's words,[3] in addition to its being a political community or an already established territorial state. Its integrative force operates even in people who live in diaspora or in tribal societies (of which the latter are probably not inclined to create their own state, or to accept the authority of any state). If embraced by nationalism, ethnicity is transformed into a total phenomenon consuming all aspects of the group's economic, political, and social life, not only the purely cultural sphere.

One cannot but agree with the crucial distinction of the concept of national sentiment or national consciousness, from the term nationalism attributed to the doctrine and political movement which aims at the creation or strengthening of a nation enjoying political autonomy. The two are, of course, intertwined, but there is no nationalism without national sentiment or national consciousness; there can, however, be such a sentiment or consciousness without it being invested in a movement and political doctrine.   In this sense, the nation is not prospectively recognizable as projected by nationalism; the real nation is not only *a posteriori* recognizable, as Hobsbawm envisages it [Hobsbawm 1990: 9]. The interplay between nation and nationalism is the same as between "nation" and "nation-state" because there is no "nation-state" without a nation, only states or "state-nations," though the nation can exist without having created its own state.

As Binder pointed out, mass and community must be juxtaposed, the formation of national communities is grasped as actual only when identity becomes a fundamental problem for individuals. That is, mass phenomena have no relationship with authentic community formation [Binder 1964: 83].   National consciousness, which is historical consciousness, is certainly acquired over the course of socialization, formal and informal; therefore, as Kohn said, it is "a state of mind, an act of consciousness" [Kohn 1944: 10], though he does not distinguish clearly between this "state of mind," and the nationalist movement and doctrine as political phenomenon.   The concept of national consciousness was well characterized by Henri Hauser, who wrote that the sentiment of belonging to a nation is a fact of the *conscience collective*, and, more particularly, it stands for a *vouloir-vivre collectif*, a collective will to live together,[4] expressed by Ernest Renan, in his famous pamphlet on the nation: "The existence of a nation is an everyday plebiscite."[5]   The deepest meaning of these explanations is that nationhood is nothing else but the ongoing self-definition of the nation which is, however, not identical with the choice of nationality or citizenship.

Many reasons have been given, since Herder, for the development of nationalism in Europe and, consecutively, in other areas of the world. Language is primarily representative as the cohesive force of an ethnic group or a nation and its principal means of communication and association. It is interesting to observe how this nineteenth-century idea concerning linguistically-defined nations was enlarged and extended to the whole human species in the twentieth century, from phenomenologists and Heidegger through the positivists and language-game theorists, to the advocates of "communicative action" or "communicative society." Nobody could deny the unique role of language as means of communication and the strong cohesive element in any human grouping or community, but it would be unreasonable to eliminate in favor of language, all other important components of ethnic belonging or of nationhood. Social communication does not generate elements of ethnicity or nationhood, but instead amplifies and maintains them through transmittal. Nation as a cultural community has a plurality of characteristics which together form and sustain national consciousness; they are the products of historical events and forces and reflect stages of the formative historical evolution.

Though group consciousness in societies is never exclusive, people do simultaneously belong to several groups without feeling contradiction between their multiple allegiances, as there is generally one allegiance that dominates over the other group-belongings. This is the case in the Arab world where submission to Islam is amalgamated with nationalism, though in the beginning, during the first decades of Arab nationalism, its main standard-bearers were non-Muslim Arabs. After the Second World War, religious consciousness became a most important and basic element of Arab consciousness. It is perhaps enlightening to refer here to the dialectical interplay of authenticity and identity, in the sense that recently formed or renascent nations seek to realize their authenticity, or freedom to be what one already is, according to one's history and cultural tradition, and to formulate that identity. In other words, acquiring the freedom to be what one wants to be even by overcoming particularities inherited from the past [Laroui 1967: 164-168], that is often a result of nation-formation.

There are some who attribute the origins of nationalism to different causes explained in terms of modern development. Ernest Gellner, for example, advances regional discrepancies in economic development, whereby certain groups suffered from a sentiment of relative deprivation in comparison to other dominating groups in a country or territory. He assumes that "uneven development" contributed substantially to some cultural cleavages. However, this argument is not very convincing, as one may ask when and where was economic development ever not uneven; or, conversely, why ethnic/national differences were present in some regions despite apparently similar economic conditions and even development. Is it really possible to say that Central and Eastern European, or Asian and African ethnic and national differences did not exist before autochthonous economic upheavals did not occur, or before such events were not imposed by foreign colonizers?

It seems more plausible to consider modernization and industrialization, as well as cultural ethnicity and nationalism, as cumulative, self-generating and *sui generis* processes mutually influencing each other in particular contexts. When one considers Gellner's thesis about the importance of general education for the rise of nationalism as a political movement and for the creation of nation-states, it is clear that his argument is much more pertinent in light of the fact that an industrialized and bureaucratized state requires a homogeneous cultural and social base (all the more so if one accepts the concept of nationality as an expression of the individual will). In a wider perspective, education and mass communication reinforce ethnic, cultural and national sentiments in the masses if the educated classes are committed to them, as Napoleon knew only too well. On the other hand, education enhances mobility and therefore weakens the ethnic and cultural ties by reducing the compactness of ethnic groups and dispersing them in accordance with economic opportunities. Conversely, if linguistic or cultural limitations reduce the mobility of members of a specific social group, then they reinforce the group's cohesion.

2. *The Discourse on Nation-State, Nation and Nationalism*

In the European context there were two roots of the rise of nationalism and the birth of nation-states. One was the creation of strong, centralized absolutist states from the sixteenth century. The other source was the revolutionary-democratic development engendered by the French Revolution which made possible the takeover of strong, centralized states by nations or citizens and gave birth to nationalism in the nineteenth century. The two consecutive developments led, with Hobsbawm's words, to the

> Equation of nation=state=people, and especially sovereign people, which undoubtedly linked nation to territory, since structure and definition of states were not essentially territorial. It also implied a multiplicity of nation-states so constituted, and this was indeed a necessary consequence of popular self-determination [Hobsbawm 1990: 20].

This equation, however, did not erase the difference between two concepts of the nation; nation as an ethnically-culturally based historical formation, and nation as constituted by the sovereign citizens who chose to be such citizens and members of the nation. In this latter case, the nation designated the difference between the people belonging together and the rest of humanity.

Up to the end of the seventeenth century Europe was dominated by great empires and national monarchies. But from the eighteenth century on a slow evolution took place, during which the latent cultural heritage of different ethnic groups was transformed into an overt consciousness of nationality with political independence and territorial sovereignty as their aim. It has been confirmed through detailed historical research that the cultural homogeneity of the European population was of major significance for the emergence of nation-states [Tilly 1975: 18-19]. This also meant that if homogeneity was not solid enough for state-creation, then a policy of homogenization was practiced in order to avoid the disappearance of the existing, autonomous state. Several other features of the European societies were also constitutive of the process of state-formation, such as the tradition of deliberative assemblies, the weaknesses of kinship structures and, most of all, the multiplicity of territorial configurations designated by Tilly as the "openness of European periphery" and the multiplicity of power structures in each society. "Stateness," autonomy, differentiation, centralization, and internal co-ordination by impersonal structures and powers, made possible through the mobilization of populations with which various authorities entertained routine relations, and the acquisition by the same populations of political rights binding governments and their agents. This was important to Huntington's hypothesis of "mobilization-institutionalization," which underlines that the stability of states depends on the right proportion between intensity of demands of political participation through mobilization, and the corresponding development of legitimate roles and structures in public life, or institutionalization [Huntington 1968: 93]. As Tilly illustrated it, this interaction was a difficult process: the suppression of rights and recurrent crises of authority prceded political participation.

In view of the evolution of European state-formation, Gellner defines nationalism as the ideology or "theory of political legitimacy, which requires that ethnic boundaries should not cut across political ones" [Gellner 1983: 1]. The formulation of nationalism as the ideology of political legitimation became predominant in the modern world, and constitutes the basic form of political legitimacy even in countries of other culture-areas. It is a paradox of the nationalist age that most European nation-states are pluri-ethnic and pluri-lingual, but in which genuine ethnical and cultural pluralism was not sincerely accepted and recognized. *Nationalism became loyalty to the state.* If ethnic groups, transformed into nations, intended to create their own state with all its political and economic prerogatives, they jeopardized, though probably without realizing it, the very culture and historic specificity they wanted to safeguard and cultivate. This was not foreseen in the nineteenth century; Meinecke's concepts of *Kulturnationen* and *Staatsnationen* were, in reality, supposed to merge into each other.[6]

The dangers were built-in to the character of the old type of territorial state existing before the eighteenth century, but came from the demographic, economic, and social evolution of the last two hundred years, which increased the state's power enormously, requiring the expansion of overwhelming bureaucracies and imposing standardization, leveling, and uniformization as a *sine qua non* condition of success. Such an evolution entailed erosion of each community's way of life, a fading away of their cultural heritage, and of shared myths and symbols; and, most importantly, a more or less complete disappearance of solidarity incorporated into the pre-existing social traditions. The new states did not become instruments of the national community for the realization of its goals, but just the opposite; they use, through nationalistic discourse, values, traditions, and cultural heritage for their own purposes [Smith 1981: 195].

The fundamental contradiction between ethnicity and cultural tradition, on the one hand, and the new nation-state, on the other hand, is well indicated by the useful metaphor of Benedict Anderson describing the modern nation-state as an "imagined community," because the original human community was gradually lost in the course of political development. This contradiction is paradoxically linked to the revolutionary-democratic idea of the nation born during the French revolution; in accordance with Hobsbawm's second equation, "sovereign citizen = people = state" instead of "state = nation = people." National self-determination was based on this change in the concept of the nation, and it brought with it the imperative of unification of all people belonging to the nation, and the need for an expansion of the nation-state through assimilation of smaller communities, regional ethnic groups, or conquered territories in Africa and Asia. The expansionist tendency appeared at the time quite natural to liberals as much as to Marxists, though for very different reasons, because they viewed the progress in history as evolving towards larger and larger scales of social organization in which the nation was the step before achieving, it was hoped, the unity of mankind. After the Second World War, countries and peoples liberated from colonial rule appropriated the principle of self-determination in the name of national expansion.

In a curious reversal of world history, when the state of sovereign citizens was firmly established, the unifying and expansionary forces were strengthened, and the nation-state needed a unique and legitimating identity. The so-called "state patriotism" which replaced national allegiance again returned to ethnical-cultural values, most importantly to language as the criteria of belonging to the nation, in order to secure a firm basis for the state's political legitimation. This was especially the case for "unhistorical" nations, for those with pluri-ethnic population, with the exception of countries like the United States, which were intentionally designed and acknowledged as a melting pot. Such nations therefore continued to represent the pure example of the citizen-state of voluntary adherence. As a final consequence of this political development, an ontological insecurity led people to search for an "identity securely anchored in the past" since everyday routine was not grounded anymore in traditional or, for that matter, in any morality [Giddens 1985: 215].

An intriguing question is the relationship between the creation of nation-states and the almost simultaneous development of capitalism. It is evident from the historical record that wide-scale merchant activities, increased production in the cities, and the consolidation of hitherto fragmented land property rights facilitating taxation by the state, all elements of the capitalist development, not only supplied the nascent states with needed material resources, but also created the opportunity for political alliance between landlords, cities with maritime or merchant activities, and other emerging economic powers. A not-always-perceived paradox of the evolution of nationalism and the formation of nation-states in the nineteenth century and afterwards was the contradiction, not openly avowed, between the liberal, market-oriented economic policies and the bounded territories of nation-states which constituted, for all practical purposes, an economic entity. In fact, the economic theory of liberal writers from Smith to Mill recognized solely the individual units of enterprise, rationally maximizing their profits and minimizing their losses in theoretical markets without spatial extension (village market, regional, national, or world market was completely left out of consideration). The central role of the market made allocation of resources its principal task, and it was assumed without evidence that the totality of individual interests, firms, or persons would represent the interest of the community or society as a whole. Contrary to this view, the market economy functioned in the national framework until the Second World War. This reality was officially recognized by List, who spoke of national economy or people's economy instead of political economy, because for him, economic policies had to "accomplish the economic development of the nation and to prepare its entry into the universal society of the future."[7]   His only condition was, in agreement with the great nationalist and liberal thinkers of the nineteenth century, that the nation had to be of a size sufficient to be viable economically.

Consequently, one can conclude that the era of nation-states became an era of cultural intolerance, an era of impatience with deeply rooted differences. Looking at the state as power monopoly explains its need to disempower communal self-management and local or corporate mechanisms of self-government, that is, the destruction of cultural and social foundations of ethnic, communal, and corporate traditions and forms of life, breaking the natural framework of the lifeworld. The transformation of the nation into a state therefore required cultural conformity, just as in Gellner's concept of the nation, the industrialized age requires a standard and uniform culture. But the idea of power-assisted culture as political emancipation is closely linked to the voluntaristic nature of the state, which can be derived from its being the exclusive holder of power. This voluntarism is known under the name of social engineering, the right of the state (in the name of the collectivity) to manage and administer existence. This facet of the modern state is the real deadly enemy of ethnicity, culture, and local or communal self-government.

3. *Nation-Building, Ethnicity and non-Western Civilizations*

The interrelated problems of nation-building and ethnicity in non-Western civilizations reveal one important example of the multiplicity of cultural worlds as well as the importance of treating these questions from the point of view of meaningful rationality. Meaningful rationality is contextual, and takes into account all relevant factors (all background information and the whole network of intentional beliefs) and the differences which separate the "Others" from the Western framework of cultural and social thought and action. It eliminates the semantic illusion that identified nations and states, and forced the independent areas of Asia and Africa to constitute themselves as "state-nations."

Nationalism as the product of European economic, social, and political developments during the last two centuries, did not and does not exist on the Asian, African, or South American continents. Nationalism there signifies the search for, and the realization of, independence from the political domination of Western countries, and from the Western mental and cultural influence, from the erosion of traditional values and ways of life it entails. Therefore, for the countries de-colonized since the Second World War, nationalism means all the above mentioned objectives: independence, nation building, modernization, and social integration. As it was well noted by Gellner, people in these countries were "united by a shared exclusion, not a shared culture" [Gellner 1983: 82]. The ideal of independence always evoked the reality, imagined or not, of the nation. Nothing else united the people in a colonial territory more than the resoluteness to chase out the foreign occupier. The nation was idealized in order to assume the function of social cohesion and integration in terms of ethnic-cultural and historical discourse. *Leopold Sedar Senghor* declared that "one country for one nation, inspired by the one and same faith, and driving towards the same aim,"[8] is the ideal.

We shall deal here in detail with the question of Islamic universalism, on the one hand, and nationalism in Muslim states, on the other, as it presents an especially interesting case in light of the opposition between the fundamental universalism of one of the great monotheistic religions of the world and ethnically, culturally, or politically motivated particularism of its parts. The concept of Islamic universalism is based on the *ummah*, which, in the *Quranic* perspective, does not represent a supra-national entity, but the *only* entity, the only nation which can exist on the earth [Gardet 1961: 28]. In contrast, nationalism is based on *Ibn Khaldun*'s famous concept of *asabiyya* (group feeling founded on blood ties) recognizing practical-political realities in social life [Ibn Khaldun 1967: 98].

The oscillation between the universalism of Islam and Arab, Iranian, or Indian nationalism is clearly demonstrated in the writings and efforts of the Islamic reform generation. *Al-Afghani*, for example, who disseminated his new vision at the time of the Ottoman empire, presented Islam as a dynamic and creative force; he recommended abandoning the attitude of blind submission to past authorities, but stressed that Islam was not only a religion, but a civilization as well. He preached the necessity to reassert Islamic identity and to reinforce Islamic solidarity in confronting the impact of Western culture and, consequently, to actively promote Islamic solutions to contemporary problems. As the Ottoman empire ruled over most of the Middle East in his time, the question of nationalism did not arise concretely (except among the Young Turks). It is evident from his emphasis on Islamic solidarity that he considered it as a commitment above all others.

The Islamic universalistic trend was much stronger among the Indian reformers, such as *Mawlana Mawdudi*, who declared that nationalism is alien to Islam and ill-suited as the basis of an Islamic state. His opposition to nationalism was based, first, on its underlying character of popular sovereignty in contradistinction to divine sovereignty as prescribed in Islam, and, second, its secular nature which, contrary to the Islamic doctrine, separates religion and the state. He determined that nationalism is in opposition to the universalism of Islam. In the same vein, *Muhammad Iqbal*, the great poet and reformer of Pakistan, stated that the religious ideal of Islam is organically related to the social order which is dependent on it; consequently, any nationalist doctrine which would challenge Islamic solidarity and the unity of religion and everyday life was unacceptable to him. The unequivocal position of the Muslim Brotherhood movement in favor of Islamic universalism as against liberal or Arab nationalism did not hinder its recognition, among the first between representatives of radical Islamism, the need for social and economic development.

In opposition to these theoreticians of the doctrine of state and nation in Islam, several others, mainly from Egypt, fought under the banner of nationalism. It is true, however, that most of them represented a small, Westernized group of intellectuals. An exception was *Rashid Rida*, disciple of the reformer *Muhammad Abduh* and editor of *Al-Manar*, who accepted patriotism and nationalism, if they do not overshadow the Islamic transnational identity and unity, and Muslims' solidarity with all other Muslims. In a moving confession, *Rida* declared:

> I am an Arab Muslim and a Muslim Arab, of the family of Quraysh and the lineage of 'Ali, of the seed of Muhammad the Arab Prophet, whose line goes back to Isma'il the son of Abraham and whose community of true belief is that of his ancestor Abraham: its base is the sincere affirmation of the unity of God and the turning of the face in surrender to God alone... My Islam is the same in date as my being Arab... I say, I am an Arab Muslim, and I am brother in religion to thousands upon thousands of Muslims, Arabs and non-Arabs, and brother in race to thousands upon thousands of Arabs, Muslims and non-Muslims.[9]

Rida's text exposes the fundamental dilemma of all Arabs between

Islam and nationalism; for the Arabs, in contrast to Muslims of other nations, Islam represented their history, their community and unity, their moral law, and the regulative principle of their society and culture. As Hourani said, Islam, in a sense, created them. How, then, to reconcile secularism and modernization with their universalistic particularism, with the fact of having between them non-Muslim Arabs who could not be treated in an Arab state as *djimmis*, or non-believers, as the *Quran* would have had it?

As much as *Rida, Mustafa Kamil* also links religion and nation, and denies that there could be conflict between Islam and Egyptian nationalism, on the condition that Islamic principles, but not the Islamic law (*Sharia*), are recognized as the basis of the national state. Contrary to *Rida*, he superimposed the sovereignty of the people on the sovereignty of God [Rosenthal 1965: 118-120].[10] *Mustafa Kamil* signals an important turning point in Arab nationalism: Islam was accepted as faith, as a system of moral principles, but not as law, as a legal system founding the state (thereby solving the problem of non-Muslim Arabs). *Abd al-Rahman al-Bazzaz*, from Iraq, also insisted that there is no contradiction between Islamic universalism and Arab nationalism. The apparent contradiction is due to the misconception of Islam as a religion like Christianity, though, in reality, it is an all-encompassing ideal and movement.[11] *Al-Bazzaz* made Islam a national religion which expressed inherent aspects in the nature of Arab people.

Sati al-Husri followed in the path of Ernest Renan, and considered that belonging to a nation is an act of will on behalf of people who identify with their ethnic and cultural group. He also emphasized that language, expressing shared history and culture, constitutes the cohesion and integrative force of nations, and interpreted this as the basis for Arab nationalism: "The idea of Arab unity is a natural idea... a natural consequence of the existence of the Arab nation itself" [Esposito 1984: 72]. He combined nationalism, loyalty to one's land, and loyalty to the state in the concept of patriotism, and thought that national religions reinforce people's cohesion, but universal religions are in conflict with the ideology of nationalism. He was convinced that being an Arab is prior to being a Muslim, and distinguished especially the moral aspect of Islamic solidarity from the idea of pan-Islamic political unity. *Sati al-Husri* concluded that the universal brotherhood of Muslims and Arab nationalism are not mutually exclusive but may co-exist together. Contrarily, *Lutfy al-Sayyid* was an outspoken nationalist who insisted that contemporary reality in the Muslim world makes pan-Islamism and pan-Arabism irrelevant. Each nation must seek to preserve its very identity and existence to gain independence [Esposito 1984: 65].

The conflict between universalism and national particularism is due to the fact that, as Ira Lapidus emphasized, "Islam was never the sole or total organizing principle of pre-modern Islamic societies" [Lapidus 1988: 880]. The integration of society and state was never entirely realized, though one could say with Binder that "the concept of the *ummah* served as a referent for the identity resolutions of individual Muslims throughout Muslim history" [Binder 1964: 131]. Therefore, evidently, there never was a clear-cut separation of religion and social life in Muslim countries, even in the last two centuries, when secularization advanced in most areas of life. The breakdown of ethnic and tribal loyalties and traditions, as well as the widening disillusion with secularism and with the achievements of modernity in economic and social life, largely contributed to the formation of a national identity and of nationalist movements, especially as the Islamic symbolism of individual and social identity was merged into national feeling. In this way, one might witness a complete reversal today, as Islamic teachings became the galvanizing force for total political commitment in the opposition against nation-states and against their policy failures in most domains of public life.

Returning to the problem of nationalism in the world of people belonging to non-Western civilizations, it seems evident that self-determination of nations or people became self-determination of states in order to safeguard the integrity of multi-ethnic states [Connor 1973: 12]. Geertz justly emphasizes that the problem that overshadows all others was the quest for a national identity in an uphill battle against the collective identities of the various groups composing the emergent states [Geertz 1971: 362]. "National awakening" was the aim, although there was no nation, but it soon became clear that the atmosphere of the revolution could not be maintained beyond the effective transfer of sovereignty. Nationalist ideologies had to be radically transformed in order to take into consideration the requirements of nation and/or state building. This meant a twofold rewriting of collective objectives. First, it had to be recognized that the task was the creation of a national identity, which, in most cases, is not yet completed, many years after the emergence of the new sovereign states. The other task concerned finding the best ways to create an economically viable entity, a community with enough material and intellectual resources to fuel a sustained, Western-type social progress. It was also discovered that once independence was obtained, a new leadership was required with qualities other than the ones that served the country so well in the struggle against the foreigner. In the age of post-independence nation building, real statesmanship was necessary, perhaps politically less dramatic, though much more essential and difficult for the new nation's or society's future development.

The main reason for this complication was that a fundamental dichotomy existed between the newly created state and the civil society. The former was an alien creation inherited from the colonizer or assumed an alien form, as it represented the introduction of an organizational model borrowed from abroad. Many of the new states, or in their parts, i.e., the Moghul, Persian, Mali, Ghana, or Inca and Aztec empires, had independent political and organizational structures centuries earlier. Those were lost and only survived in memories and myths, or not at all.   There was no historical, only mythical, consciousness in the nationalist movements striving for independence. The Chinese empire, though it survived formally and represents an almost homogeneous entity possessing one of the oldest civilizations on earth, faced a powerful culture shock at the time of modernization in a totally different international environment redesigned by technological developments in transportation and communication, by worldwide trade and competition, and by emerging, politically and economically powerful states.   Hence the difficulties inherent in the nation-building processes and the urgent need to copy foreign models without considering their aptitude to resolve the ethnic, social, and cultural problems of the new state-nations.

The events of the period after the Second World War show an example of tragic errors in history, under the impulse of the universalistic tendencies of Western culture. A "timeless" concept of global culture gained total predominance, and it was supposed that in the wake of the movement of de-colonization and emancipation all countries on earth *must* adopt and absorb this culture.[12] There is here more than a paradox; the basic elements of other cultures simply resist. Traditional social structures (though damaged) are still there, and the implantation of the universal civilization ("the world revolution of Westernization") does not progress. Particular cultures (which do not correspond to existing states, federation of states, or any other organizational entities) are timebound and expressive, with symbols and imagery deeply rooted in historical experiences and social patterns evolved over centuries. Culture by definition is specific and historically defined, containing strong emotional connotations and symbolic forms;

the essential question therefore is whether the other, non-Western cultures are able to adopt all technological innovations and also selectively borrow institutional and organizational forms from the West. Yet safeguarding at the same time, their cultural heritage and social structures as well as their traditional ways of life, as far as possible in order to survive.

The whole argument on universal civilization is important because the problem concerning the adoption of the organizational form of the nation-state represents the first encounter with this dilemma.   An extensive analysis of the recent evolution of the non-Western world clearly shows that the nation-state as basic political entity is not convenient for most other "cultural worlds." It does not correspond to their way of being, especially to ethnically based structures of life. It is a real drama that even the creation of international organizations such as the United Nations, pressured the emerging nations into accepting the imposed institutional system of the European-styled nation-state. The formation of European nation-states teaches us that when they were firmly established they constituted a state-system guaranteeing each other's existence. Thus, the evolution in the newly sovereign states and their societies follows more or less, an already well known model. After decolonization, the leaders and social groups in the independent states of Asia, Africa, and (much earlier) Latin America, turned outward, placing the blame for the difficulties they encountered in the course of modernization on the colonial power or on the other developed, by definition imperialist countries. The result was short-lived social integration, due to the unity reached on the anticolonial theme; after a couple of years, divisive internal conflicts appeared.

The problem of ethnicity, culture, and state is, consequently, entirely intertwined in non-Western countries with the complex historic process of modernization.   In its non-technical and non-economic definition, modernization can be captured as "an increase in the range of techniques and possibilities open to men, as well as in their awareness of alternatives and choices" [Smith 1983: 97-98]. This definition does not exclude an interpenetration of tradition and modernity in a reasoned framework of thought and action, an integrative revolution. The universal Westernization process not only creates *state-nations* instead of nation-states, but also offers a striking example of economic determinism, which in the perspective of meaningful rationality is unintelligible. This amounts to the negation of the collective identity of people, of the ethnic or religious groups concerned. Mass media magnifies this ethnocentric economic-technical determinism and negation of Others' identity, as it reflects current and generally accepted assumptions in the Western world. It is not taken into account that information and communication do not modify situational and contextual beliefs and interpretations, shared values, and traditions, because the tension is between social institutions carrying with themselves discordant cultural meanings. The extremely slow changes, if any, happen through gradual diffusion and adjustment over a long period of time.

The repercussions of local conflicts on the international order, the state-system, can be important. In any case, as states and, per force, governments, are members of the representative institutions of the system, one government replaces the former (note the marked difference, nay, a real incommensurability between these forced changes, mostly *coup d'Etat*, and the governmental changes and crises in democratically governed states). This process continues endlessly without disturbing, only discrediting, the functioning of the international system.

CHAPTER SEVEN

POLITICAL ACTION AND THE STATE

The modern nation-state is a product of evolution in the West, shaped entirely by Enlightenment ideology, the consequences of the Napoleonic wars and the development of the market-oriented private enterprise system. It obtained its present form after the First World War through transformation into a welfare state and the creation of an international system of states, thus reflecting the growing interdependence between these sovereign entities. In considering political action and the state as its framework, one cannot deal with all related and inherent problems. Therefore, aspects of political action and government which will be discussed here are those particularly essential in the perspective of a civilizational dialogue, — because of their overwhelming importance in contemporary Western culture, — such as political participation in democratic processes, the role and accomplishments of the welfare state, as well as the especially crucial theme concerning the modern state's bureaucracy.

1. *The Differentiation of the Political Sphere*

In the course of the social process of differentiation, as outlined by Weber, Parsons, Habermas and Luhmann, a disjunction of the sphere of political activities from other sectors of society gradually took place. In Luhmann's terminology, the functional specification of the political sector concerned the formation of a distinct and autonomous power governing social relations which issued binding decisions and whose acts were generalized as well as reflexive. This isolation and autonomy of the political and other sectors of society is reflected in role-differentiation, or, properly speaking, in the changing combination of roles which constitute the social structure.   The integrated role-ensemble vested in an individual in traditional societies disappears; the role-performance is relativized to partners in the same context in which they motivate and check each other.   Consequently, the relationship between roles is characterized by a great mobility within this differentiated social background. In such a situation, variability, or the possibility of change is the condition of stability. Differentiation and versatility in roles, however, require a pronounced orientation to universal or neutral criteria without regard to persons and their relationships, conceived in terms of causal, not cosmic or symbolic, explanation of human action. Thus, the universalistic orientation is imposed by the differentiated character of society.   The causal explanation of actions leads to the rationalization of roles interacting between them in accordance with the regulative standards of the political sphere. Differentiation is based on clearly demarcated external boundaries between actions issued from various sub-systems, and further internal differentiation permits a better specification and stabilization of external as well as internal boundaries.

The first example, for Luhmann, of a differentiated political sector in society is the appearance of the nation-state in Western Europe. Its environment is constituted by other societal collectivities that are expected to meet the specific needs of the political sector. The state as supreme authority issues binding decisions signifying that based on whatever legitimacy, the state-power imposes its will on the population, thus acquiring "legitimating legality" (as Weber would have said) through the effective monopoly of making decisions about the use of physical force. The creation of states was linked to the idea of establishing an impartial power with anonymous structures, constituting the supreme political authority in the boundaries of a given community, an authority based on publicly-approved legal arrangements and possessing functional competence in all fields relevant to the conduct of public affairs.

After the appearance of the state, the successively formulated concept of citizenship expressed that members of a political community, the state's citizens, were bestowed responsibilities, rights, duties, and powers, as well as constraints and liberties; as a result, the unresolved issue of equitable balancing of authority and liberty between rulers and ruled first appeared.

The process of differentiation of the political sphere from the lifeworld reinforces the power of control of the central political institution, the state, over its subjects; it meant that the regulatory influence of moral principles in social life vanished. In the modern age, consqeuently the state ensures the legal framework for all social activities as an impartial arbiter, thereby gaining its legitimation in the eyes of the population. But it is also expected to assure the smooth functioning of another differentiated sector, the economy, through its position as impartial guardian of the general interest and societal harmony. Through a further differentiation the political power structure of the state was separated from the power structure of economic entities (corporations, etc.) which led to a compression and restriction of the public space created during the first phase of the existence of the modern state. This took the form of a doubling of the parliamentary democratic system, that is, a determinate political sphere legitimated by scientific progress and rationalization but effectively not subject to decisions taken by bodies under the control of popular sovereignty [Beck 1992 184-185]. In this situation, bureaucratic rationality and management is combined with the Habermasian "technocratic consciousness" which dictates decisions in accordance with "the logic of scientific-technical progress;"[1] therefore, technology-induced social changes vary inversely with democratic legitimation. It may be justified, in the sense of the state's contradictory functions and the consequent disillusions and unfulfilled expectations of people, to speak of a legitimation crisis in view of the waning mass loyalty of populations toward the state.

Precisely for this reason, the full development of the modern state brought also with it the phenomenon called by Giddens the *sequestration of experience* [Giddens 1991: 149]. The institutional sequestration of experience, that is, the deliberate concealment of certain basic life experiences by the powerholders in the state, is a fundamental fact in the life of contemporary modern societies. It is not only the consequence of the extension of administrative power which, through its surveillance system, creates strong asymmetries in power relationships, but also of the increased institutional reflexivity of the political sphere and its principal agent, the state.

The appearance of the modern state led to a further differentiation in the political sphere between state and civil society. Civil society is defined as the totality of social institutions and activities, formal or informal, which are not related to the state power, any bureaucratic or other power structures, or power centers constituted in the private sphere, such as multinational corporations. Thus, *civil society is conceived as the opposite of dominant power structures and, beyond that, as expressing the totality of the lifeworld aspirations and constraints.* As an aspect of the lifeworld, civil society is certainly antecedent to the state. It includes not only grass-root initiatives and actions to obtain local autonomies, but also all collective and individual efforts deployed for the protection of the cultural and physical environments. Civil society, consequently, represents people's desire for an extended autonomy from encroachment in their community's life by any and all powerholders, political or otherwise.

The differentiation of various spheres of social life and the consecutive differentiation of state and civil society, enhance the importance of political action as an all-pervasive force which is present in various differentiated spheres and segments of society [Held 1989: 1]. Politics is always related to power, that is, to the capacity of intervention into public matters with a view to transform existing relationships, as well as the possession of resources needed for the attainment of such objectives. Power relationships are rarely unilateral or hierarchical for most power positions in modern pluralistic democracies, there is a countervailing position opening possibilities for competition, bargaining, and joint decision-making. It depends, of course, on the rules of the political game (such as the rules of democratic processes) to ensure that the competition and bargaining are fair, and on the resources acquired by the participants in political activities, whether there will be real conflict or achievement of consensual decisions. The "socially consequential exercise of power," as Bowles and Gintis define it, depends on rules regulating social action through: forms and rewards of participation in a particular practice; the limitation of a socially feasible ranges of alternatives; and the socially mediated effectiveness of different practices [Bowles-Gintis 1986: 98].

In a highly differentiated political sphere, positive law reigns, that is, legality is conformity with procedures. The definition of values guiding actions is institutionalized in varying ways. The formal-legal institutionalization of the state is, to a great extent, time and culture bound; the good functioning of the legal mechanism presupposes a congruence with socially accepted and internalized norms. The most important conclusion of Luhmann's examination of the functionally differentiated political sector of society therefore is that *there must be a congruence between the level of complexity of the political sphere and that of its social environment*; and, especially if power exceeds a certain threshold, the complexity must be complemented by reflexivity [Luhmann 1982: 152]. The high differentiation of the political system necessitates a marked flexibility, a certain degree of indeterminacy or the possibility of contradictions, dissent, and conflictual situations in the institutionalization of established or nascent structures. It is, however, extremely difficult to institutionalize the required degree of indeterminacy in any political system; therefore, complexity and the drive toward change and variability create the danger of instability, especially if political rigidity impedes the realization of the most important change, the redistribution of political power. It is for this reason that de-centering or fragmentation of social experiences, or, using Keynes' words from *The End of Laissez-Faire* [Keynes 1963: 313-314], the creation of "semi-autonomous bodies" within the state located between the individual and the centralized power, offers the best solution for maintaining stability in political systems.[2]

Differentiation of spheres of social activity and internal differentiation of sub-systems do not exclude the substantial role played by sub-collectivities which represent meaningful stratification structures [Etzioni 1968: 441]. Consensus as the "congruence in the perspectives of two or more actors" is indispensable for effective action. Etzioni refers to *consensus-formation* when the process is upward and to *consensus mobilization* when the process is downward, but to *consensus building* when it encompasses both upward and downward processes. Less extensive social bonds make reaching a consensus much more difficult. In order to reach people through direct mobilization to replace vanishing social bonds, the category of citizenship encompassing all inhabitants of the state appeared at the end of the eighteenth century, complemented, as necessary, by some measures of coercion. Citizens are simultaneously subject to control and to consensus-building incentives. The nation-state assumed more and more responsibility in the course of the last centuries, until it reached the full extension of its power in the form of the welfare state.

2. *Ideology and Civic Culture*

There are many definitions of ideologies as collective belief systems aiming to stimulate action of its adherents in a desired direction. Modern ideologies mostly try to justify a claim to or about power; ideologies may be represented as the combination of a "particular definition of reality" with a "concrete power interest" [Berger-Luckmann 1966: 113]. It is obviously possible to speak of ideologies in the plural, as they represent collective belief systems which show some common patterns, formal or not, accommodating belief-structures to different environments. Ideologies are frequently designated as belief systems representing group interests in a given social order, such as Marxism-Leninism, which was designed to be the ideology of the industrial working class. However, Gouldner was right in writing that ideologies legitimate themselves by reference to "the imputed interests of the *totality* and the good of the whole. It is on this claim that the moral authority and suasion of ideology grounds itself" [Gouldner 1976: 276]. Persuasiveness implies, even if not simultaneously, a prescriptive perspective, and this is necessary for any ideology's accomplishment of its mission in obtaining the expected results. Ideological methods of covering their real aims and actions with a "veil of apparent ignorance" give the impression that they do not have prescriptive intentions or that they submit themselves willingly to a critical scrutiny, which, in truth, is very rarely the case.

The same Marxism-Leninism, that led the struggle against the oppression of the working class pretended to lead not only the working class, but also all humanity toward a bright future. In contrast to such pretensions, Ricoeur's examination showed that an ideology is condemned to remain fragmented because all objectifying knowledge is based on *belonging* to a social class, to a cultural tradition, or to a historical circumstance from which, even in critical discourse, one cannot distance oneself, as one can only reach a relative autonomy through belonging. Therefore, the critic of ideology cannot free himself from this underlying primordial tie; if he pretends to do so, he errs in illusion [Ricoeur 1981: 243-245]. Plamenatz adds that ideologies must be functionally related to those who are their bearers, in fact justifying the latter's attitudes and actions, "regardless of whether or not its constituent beliefs satisfy the criteria of truth" [Plamenatz 1970: 31].

Ideologies are undoubtedly social and cultural phenomena. They use symbolisms as well as social rituals, enacting the reconstruction of social reality and integrating their own principles and beliefs into social behavior patterns in order to persuade men and drive them to realize the aims spelled out in the ideological credo. Belief systems related to the creation and development of nation-states and to the principles of political participation and democratic politics are, without doubt, ideologies which, through institutionalization in Western civilization, became culturally, socially, and politically constitutive of the modern lifeworld.

Culture in the evolutionary perspective is an action-oriented information system, and culture patterns play the role of programs, templates or blueprints for social and psychological processes: this is necessary because of the extreme plasticity of human nature. In this context, should the role of ideologies be inserted into the concept of political development, it frees the political sub-system from "governance of received traditions," (religion, moral conventions, etc.), and developing an autonomous cultural model of political action [Geertz 1973: 218-219]. This characterization of the role of political ideologies as means of political mobilization and legitimation is particularly valid in periods of social upheaval and cultural change. The disorientation of the leaders of formerly colonized countries at the moment of independence or of those which recently liberated themselves from Soviet domination led them to look for templates or blueprints they could follow in constructing a new reality in their countries. The various ideologies offered by the West filled in this role; recourse to the religious-traditional belief systems and their concepts of how to construct society and the state only took place when the borrowed formulae proved disappointing.

Ideologies also play an important part in political *rituals* that serve the elaboration of determinate power relationships in the framework of the dynamics of social interactions. Political ideologies, therefore, are generally part of the so-called political or civic culture. Today civic culture designates the *democratic culture of political participation*. As this particular form of political ideology and action, called "participation explosion," spread around the whole world, ordinary men took their destiny in their hands and the government with the consent of the governed was born. This active participation of citizens in civic affairs necessitates a certain political culture and an understanding by people of how democracy works, at least in its essentials, of what they should decide through their votes on party's and policy platforms. The adoption of civic culture in most countries belonging to non-Western civilizations requires, therefore, not only an education of the common man, but also a complete transformation of the social and cultural environment. The *participant political culture* of the democratic system is contrasted by Almond and Verba [Almond-Verba 1989: 18-26] with the following: the *parochial political culture* (or traditional-despotic), in which affective and normative rather than cognitive attitudes dominate, differentiation of political roles is non-existent, and no expectation of possible change in the social and political worlds due to internal processes is manifest; and the *subject political culture* (or constitutional-absolutist), in which high expectations are related to differentiation in the political system and to its results, and in which the subjects do not show any orientation towards changing the processes, especially through their own participation.

If the political culture is incongruent with political structures, a mixture of the above characteristics is produced. From these mixed categories of political cultures, two are most relevant to the contemporary situation. The first is the *parochial-subject culture*, in which a substantial portion of the population feels freed from the exclusive claims of tribal, village, or feudal loyalty and accepts the formation of a more complex political system built around strong, central governmental structures. The second is the *parochial-participant culture* that represents the most widespread type of political organization in the new state-nations. In these, the underlying structures are democratic or participant, but congruence requires the development of the corresponding political culture with responsible and competent citizens whose consent is necessary for high-level decision-making by governmental authorities. This not only refers to the problem of education but to the proper mobilization of the population as well. This includes setting up the necessary infrastructure, party machines, and political operatives, but, also the adequate and simply worded ideological stimulation of the public's political interest, instead of building on personalities and their emotive and ascriptive merits. In this combination of parochial and participatory features, fragmentation and instability are frequent, reinforced by the general cultural and social fragmentation and by concurrent economic instabilities.

3. *Participative Democracy and the Welfare State*

The evolution of the political realm in the Western cultural orbit during the period we call modernity, was characterized by two major developments. First, the adoption of the ideology and practice of political participation, and, especially, the predominance of the state governed with the consent of the individual citizen, as in our contemporary democracy. Second, the transformation of the state into a welfare state which, following the ever-increasing numbers of the population and the ever more complex problems and difficulties of industrial societies, intervened to an increasing extent in the functioning of the hitherto autonomous or quasi-autonomous spheres of economy. Society and culture therefore became subordinate to the collective individual, the sovereign people.

In a definition reflecting the modern evolution of the democratic concept, Huntington and Nelson define political participation as an

Activity by private citizens designed to influence government decision-making. Participation may be individual or collective, organized or spontaneous, sustained or sporadic, peaceful or violent, legal or illegal, effective or ineffective. Effective support for a substantial shift in economic and social policies is most likely to come from organized collective participation, which can assume a variety of forms [Huntington and Nelson 1976: 3],

and constitutes the aim of party activities in Western democracies. Political participation, if not autonomous, may be induced; people are mobilized, by whatever means, to take part in specific activities. This means, of course, that democracy cannot be achieved but by deliberate constitutional engineering to ensure freedom of the citizens and participation in the decision-making process. It is, however, also clear, as the Athenian case attests it, that democracy can only survive in societies capable of sustaining it.

Thus, the modern democratic state exchanged the sacred foundation of legitimation to a foundation on a common will. Democracy is a combined result of the rationalization of worldviews (the "disenchanted" world), the generalization of some legal and moral norms (replacing the ethical views of yesteryear), and the growing individuation of individuals (without being integrated into an organic community). Yet when rules governing the social and political order are simply inherited from the past, rights codified in texts written and approved by preceding generations, what kind of moral or other sanctions rooted in the community's lifeworld lead individuals to comply with them since laws and decisions made by a collectivity of individuals which may or may not be respected if not physically enforced [Buchanan 1975: 74]? Democracy, in Dahl's interpretation, is *polyarchy*. It is not only the equality of individual citizens in respect of their rights and their participation in decision-making through the electoral process, but it also means the respect of citizens' preferences by their governments. The governmental responsiveness evoked by Dahl concerns all preferences political, economic, and social, meaning that the concept of political equality was extended to the economic sphere, and *the idea of economic equality became constitutive of democratic-participatory ideology*. Thus, from equality before the law, the idea evolved to the requirement of equality of opportunity, finally reaching the extended notion of equality of result among any and all participants in a democratic process. This evolution nonetheless meant that the much-evoked Weberian-Luhmannian differentiation of the political and economic-social spheres was progressively eliminated, and the public-private distinction gradually disappeared as well. As a result, the evolution of the modern state tends to re-unite, with the exception of the expressive-artistic sphere, most of the domains of the lifeworld in a centralized, powerful, and bureaucratic framework.

The state thus undertook intervening more and more in favor of the disinherited and poor strata of the population, as poverty and indigence produced by the demographic explosion and the growing pains of industrialization and social disintegration grew at an alarming rate. The welfare state assumed responsibility for providing economic security for the poor, old, and sick segments of the society in the name of social solidarity through the redistribution of income and other resources to those strata. It intervenes in the management of the economy as well, through indirect measures that ensure minimum prosperity for low- and middle-income earners. The welfare state, in consequence, is characterized as a specific version of democracy and of the capitalist economy, "a state democratic in form, interventionist by inclination, and eager to manage the capitalist economy to achieve steady economic growth and maintain full employment" [Logue 1979: 69].

The perseverance of inequality is partly due to genetic factors according to modern biology; that is, every individual is endowed differently by nature [Rae 1979: 38-39] — in the sense of differential endowment which does not mean either inferiority or superiority. In addition, each individual also participates in a differential way in the socialization process. The ideology of democratic egalitarianism is culturally and historically specific; there is no universal legitimation sustaining its requirements. Inequality thus has a double source of origin, biological and cultural; therefore, equality in the economic and social spheres is more plausibly a relational idea. It is not additive, but as it is relational, it embraces all concerned at local, national, or even international levels.

In Walzer's formulation, the state's policies tend toward economic equality and should obey "pluralistic equality" or "distributive pluralism," based on universalistic but, at the same time, pluralistic principles. Pluralism here is understood as respect for the principle according to which "different goods to different associations of men and women for different reasons and different procedures," thus admitting the survival of inequalities in certain domains though recognizing that democracy means equal rights or entitlements for all [Walzer 1983: 64-65]. What is important in Walzer's conceptualization of pluralistic egalitarianism is his opposition to reductionist approaches. Walzer also privileges complex versus simple equality in accepting the reality of unequal possession of certain goods. That means that the owner of some goods cannot be entitled, because of this fact, to privileged access to other goods. Walzer's suggestions concerning the problem of economic equality amount to a contextualization or relativization of the distributive principle to a situational logic, which opens up much larger perspectives for equitable economic policies than rigid egalitarianism. It is questionable whether perfect egalitarianism is achievable in view of the influence of "distributive coalitions," to which Mancur Olson called attention [Olson 1982: 175]. These coalitions are not isomorphous with inherent productive abilities of people and, as history proved, are not instrumental in reducing social and economic inequalities.

The advantages of Walzer's approach are more evident when one considers that for an egalitarian state and for a government pursuing egalitarian policies, the great dilemma is whether it should treat different people differently in order to treat them equally, or to treat people identically, although they may or may not be different, in order to treat them equally. Contemporary welfare states follow the second, "uniform" solution, as the first one is technically impossible to carry out by a state bureaucracy, in view of the wide and continuous need of updated information on individuals and the extremely difficult task of administration in actual situations. In the same vein, the equal-opportunity concept reveals a fundamental antagonism between the egalitarian and utilitarian aspects. In order to realize equal opportunity, the method of impersonal competition is normally used, which is less egalitarian than capability-oriented competition; to achieve equal prospects of success, no chance is given to individuals with different capabilities to benefit from competition, but it is rather similar to a lottery, where everybody is given an equal chance. This way of proceeding is, of course, more egalitarian, but seems unjust and is definitely less useful from society's point of view [Rae 1979: 48-52].

In fact, the modern state cannot survive without its welfare activities, as the slowly disintegrating society will produce more and more people dependent upon it for their survival. It is possible that a "spiral of constantly re-induced forms of 'relative deprivation'" will lead to an increasingly overburdened state, to a permanent discrepancy between claims made by individuals and the state's performance capacity [Offe 1984: 68-69 and 76]. This perspective of the evolution of the welfare state is cogently argued by Offe and other economists, in light precisely of the rational expectation doctrine of contemporary economics. Rational expectations are fatal to Keynesianism, as soon as the economic actors expect state intervention to be made regularly and routinely in their rational programming of operations. In this sense, Keynesianism is a self-defeating policy whose disastrous effects can already be seen in many sectors of national economies and even at international level.

To conclude this section, it is necessary to call attention to some grave deficiencies in the functioning of the participatory form of democratic political action. In democracy, ordinary citizens exercise control, in principle, over the elite, who is in charge of the conduct of public affairs as well as of the executive machinery of the bureaucracy [Weber 1978, Vol. II: 985]. This control is reduced to the mode of choice of those who govern and the electoral system of one man one vote, but does less and less to control how the elite rule while they are in power. Therefore, even if such control by the ordinary man is considered legitimate, political and economic decision-making is concentrated in the hands of a few. Citizens as much as public opinion cannot make policy and master all the intricate and complex technical problems involved in the management of contemporary society. The importance of the political party system as an intermediary between citizens and the social groups in power, together with the representative role of elected bodies and corporate institutions such as unions, is declining in the entire Western world. The complexity of problems is such that it surpasses the capacities of those whom the electoral system puts into power; the people, the ordinary citizens consequently lose their confidence in the ruling strata (politicians, officials, bureaucrats) because of their incapability to resolve the growing and increasingly menacing problems of society. The question therefore is, as Dunn put it [Dunn 1979: 23], whether political participation and democracy is nothing more today than "an abstract moral standard" which cannot yield any more reasoned expectations for the future of mankind. And if this may be true for countries in the West, how can democratic pluralism and participatory democracy be congruent with traditional cultural patterns in countries situated in other civilizational orbits?

There is a tension between governmental power and responsiveness and between citizens overwhelmed by the conflicting demands made upon them by the democratic system. This means that citizens must be involved in politics and remain influential, knowledgeable, and aggressive enough to enforce responsible behavior by the elite. The question still remains open whether the citizens' active participation leads to a tyranny of the majority or to a tyranny of a minority: the first resulting in radical egalitarianism (according to Tocqueville), the second resulting in the disintegration of society into heteroclite minorities having few shared cultural values. It goes without saying that these tensions become most apparent in times of crisis. The loss of confidence in the governing elite shows such a crisis looming on the horizon, as "bureaucracies create profound inequalities of power" [Blau-Meyer 1971: 166].

4. *Bureaucracy: Ideal-type and Reality*

(a) THE WEBERIAN CONCEPTUALIZATION

It may be questioned why the organizational form of bureaucracy is dealt with in a study concerning the dialogue of cultures. However, it is without a doubt the organizational form that dominates the national as well as international scenes today and plays a more and more criticized role in the relations of different civilizations. This is not to say that bureaucracies are not at all necessary; the evolution of the modern world made them unavoidable.   But even the large, contemporary bureaucracies are, simply unable to handle the problems of the multitudes produced by the demographic explosion.   They are also unable to deal with the questions raised by technological evolution, which makes management of the collectivity's life incredibly complex and unwieldy.   What is truly remarkable is that all functional theories of bureaucracy repeat the Weberian definitions and explanations of the necessity and efficiency of bureaucracy in the modern world.   Though many describe bureaucracy's numerous shortcomings and deviations from the Weberian ideal-type and assume a critical attitude toward the bureaucratic phenomenon, no one even tries to investigate how the functioning of bureaucracies over the course of the last half century could be remedied in view of their catastrophic performance.   It therefore appears necessary to examine the bureaucracy's functions and its shortcomings (not always admitted) and their harmful effects on the civilizational dialogue as well as on economic and social development.

The problem of bureaucracies is not new.   The bureaucracy of the Ottoman Empire was well known by its "ossified functionalism,"[3] long before contemporary mushrooming bureaucracy was extensively studied by Max Weber at the turn of the century [Weber 1978, Vol. II: 971-972].   As the main factors operating in the direction of bureaucratization, Weber noted society's desire for order and protection as well as the need to implement social and economic policies such as welfare policies in the interest of the collectivity.   He knew that one of the most important reasons for growing bureaucratization was the rapid development of modern means of communication, including the creation of a necessary infrastructure which, through a feedback effect, also represents the essential prerequisite for "the possibility of bureaucratic administration" [ibid. 973].

Weber was surely impressed by the performance of the Prussian state's bureaucracy, but also modeled his description of bureaucracy's function on what he saw in the United States.   He appears convinced that a bureaucracy offers the optimum solution for: "specializing administrative functions according to purely objective considerations," assuring the respect of the principle of impersonality in recruitment and functioning, as well as in leveling of social status or class differences; and functioning on the basis of calculable rules demonstrating consequently a purely technical superiority [ibid. 975].   In fact, Weber praises the monocratic form of bureaucracy, that is, the total control of the bureaucracy by its head, a type of new despotism.   He is, however, lucid enough to note that although the formalism, formal rationality, and rule-bound coolness of bureaucracy satisfies in principle such requirements as "equality before the law of all citizens" or "guarantee against arbitrariness," if people are ethically motivated and ask for substantive justice, then the bureaucratic administration must be on a collision course with them [ibid. 78-80]. Bureaucracy, in the Weberian perspective, is a corollary of mass democracy and is antithetic to self-government; but it is an inevitable instrument to ensure, "through the abstract regularity of the exercise of authority" [ibid. 83], indispensable efficiency and equality before the law, and to avoid all the sins committed during the *ancien régime*. For Weber, democracy could not exist without bureaucracy, and even if sometimes democratic forces oppose bureaucratic rule or create impediments to its functioning, they are unavoidably yet unintendedly increasing bureaucratization, because democracy cannot exist without it.

Weber recognizes that the bureaucratic official is chained to the organization economically and ideologically, and identifies himself with his colleagues in defense of their common interests. He knows, therefore, that to destroy a bureaucracy is difficult [Weber 1978, Vol. II: 1401] due to the resistance of those who have a vested interest in it, either officials who have acquired a certain mentality, or politicians, groups, or parties who make use of it. Weber clearly thinks that the economic or social effects of a functioning bureaucratic organization are not visible and concretely experienced; it is therefore an instrument that can be used to promote any interest, to serve any power [ibid. 987 and 1402]. The common man, the ruled, cannot oppose bureaucracy, nor can he try to modify its underlying principles, rules, and regulations, as his own existence depends on the smooth functioning of the administration, on the latter's expertise, specialized work, and action in maintaining an orderly state of affairs.

It is most noteworthy that Weber realized that even officials of the bureaucratic administration, if not in the highest grades, cannot influence the evolution of their organization (except in defending the common interest), and he did not deny the fact that among officials, there is always a "mostly silent critique," not observed by outsiders, or a "profound scepticism about the wisdom of appointments" [ibid. 1449]. But powerholders' influences and the bureaucracy's usually monocratic structure rule out any changes initiated from inside the organization.

(b) CONTEMPORARY CRITICISM OF BUREAUCRACY

All recent conceptualizations of the ever-growing bureaucratic system throughout the world are built on the Weberian foundations. For example, a pathbreaking study was carried out by Blau and Meyer in the fifties [Blau-Meyer 1971]. Their critical comments on the function of bureaucracies' can be grouped as follows:

Policy-making and policy-implementation: A major dysfunctional factor in bureaucracy's operations is the completely blurred distinction between policy-making and policy- implementation. It is normal, in fact, that bureaucrats make decisions not only of a technical nature, but related to political issues or, rather, guiding the organization's activities ("organizational policies"). In many cases, guidelines and action-frameworks allow officials to decide between alternative courses of action, though they nevertheless generally proceed in consultation with the organized interests most directly concerned. It is, of course, always possible that what the public or its representatives want or request becomes what the public or its representatives are expected to want or request. Therefore, according to Reinhard Bendix's formulation, a sort of interaction between national bureaucracies and society takes place [Bendix 1977: 165], though Merton's remark concerning the conflict of the public with bureaucratic authority is more to the point, any bureaucrat, whatever his position in the hierarchy, represents the power and prestige of the organization, he feels vested, and is considered vested with authority, which entitles him (or so he thinks) to a domineering attitude [Merton 1968: 257-258].

Authority and submission to the organization: Authority appears, as an observable pattern of interaction and not an officially defined social relationship, partially constituted by complementary role expectations of superiors and subordinates. Officials depend on the good will of their subordinates and the public [Bendix 1977: 24]. Even if authority partially rests on sanctions, frequent resort to such sanctions weakens it disproportionately, in comparison with the sanctions' positive effects. It is true, as Blau and Meyer point out, that officials and employees frequently internalize rules, regulations, or other normative standards of the bureaucracy, in order to unconsciously convince themselves that they carry out tasks corresponding to their own convictions and to the community's shared values and norms. This, of course, amounts, in many cases, to nothing more than self-deception. Often, a brutal change in the orientation of the bureaucracy provokes a total collapse of the internalized normative and value-systems (e.g., in the former Soviet

Union, where old party cadres are unable to adjust to changes).

Staff and technical responsibilities: A new internal contradiction developed in the bureaucratic organizations with the increasing role of experts, whose professional competence and activities lead to a collision with staff responsibilities. This is easily explained by the traditional concept of gradation of levels of authority corresponding to similar degrees in competence. Higher officials are presumed to be more competent than their subordinates, whereas the head of an organization is expected to possess the most impressive technical knowledge, in addition to its managerial capabilities. The increasing use of specialist experts familiar with advanced technology which staffers and high officials do not even understand eliminates the presumed identity between expertness and hierarchy. This discrepancy between expected and actual authority thus constitutes one of the most potentially destructive conflicts in a bureaucratic organization. Such contradiction between professional expertise and bureaucratic staff was underlined in the last decades when the latter category started to be called administrators, as if this term could have meant a special professional skill (contrary to the professional managers). This term, in fact, covered staff who was making their whole career, or a good part of it, within the organization.

Efficiency: It is a good question whether highly praised bureaucratic efficiency refers to the effectiveness of the services rendered by a bureaucratic organization to the public or to its clients, or if it relates to the cost-efficiency of its operations. As Beetham said, measurement of effectiveness consists of nothing more than qualitative and political judgements in relation to the definition of the objectives and the distinctive practices and operations of the administration concerned [Beetham 1987: 34-35 and 39]. Most authors recognize that hierarchical supervision is not enough for effective coordination, but a rigorous discipline is needed; this is established by the rules and regulations that govern the organization's operations.

Coordination: Merton called attention to both functional and dysfunctional aspects of bureaucracies, one factor enhancing their efficiency, but another counter-balancing this effect by reducing it. This vicious circle has best been explained by Herbert Simon who juxtaposed the requirements of specialization and the division of labor based on specialization, and those of coordination necessitated by overlapping functions or conflicts due precisely to specialization and the division of labor, but which, in practice and not only in principle, are incompatible with specialization.

Communication: Another shortcoming of bureaucracy, evidenced in its long history, is the one designated in organization theory as the problem of two-way communication, that is, the necessity of communication between organizational levels from bottom up and not only downwards from the head. Heads of large organizations, including the state, are frequently ill- informed of events because information originating with those who are in touch with operational problems daily tends to be neglected for the very reason that it comes from a subordinate. Formal rules and regulations, by stating the goals of the organization and setting performance criteria for the whole staff, are much more important in a decentralized model combined with multiple levels of hierarchy (vertical differentiation). They are assumed to guide decision-makers and to ensure that decisions are made which are consistent throughout the whole organization.

Blau and Meyer are certainly correct in saying that Weber's ideal-type of bureaucracy is built not only on conceptual definitions but also on implicit assumptions and generalizations such as, for example, the hypothesis that the imparted characteristics of a bureaucratic organization enhance efficiency. Those hypotheses have been falsified since Weber wrote about bureaucracy, but the Weberian reminiscences still predominate and no efforts were really made to correct those failures and adopt the lessons learned from the past.

(c) THE HYPOTHESIS OF BUREAUCRATIC RATIONALITY

According to Weber and most sociologists and political scientists succeeding him, social rationality does not often coincide with individual rationality. In fact, it often suppresses it. Bureaucratic rationality is closely tied to the impersonal character of bureaucratic activity as it relates to the clearly- defined pattern of activities in which every series of action is functionally related to the purposes of the organization. This functionally-related nature of an administrative organization is expressed by the hierarchical linkage of status and the more or less integrated setup of offices for which the rules and regulations specify obligations and privileges, rights and duties. Thus, the Weberian conceptualization of bureaucracy itself represents what one generally considers as the bureaucratic or administrative rationality. In a narrower sense, Weber's idea of social rationality concerns the application of general rules to particular cases; it constitutes a clear-cut example of instrumental-purposive rationality aiming at safeguarding public interest from encroachments of subjective values and desires, of egotistic convictions and actions because values and valuations are deemed non-rational.

In this perspective, bureaucratic rationality is specific in the sense that, first, it is bound to rules which can be analyzed and argued on objective grounds in public discourse; and, secondly, it is expected to show a high degree of consistency or, by reversal, to reduce to a minimum discrepancies between decisions and operations due to personal idiosyncrasies and interests. It is generally considered that discretionary decisions not responding to criteria stated and discussed in public cannot be assessed reliably and objectively. However, the major problem in respect to the functioning of bureaucracies is that, despite the principle of separation of policy-making and policy implementing in the rational bureaucratic structure, the interests of the state and the interests of the bureaucracy became identical in the affirmation and praise of bureaucratic rationality. In consequence, then, one can say that the Weberian conception of bureaucratic rationality is dysfunctional because it imposes successive examination and evaluation of general principles and rules on which criteria and corresponding decisions are based. This procedure must lead to a regress and, most importantly, back to value-judgements, beliefs, and interests motivating the assessment of principles and rules.

5. *Political Participation and Democracy in Other Civilizations*

In investigating the possibility of establishment and the actual role of the participatory democratic form of political action in other civilizations, it is useful to look at it from Giddens' interpretation of modern history emphasizing temporal disjuncture between pre-modern and modern. In this perspective, participative democracy is not seen as the last and perfect stage of progressive development of humanity, but as a radically-distinct social and political configuration, in comparison to all prior forms of political order [Giddens 1985: 32].

In traditional societies, political relationships were largely determined on the pattern of social and personal relations. The fundamental framework is generally a communal one corresponding to ethnic and cultural identity, including mythic and religious consciousness. Even today, the political sphere is not clearly differentiated in most societies, in spite of the impact of Western conceptions. Correspondingly, political parties channeling participation frequently represent non-secular worldviews and ways of life and usually become social movements. On the other hand, in most Western or non-Western contemporary autocratic states, structures and institutional controls do not involve cultural homogeneity between rulers and the ruled, but on the basis of strong power relationships between dominant social groups and a corresponding enforcement apparatus. A dialectic of reciprocity and autonomy then operates; the state extracts as much revenue as possible from subjects who benefit from protection from external enemies or from the oppression from internal oligarchies.

It is an important difference between Western societies and Islamic, Oriental, and African societies that the latter are kept together by ethnic bonds, whereas the former are based on legal structures. In the Islamic civilization, a certain specific, legalistic approach prevails in the sense that in Islam, both state and society are based on God's unique sovereignty. The non-Western type of political practice presupposes the underlying identity of apparently irreconcilable phenomena and endeavors to resolve conflicts through arbitration and compromise, while the Western type is based on an acceptance of pluralism, which accentuates antagonisms and distinctions such as church and state or polity and civil society; this phenomenon partly explains the emergence of the uniquely-Western liberal tradition since the eighteenth century.

From the point of view of contemporary non-Western societies that desire to modernize, it is important to understand what Huntington and Nelson clearly showed and what is also fully applicable in the West, that political participation is "a function of the priorities accorded to other variables and goals and of the overall strategy of development, if any, that the leadership of the society has adopted" [Huntington-Nelson 1976: 17]. The general outcome is an orientation towards either a bourgeois or an autocratic regime but, as the O'Donnell study demonstrated, there is an "elective affinity" between modernization efforts and bureaucratic, authoritarian rule [O'Donnell 1973: 90].

If the country turns toward the bourgeois model, the practice of an electoral system and parliamentary institutions is introduced providing some short-run political stability; the middle class participation in power is extended at the expense of the lower strata, whose economic situation is declining. Eventually, however, economic growth proceeds relatively rapidly. If the introduced socio-economic changes continue to produce their effect, the lower strata begin to benefit moderately from them and are increasingly mobilized socially and politically though the demand for opportunities in political participation and access to political power. If, alternatively, the autocratic model is accepted by the ruling elite at the state's helm, economic growth may be enhanced, the participation of the middle class in political activity is restricted or suppressed, and the government may have recourse to measures, principally land reform and change in rural social structures, to promote socio-economic equality in order to receive the support of the most numerous segment of the population, the peasantry. The outcome of this model is the same as of bourgeois orientation, in which the lower classes having their positions strengthened demand meaningful access to and participation in the political system.

In both cases, in accordance with Huntington and Nelson, the groups in power can either envisage the technocratic solution or the populist one. The first signifies more growth and investment, restricted political participation in the name of efficiency, and increasing economic inequality for the sake of economic progress. The reverse picture is shown by the populist regime, with high levels of political participation concomitant with expanding welfare policies and governmental handouts as economic equality slowly increases, but the rate of economic growth is much lower. This evolution leads toward social conflict and the polarization of society, as more and more people demand equality through sharing the results of growth and a better quality of life. In the bourgeois and technocratic regimes, a conflict develops between expanded political participation and the requirement of socio-economic equality, whereas in autocratic and populist models conflict opposes larger political participation and more rapid economic growth.

In respect to the variables specified by Huntington and Nelson, it is necessary to point out that they reflect a typically Western approach to problems of non-Western countries. Political participation and stability, socio-economic development and equality are considered, but they ignore all other social and cultural factors. Political modernization depends, after all, on fundamental changes in the social structure: a pluralism of roles, the dominance of crude interests not hampered by old values and conventions, as well as more aggressive claims for political participation and for access to decision-making levels. At the same time, it multiplies the opportunities for restrictive and authoritarian political solutions. For that reason, and independently of the ethnic-cultural diversity, the political systems of the new state-nations mostly fall into the *autocratic-cum-populist category* (though showing some technocratic interest), consisting of weak parties and characterized by a *parochial-participative political culture* as described above. This is what Kohli calls "uncontrolled politicization" within both the State and civil society in India [Kohli 1990: 196].

The main problem in the political domain is that one cannot automatically presuppose the applicability of Western ideologies and principles of political organization in non-Western societies. This is, of course, a *Leitmotif* of the present study and, therefore, it may seem that it is repeated concerning each problem area. But it must be understood that in many cases either a definite adaptation of our ideologies and principles has to be carried out by force, in order to insert them into the local and civilizational context, or the countries concerned have to go through a painful and difficult social and cultural process of change until the new, renascent structures are able to accommodate the requirements of the Western way of life.   To demonstrate the above pattern, examples of differential civilizational approaches to the problems of political interaction will be considered.

After the disappearance of the "sacral kingship" of ancient India, or the empire of *Ashoka*, the *Mughal* empire represented, in Heesterman's words [Heesterman 1985: 15-18], segmentary political units between which power relations were constituted by ever-shifting alliances and deadly rivalries either through total dispersion of power among component parts, or centralization by a large-scale administrative apparatus.   This type of power relationship was based on the loyalty structure of personal ties of kinship and dependency reigning in a segmented society, reflecting the feudalistic structure of land distribution but not residence or belonging to a specific territory. Because of a potentially unending interwovenness and overlapping of units relating wide areas, the power structure could not easily be broken and latent conflicts and tensions were diffused without requiring a central intervention.   But in a dialectical play, the shifting weight of power between regional and local centers encouraged efforts of concentration through seeking a transcendental legitimation of a universal polity, which sometimes succeeded to break up structure and to create a center of power and influence, though the destruction of the entire network of concatenation was almost impossible.   The strongly centralized power of the British colonizers was imposed on this segmentary political network; therefore, the federalist-centralized power structure of independent India did not represent such a break with the past, as in many other countries of the non-Western world.   However, it can be questioned whether the former, looser system of power relations was not more responsive to the realities of such a continent-wide state and whether the symbiosis of the two systems is viable.

For political modernization, collective inspiration based on shared belief and value structures is essential. This function was accomplished by nationalism for the first time among non-European modernizing states in the case of Japan; though it is important to point out immediately that it was coupled with the move to discard *joi*, or the hate of foreigners. This enabled Japan to absorb all foreign input; intellectual, technical and technological, with a view to serve the interests of Japanese nationalism. This integral Japanese nationalism is best described by the word *kokutai*, which means a "concept of the state in which religious, political and familistic ideas are indissolubly merged" [Bellah 1985: 104], a concept which was correlated with *bushido*, "acting in moral integrity." Modernization in Japan was government-led, but its bearers were the members of the lower *samurai* class (and not the merchants or artisans constituting the nascent bourgeoisie) who lost their former status in the feudal courts but were perfectly apt, due to their talents, skills and ethical excellence, to assume the duties of reshaping national life and lead the nation into a new age. However, the introduction of participatory democracy was not possible except by imposition of the victorious power after the Second World War, as it did not correspond to the social and cultural belief and value system.

As far as modernization in China is concerned, Fairbank noted that the relatively advanced state of Chinese industrial and commercial activities at the beginning of the nineteenth century, coupled with a demographic growth unprecedented in the Western world at the time, was a crucial factor in obstructing further Chinese moves toward modernity Western-style. With a felicitous expression, Fairbank wrote that China achieved in the nineteenth century "the capacity to persist in a steady state" [Fairbank 1987: 50], but he also recognizes the role played, for example, in the 1860 *Ch'ing* restoration, by official corruption and bureaucratic capitalism.

The reigning Confucian view inspired an approach of respecting power and those who were bearers of it; according to this view, good government reflects a natural harmony between the interests of the rulers and their subjects, expressed in the progress of the affairs of the state, which guarantees order and the good life for its people. *Sun Yat-sen* introduced, in conformity with contemporary foreign ideologies, the so-called *Three People's Principles*, which stood for the following: first, people and race forming a nation; second, people's rights or power; and, third, people's livelihood. In Western parlance, these principles could be translated as nationalism, democracy, and socialism. These slogans (because they were not much more) were supposed to create a collective stimulation and the integration of the will of the people to modernize the country. Their success was limited, however, as "imperial Confucianism" opposed strong resistance to ideas imported from the West.

The problems encountered in Islam were related to the universalistic versus particularistic tension inherent in the Islamic teaching of total way of life, or the unity of religious and public life. As since the epoch of the Abbasid caliphate, state institutions and religious entities diverged more and more, two conceptions survived simultaneously: first, that the Islamic State embodied the whole of Muslim society and, second, that Islamic society was divided into separate states and other public institutions as well as into religious associations and bodies.[4] Therefore Islam can as easily be referred to as a legitimation of power or as an ideology of opposition [Tibi 1990: 129].

There was, however, a historical precedent of the conciliation of the bifurcating ideal juridical system of the *Sharia* and the actual legal practice in Muslim countries, the doctrine known as *siyasa shariyya*, or "government in accordance with the precepts of divine law." The so-called *mazalim* jurisdiction was based on this development, which recognized as judicial authority the power of the political ruler.

As far as the state and the political realm were concerned, the Indian reformer, *Mawlana al-Mawdudi*, was the most explicit in his critique of the borrowed Western forms. He viewed the Islamic state as the "very antithesis of secular Western democracy."[5] In his explanation, the basic principle in Islam is *hakimiyya*, which means that God is the absolute and ultimate sovereign of all creation. As God created the whole world, He is its owner and master and, therefore, commands absolute obedience. *Al-Mawdudi* objected to the Western ideology of democracy, as it is based on popular sovereignty, in which people are vested with absolute power to legislate and vote for laws which are against God's will, religion, and morality. The state is created by God, and given to the faithful by Him as the framework in which the latter can fulfil his moral duties by adhering to the law and divine order. Sovereignty belongs to God only. However, as the law, the manifestation of God's will and the political power structure, caliphate and sultanate, were clearly separated, any rebellion or seizure of power could be legitimated if the new ruler submitted himself to the divine legal order [Sharabi 1966: 16-17].

The conflict between the Western political ideology of political participation and democracy and those of other civilizations is real; the chronic instability of many non-Western political regimes proves this. One of the factors contributing to this instability is the fact that these countries had to accommodate the co-existence of political equality with economic inequality for a long period and practiced a wide-scale interventionism inherent in the design of state-led economic and social development (interventionism was also the instrument in the construction of the Western welfare state, but this happened in the West in a much more advanced state of economic development).

In search of a solution compatible with modernization, non-Western countries appear to try one of two possible ways out of their situation in which social, political, and economic developments are inextricably woven together and mutually obstruct the course of change. One of the solutions pursued is the recourse to a charismatic personality; the other is an endless series of revolutions which never initiate the desired betterment of life and stability required by a sustained developmental effort.

As Weber pointed out, charismatic power manifests itself when the collectivity faces extraordinary circumstances and finds itself in a critical situation. The charismatic leader disrupts all rational procedures and transforms tradition at his will. He follows his inner voice, an unprecedented and unique inner guidance in the fulfillment of a mission. For this reason, charisma, for Weber, represented in history a proper revolutionary force. Several charismatic leaders appeared in Asia and Africa during our century: Nasser, Nyerere, Nkrumah, Gandhi, Nehru, Mao Tse-Tung, and others. However, none of them did succeed in leading their countries to adapt to modern conditions without abandoning traditions, values and the proper lifeworld of their people, nor did they completely overthrow old structures and beliefs and implant new ideologies, ways of life, and forms of political organization.

The other solution available to modernizing state-nations is that of recurrent revolutions, replacing one regime or government with another without reversing their destinies. Revolution as such is a modern phenomenon; modernity was identified with a rationally constructed destiny of man, with the absolute confidence in the so-called progress of human spirit. Revolutions, therefore, are always perceived as mutations or the triumph of reason against the Old World, traditions, stagnation, obscure forces of reaction and absolutisms, anything which is designated as irrational. Applying Touraine's distinction between revolutions and social movements [Touraine 1990: 130-131], we can say that revolutions in modernizing state-nations did not succeed because they were limited to the state, the central agent of mutations in modernizing perspectives, and revolutionary action aimed at seizing control of the state in order to impose change as dictated by borrowed formulae. Social movements, on the contrary, embrace civil society; they become actors within this society, slowly preparing in undercurrents below the agitated surface, the historical mutations of the future. Revolutions always destroy themselves because they negate the other, the different; in consequence, they are invariably followed, as in the case of the French Revolution, by chaos and tyranny. Unfortunately, the recent history of state-nations in the non-Western world proves this historical analysis, as the endless series of revolutions failed to play the role either as agents of modernization or as agents of social integration combined with economic and social development.

It is even possible to question whether some of the state-nations are effectively states in the sense of theories of international law and international relations, notwithstanding that they are admitted in international organizations. The disparity between outward forms and inward substance of some sovereign states or the possession of juridical statehood even if not much evidence of empirical statehood exists, undoubtedly sustains this assessment. These quasi-states, as Jackson calls them [Jackson 1990: 24-25], were creations following "changes in the rules of membership and modes of operation in international society which were deliberately made to replace the institutions of European overseas colonialism" [ibid. 26]. This meant self-determination for countries formerly colonized and, at the same time, entitlement to development assistance for impoverished countries (an international distributive justice) but, most importantly, freedom from outside interference.

6. *Bureaucracies and Development*

The crucial problem of bureaucracies' impact on modernization in countries belonging to non-Western civilizations was more and more frequently indicated in sociological writings in recent years, but not in those on development economics. Beetham, for example, raised the question whether the bureaucratic system could operate effectively in the context of other cultures, in other worlds, where cultural beliefs, social structures and public attitudes do not support it in some of its essential features [Beetham 1987: 42]. He mentioned, among the latter, the requirements of appointment by merit, of impersonality and rule-governed procedure, and emphasized the impact of the bureaucracy's functioning on traditional social structures such as kinship or ethnic ties. In addition, Beetham also pinpointed the effect of unemployment that led governments to became the largest employer in most non-Western countries, in contradiction to the bureaucratic rationality. This, of course, overburdened the states' already insufficient budgets.

It is evident today that the responsibility of bureaucracies is considerable in the lack of success of modernization and development. To deal with this question, it is necessary to differentiate between national or local and bilateral and multilateral bureaucracies, whose work is related to the promotion of economic and social development. My thesis in this respect is as follows: *the lack of success of efforts to help the countries of Asia, Africa and Latin America in their economic and social development, the lack of success witnessed during the last third of this century, is, to a great extent due, to the bureaucracies which are responsible for these efforts.* Local governmental bureaucracies are responsible, without any doubt, in the largest extent, as they are in charge of the development of their own countries and are accountable to their own people. Bilateral donor countries' bureaucracies are organizations that handle all kinds of assistance given by governments to governments. Finally, multilateral or international bureaucracies such as the United Nations, the United Nations Development Program, and so-called specialized agencies such as the World Bank, the International Monetary Fund and regional development banks, are also responsible, to a considerable extent for the lack of success of development assistance. As the impotence of developmental efforts is partly due to the activities of these bureaucracies, there must be particular reasons, beside specific motives in each particular case, for their poor performance.

The first of such reasons appears to be the noticeable change in the practice, if not rules, governing recruitment in these bureaucracies. In national administrations, recruitment is done on the traditional basis of social links, that is, tribal and ethnic affiliations, clienteles, and so on. This is a fact of life in non-Western societies, and if there will be a change, it will come very slowly, when economic development and social re-structuration are already well advanced. It would, of course, not be true that there is no recruitment of officials with good technical knowledge or with the necessary dedication to ideals of development, but their numbers are limited. As for bilateral and multilateral aid and assistance bodies, their method of recruitment is more and more based on ascriptive characteristics and not according to merit, showing the general degeneration of the Western bureaucratic system (if there was ever one approximating the Weberian perfection). Thus, today's bureaucracies show signs of a *bureaucratic feudalism.*

In multilateral organizations, particularly in the United Nations system and its various organs, the problem of non-ascriptive recruitment is perhaps the most serious. Official rules foresee that staff should be recruited according to a geographic quota in order to avoid, justly and reasonably, that nationals of Western countries should take up all posts. This rule was mainly established for political activities, and even there, it is considered that it should be taken into account in case of equal educational background and technical competence only. Nevertheless, the rule is applied in all sectors; this leads to anomalies that are unacceptable in any administration. For example, technical assistance personnel are placed to perform duties in their own countries (when the country itself could employ them for the same purpose on government funds but with lesser salaries). Or, in the case of groups of similar countries, especially if they speak the same language, people are moved from one country to another, from one post to another, in internationally funded programs and assistance activities. This could, of course, not be a major problem if the criterion of recruitment was not carried out on the basis of ethnic solidarity, knowledge of a language or other ascriptive and political reasons, but technical excellence and widespread professional experience. The ascriptive trend in filling posts in national administrations and bilateral and international aid bureaucracies is overwhelming; one could almost say that instead of the introduction of the Weberian principles into non-Western administrations, the traditionally sanctioned, ascriptive criteria more or less dominate Western, especially cooperation bureaucracies, and first of all, the multilateral bodies.

The second major defect is the saddening and profound disinterest in the goals of economic and social modernization, not only on the surface of activities, but also in the essentials of the bureaucracies' objectives. Local administrations in any country are responsible for the collective destiny of the nation, for carrying out what people want and prefer. But they largely implement what the ruling strata think is the best for the country. The fundamental problem is that objectives, strategies, future tactics change periodically, but regularly, indicating that no serious effort was made by any of the participants in their definition and formulation, no objective and sincerely committed will to the welfare and progressive improvement of conditions of life is evidenced in the preparation of such programs. Officials of national, bilateral, and multilateral bureaucracies frequently appear to be disinterested in the goals pursued, strategies prepared, and, most importantly, results and performances obtained through the operations of their administrations. In this way, the principal objectives of economic cooperation and technical assistance activities are ignored, pushed aside. The words are, of course, there, but not the careful action or, in many cases, the intent.

To close this chapter, an especially important effect of the national, bilateral, and multilateral bureaucracies' intervention in developing countries should be noted that which is mostly responsible for the failure of modernization and developmental efforts. *All three types of bureaucracies involved in these activities, either on the receiving and implementing side or on the donor and executive side, are the most important vectors of the transmittal, without any effort of critical evaluation as to their suitability or without any effort for their adaptation, of Western social and economic beliefs, concepts, structures, and policies to the non-Western world.* Again, the largest responsibility must be laid on the shoulders of the bureaucrats and managers of the receiving countries, because it cannot be a foreigner's duty, as it is beyond the bounds of his competence and his understanding of the local cultural context, to adapt beliefs, concepts, structures, and policies borrowed from abroad to the respective countries' cultural, spiritual, and social traditions and lifeworld. It is well known today how the elite of developing countries educated abroad were isolated from the masses once they returned home, isolated particularly from the rural masses.

The Western-oriented bilateral and multilateral bureaucracies behave, in truth, as the missionaries of other ages, who brought to the poor and destitute populations of the world their own Gospel. It is justified to designate their doctrine as such because, in many cases, it is not even allowed to question or discuss it. Acceptance is expected to bring the desired results of improved quality of life and, first and foremost, material riches. It should be clearly stated that the efficiency of Western methods of economic development and modernization achieved phenomenal results in the West in improving human life and, especially, the life of the lower strata of society. But this still does not justify the supposition that "all things being equal," which they never are, the same concepts, methods, structural changes, and cultural transformations are applicable anywhere in the world. Such an attitude shows an unbearable self-sufficiency, an inadmissible ignorance of the existence of other cultural worlds, and a deliberate annihilation of the wonderful human diversity.

CHAPTER EIGHT

MODERNIZATION AS FRAMEWORK OF ECONOMIC DEVELOPMENT

The eventual dialogue or conflict between the Western and non-Western civilizations may have considerable influence on the domain of economic activity in the world, in general, and on the interaction between these civilizations, in particular. The problem envisaged from this angle could best be formulated as the interplay of modernization and development. After more than three decades of efforts of cooperation between Western and non-Western countries, and after provision of huge amounts of financial aid as well as technical assistance to the latter, the results of these efforts appear, in many cases, disastrous. Often, the countries to be modernized are less better off now than they were at the beginning of the period when cooperation and assistance started; one might even say that their situation is desperate, from the point of view of their lifeworld, as traditions, social structures and the everyday way of life were destroyed without having been replaced by new ones adapted to their cultural heritage and natural environment.

In some instances, there is much-heralded success due to particular circumstances which explains why these countries were able to affect the "cultural switch;" to slowly erase the inherited values and beliefs from people's minds, to gradually change social and communal structures of life, and adapt, step by step, the Western way of life correlated with efforts of modernization and development. In most countries, however, a situation prevails which could best be called schizophrenic; some economic changes were introduced, and social stratification was somewhat modified without replacing the mental and cultural world which hitherto sustained economic activities and the traditional differentiation of society. As a result, people in these countries live in two completely different worlds: the world of modern economic and political activities, and the world of inherited cultural and mental realities. This situation is reflected in uprooted ways of life, urban and rural maladjustment, new differences in social status, and discrepancies in belief and value systems. Simply, many of the modernized groups of society live in a cultural vacuum, without an all-encompassing worldview constituting the framework of everyday life. Hegel would have considered these people as possessing consciousness in two separate worlds through estrangement from their inherited institutions and cultural surroundings.

The situation thus produced in countries belonging to non-Western civilizations is dramatic, not only because vivid hopes stirred by the movement of decolonization after the Second World War faded away, but also because no political independence can be complete without (relative) economic independence, or at least the hope of reaching it in a foreseeable future. In addition, such a situation cannot be sustained for another half a century, and who could say that this is not to be envisaged in light of the results of the past three decades? It appears that the industrialized and democratic countries of the West will run into greater and greater economic and social difficulties in the future for reasons inherent in their proper evolution, and all the more so as people from other continents try, by every means possible to migrate into the richer areas of the world in the hope of a better livelihood. Populations of Western countries will therefore not be willing and able to continuously deliver ever-growing volumes of financial aid and technical assistance, not even the humanitarian aid necessitated by the terrible sufferance resulting from political troubles and uprooted social structures, the disintegration of communities, and cultural disorientation.

In exploring aspects of modernization and development in the framework of inter-civilizational relations, the methodology of contemporary mainstream economics will first be analyzed here.

Significant trends of economic activities in non-Western countries will be traced before examining and, finally, with modernization and development in the cultural context.

1. *The Methodology of Contemporary Mainstream Economics: A Critique*

Our critique of the methodology of contemporary mainstream economics will be limited to those features of it which, despite an apparent domination, were fundamentally questioned by outstanding representatives of the economic profession during the past two decades.[1] All these critics attacked economic theory's and methodology's formalism ("an aestheticism of mathematical *technè*" [Rosen: 1989: vii]) and the tendency toward unrealistic assumptions and arbitrariness. In more or less the same vein as the above-mentioned critics, this text deals with such problems as linking economic theory and reality, that is, laws, generalizations, and assumptions, and the methodology of individualism with its implication to ignore social forces. *These are issues which, par excellence, show why economic theory and practice developed in the intellectual framework of Western civilization cannot be automatically transplanted to areas belonging to other civilizational worlds like China, India, the Muslim states, or African countries.*

(a) ECONOMY AND REALITY: LAWS, EMPIRICAL GENERALIZATIONS AND ASSUMPTIONS

The designation of the style of argumentation of contemporary economic science by a German author as "Model-Platonism"[2] best illustrates what one could qualify as the confusion of logical presuppositions with empirical conditions: the elaboration of idealized, pure theories, non-verifiable and sometimes tautological hypotheses, which have no relevance for substantive, empirical generalizations. Thus, propositions are deducted from a series of postulates, and these propositions, according to Lord Robbins, "are so much the stuff of our everyday experience that they have only to be stated to be recognized as obvious" [Robbins 1984: 79]. However, Blaug is right when he says that economics hardly produced any laws until now, if we define laws as "well-corroborated, universal relations between events or classes of events deduced from independently tested initial conditions" [Blaug 1980: 161].[3]

Most exponents of neo-classical economics are protagonists of the hypothetico-deductive method, since John Stuart Mill,[4] who rejected empirical generalizations because these can only be based on a definite series of observations among an infinite number of possible ones. This series of observations follows a principle of selection, and the selection process must be based on a hypothesis. For many economists, however, economic generalizations are thought to be equivalent to laws in the natural sciences; Robbins requires only that such generalizations be stated exactly and be related not to vague notions, but to definite concepts such as price, supply, and so on [Robbins 1984: 66-67]. This, of course, implies valuations and value-relationships. It is, nevertheless, evident that examples of economic laws given by Robbins, such as the laws of diminishing returns or individual preference ordering, are not laws, but generalizations. They signify functional relations between variables, valid under certain circumstances only, whereas "causal laws are inductive generalisations of observed correlations" [Hollis-Nell 1975: 71]. Economic laws cannot be tested as laws of nature, but solely through their applicability in a given situation; if derived propositions-generalizations are realistic, they may have inevitable implications but are only valid *ceteris paribus*, that is, "other things being equal" as Duhem's irrefutability thesis showed for laws of natural sciences long ago [Blaug 1980: 17].

This critique also covers Samuelson's tentative to break out of the vicious circle of analytic thought through the claim of "operationally meaningful theorems" completed by the correspondence principle [Samuelson 1983: 3-5], or Machlup's "indirect testability hypothesis" [Machlup 1978: 192-194]. It would be much more reasonable to accept Blaug's proposal that in economics, in a state of uncertainty and ignorance about the world, there is nothing else but "tendency laws" or, even better, "tendency statements" which can be regarded as promissory notes "only redeemed when the *ceteris paribus* clause has been spelled out and taken into account, preferably in quantitative terms" [Blaug 1980: 69]. The proposition of using in economics and the social sciences "tendency laws" is all the more justified as empirical success depends on contingent truths or statements which depend on the truthfulness of other statements, i.e., the truthfulness of *ceteris paribus* clauses or the givens included in the economists' universe of discourse. It is evident that this method serves the purpose of isolating economic propositions from real-world conditions by formulating the givens comprised in the universe of discourse in such a manner that they exclude any counter-examples and make attempts to disconfirmation or falsification void.

The most criticized assumption in economics is the maximization-under-certainty postulate (maximization, that is, of net advantages, not only of monetary gains). That this postulate is so indispensable for economic theorizing and modeling as Hutchison pointed out [Hutchinson 1977: 80], stems from the fact that no other generalizing assumption with such an oversimplifying power has yet been invented to replace it. Frequently used assumptions are not infrequently self-contradictory. For example, the adoption of intra-personal comparison of utilities as the warranted basis of consumer theory, whereas comparison of inter-personal utility as a guide to welfare economics is not accepted [Hutchison 1965: 138-139]. Most importantly, assumptions are often untrue.[5] But this unreality of assumptions was easily accepted in accordance with the most popular but epistemologically unacceptable view, which was first proposed by Friedman, that assumptions or postulates do not matter, as the principal function of propositions is not explanatory. Therefore, the only thing which matters is the correctness of the prediction based on these assumptions [Friedman 1953: 14-15]. Friedman treated, in an instrumentalist vein, any assumption as a kind of approximation (without even caring about their initial conditions, core hypotheses, and boundary conditions) useful for the purpose of the modeling theorist to depict the conditions in which the theory is expected to be valid. Hollis and Nell [1975: 95 and 111] found a fateful resemblance between this Friedmanian positivist conception of prediction and the procedure of Zande oracles studied by Evans-Pritchard. Thus, statistical correlation replaced causal explanation, truth or falsity was thrown out together with disconfirmation, and falsified predictions led to changes in the model's postulates or assumptions until its predictions were proven correct. Predictions were thus transformed into "covert" analytic statements [Caldwell 1982: 181-182 and Hollis-Nell 1975: 37-38] or tautologies, showing a definite circularity, predicated assumptions assorted with *ceteris paribus* clauses yielding logical implications.

There are, of course, more elaborate theories of assumptions than

Friedman's (sleight-of-hand) treatment. Archibald, for example, distinguished five kinds of assumptions: statements of motivation; overt behavior of economic agents; the existence and stability of determinate functional relationships; restrictions on the range of relevant variables; and, boundary conditions of the theory under which it applies [Archibald 1959a: 64-65]. Melitz, on the other hand, distinguished between auxiliary and generative assumptions [Melitz 1965: 42], *ceteris paribus* being a typically auxiliary assumption, while profit maximization is a generative assumption *par excellence*. Melitz believed that a lack of realism relative to auxiliary assumptions can have more pronounced effects than those relative to generative assumptions, as the latter may be given different interpretations when required.

(b) METHODOLOGICAL INDIVIDUALISM AND SOCIAL FORCES

Methodological individualism[6] in economics had, undoubtedly, disastrous effects although most economists still advocate it, perhaps not so much by conviction but by the inertia of routine. The best definition of this methodological view was given by Boland: "*Methodological individualism* is the view that allows only individuals to be the decision-makers in any explanation of social phenomena" [Boland 1982: 28]. Not only is this methodology erroneous because it ignores society's institutions, but also because it ignores the profound interplay between the individual and the community in which he lives, or the cultural and social conditioning of individual intentionalities. This interplay (which is far from being, as sometimes characterized, a constraint) means that the individual himself is a common creation of biological factors and social and cultural influences, on the one hand, and that social institutions are a result of the actions of individuals as well as social forces and cultural traditions, on the other hand. Therefore, it is as false and unbelievably reductive to consider institutions, the culture and society of the lifeworld, as exogenous variables in economic activities, as it is an unacceptable reduction to identify individuals with their utility function or consider them only as bearers of their own revealed preferences. The opposite view, purported here, has been expressed by a few economists, among them Thurow, that mainly social choices and social preferences guide economic activities [Thurow 1983: 222-223], if one admits that fundamental interaction between individuals and their community remains a decisive factor in forming these social choices.

One could, of course, say that mainstream neoclassical theory recognizes some endogenous institutions of the market economy, such as the price mechanism, which links the individual to others in responsiveness to modifications of individual choices. It signals, at the same time, to every individual decision-maker, decisions or wishes of all other individuals living in a society. The correct functioning of the price mechanism is linked, in Arrow's theorem, to the equilibrium state of the economy. But this leads reasoning into a vicious circle, because maximization by individuals and market equilibrium are interdependent. Markets, on the one hand, cannot be in equilibrium if some individuals only are maximizers, and any incentive to change behavior therefore upsets the equilibrium, for example, extraordinary profit expectations. But all individuals cannot maximize their utility functions if markets are not in equilibrium. Perfect competition and the assumption of a given combination of exogenous variables is then a *sine qua non* condition for the maintenance of the Walrasian general equilibrium state (unchanging prices and production patterns). Disequilibrium means the possibility of obtaining gains and increasing returns to scale; disequilibrium, consequently, as a result of imperfect competition, creates a conflictual situation between the individual decision-maker's profit maximization and the optimum outcome for the society.

It is also due to methodological individualism that *macroeconomic* considerations are based on conclusions derived from *microeconomic* theorizing, as Thurow and Boland recently reminded us. The essential error is that the distinction between individual decision-making behavior and market price-determining factors is lost from view or, put another way, attributing economic decisions to individuals is only justified if the overall stability of the market and of the environment is ensured.

The relative ignorance of the *temporal perspective* is also directly related to this methodology. In the image of the natural or experimental sciences, initial conditions and exogenous conditions are always supposed to be constant over time. The situation is considered in a steady or static state; if at least one of the givens is allowed to change over time, it is a dynamic state that is encountered. But time as a constant factor really means that there is no "real-time" perspective envisaged, but a sort of pale, theoretical temporality, the concept of which is justified by the timeless character of the models' logical validity. But such a concept of temporality cuts off entirely the theoretical, imaginary situation from reality, and makes it impossible to link the two together by any kind of correspondence or other principle, because the values of endogenous and exogenous variables supposedly consistent at a given point of time, and may not be the same at another moment in the temporal progression. Everything in economic reality is situated in real time; everything is inserted in a historical sequence. There are no timeless economic facts.

2. *Dual Economy and Unbalanced Growth*

(a) CHARACTERISTICS OF DUAL ECONOMIC STRUCTURES

Economic growth and social development[7] implies dual or hybrid *economic structures*, the juxtaposition of more or less modernized and entirely traditional sub-sectors of the economy. These dual structures are the result of *non-proportional* rates of change: in economic magnitudes; in the multi-dimensional differentiation of the economy's sectors; and in the concomitant changes in other spheres of society. In this process, each sub-sector is totally interdependent. Non-proportionality, in both the short and the long term, is the linkage between dualistic structures and unbalanced growth. Both are based on the facts, first, that most countries passed through the historic process of underdevelopment in Celso Furtado's sense [Furtado 1964: 129]; and, second, that many of the factor inputs are not endogenous, as supposed by the development models, but of exogenous origin.

The dualistic character of economic growth shows how important it would be to adapt *imported* economic principles to the environmental and cultural context of a country where growth is stimulated, instead of initiating society's development through foreign concepts, methods, and processes. There is a mutual reinforcing or weakening dynamic inter-relation between factor supplies, production increase, structural differentiation, and institutional transformation, if economic concepts and methods applied in a specific context are pre-selected in accordance with the environmental, cultural and social parameters and, afterwards, integrated into this context.

It was demonstrated long ago that determinants of supply, among them labor productivity, exert the most crucial influences on economic and, especially, industrial growth patterns, if attention is paid to sectoral shifts of comparative advantage and factor costs corresponding to non-proportional rates of change in the relevant sectors. But even if factors influencing production processes are more important from the point of view of economic activities proper, they are not more influential than such non-economic factors as demographic behavior, cultural conditioning, or spatial determinants. It is, however, crucial that though the economy and its sectors or sub-sectors are characterized by a dual nature, all the endogenous or exogenous elements operate in an *interactive* fashion.

The dualism between agricultural and industrial sectors, reflected normally in the dualism of the spatial divide (the rural-urban differentiation), is essential from the point of view of economic growth. It is essential because for decades, politicians and their advisors promoted the manufacturing sector and urbanization with all possible means, except for Meiji Japan, where no agricultural revolution took place, but a concurrent growth of the agricultural and industrial sectors, supported industrialization and the ever-growing urban population through revenue transfers from the countryside. Those policies resulted in the growing impoverishment of rural regions and a disastrous decline of agricultural production and food supply.

Countries which were previously self-sufficient in the main crops of local consumption and exporters of other industrial crops, became net importers of most foodstuffs, especially as local consumers' tastes and requirements changed and underwent considerable diversification as a result of the often questioned "demonstration effect" (that is, inducement to replicate habits of others). It was also proven during the past decades that mainly agriculture and services, and the rural informal sector, not manufacturing, are able to absorb the so-called surplus labor, which in fact is not surplus, but unemployed labor, due to the high rate of demographic reproduction. Therefore, growth of the agricultural sector should be the primary goal of development efforts. An outstanding example of agriculture or, rather, of the rural world's absorbing capacity was the acceptance in Ghana, at the beginning of the eighties, of more than a million Ghanaians thrown out from Nigeria. These refugees found a place to live, principally in the countryside, through extended families and kinship ties, religious organizations, and other socio-cultural associations.

During the period after the Second World War, the main economic emphasis was on the most efficient allocation of capital as the engine of progress and growth. Today, though many people still cling to this belief, even if it is proven wrong, it becomes clear that it is only a proper proportionality of factor supplies and their interaction, as well as profound changes in the cultural characteristics and mentalities of the countries concerned, that can enhance economic growth. The problem today is no more a question of resource allocation but *resource creation*, which is a completely different proposition. Real wealth in countries belonging to non-Western civilizations is not constituted in liquid assets, or in assets which are easily transferable or negotiable, it consists of land and buildings, livestock, and inventories of goods including foodstuffs, traditional valuables, consumer goods, and tools for work. Such capital assets, which are exposed to risk and uncertainty, assure at the same time the social status of those who possess them, who do not easily sell such wealth in order to invest in negotiable and transferable values. Even the establishment of modern-type financial institutions can only change such habits very slowly, though they provide increased incentives to mobilize savings for investment. The question is not whether capital market imperfections as encountered in industrialized economies, or information costs or absorption capacities and such niceties of developed market economies are relevant. The need of means for resource creation obliges most countries to try to achieve economic growth finance their investment mainly from foreign sources, through Official Development Assistance (ODA), loans fromthe World Bank and its affiliates, or credits from foreign financial institutions. But how long can this situation endure when, in most cases, even the recurrent costs related to the investments realized are not locally mobilizable? What is the sense of gaining political independence when many dual economy countries are not even able to cover a small part of their capital requirements?

(b) UNBALANCED GROWTH: THE ONLY POSSIBLE WAY OF GROWTH

In any dual economy, *economic growth is unbalanced*, as the two concepts are strictly interrelated through the non-proportional rate of growth of different parts of the economy. Balanced growth, a simultaneous, multi-faceted process in an equilibrium context, cannot lead to real growth, because it aims at the superimposition of a foreign model, that of a self-contained new economic structure on an equally self-contained traditional sector which reflects an entirely different worldview. In a situation of unbalanced growth, there are always some leading sectors and some lagging sectors which bring about a seesaw advance of the economy: one sector communicates impulses to others, to leaders, or to those left-behind. This conceptualization of unbalanced growth is in conformity with the so-called Heisenbergian paradigm in economics (Weisskopf), as the emergence of oligopolies reflects an indeterminateness, giving place to an infinitely varied pattern of possibilities. Economic processes in underdeveloped countries are unbalanced because *it cannot be otherwise.* Balanced growth and equilibrium situations are ideals, probably never realized, and unbalanced or disequilibrium growth represent reality, apparent today in Asia, Africa, and Latin America.

In conditions of unbalanced growth, a sequential orientation is desirable when there is a possibility to establish strategies based on priority-ordering with a view to build up a country's infrastructure and public services indispensable to productive and market activities, such as power and water supply, transportation, storehouse networks, communications, irrigation and drainage systems, education and public health services. But it is due to the specificity of these investments that they cannot be governed by the usual criteria (capital/output ratio, profitability, etc.) on the basis of which private investments are evaluated. The real importance of the unbalanced growth process is that it allows for a parallel investment activity, simultaneously undertaken by the authorities and by private entrepreneurs, in which the former can start constructing the indispensable infrastructure of public services, whereas the latter exploit, here and there, easy-to-actualize investment opportunities. In the case of private investments, forward and backward linkages may play a useful role, but not to such an extent as imagined during the past decades, simply because these linkages presuppose an already advanced context, with some industrial structure showing a limited cumulative tendency, as well as because of the lack of perception of linkage-indicated investment opportunities.

3. *Modernization and Development in the Cultural Context*

The main error in the twentieth century development process was, first and foremost, *the belief in the universal validity and applicability of the liberal-market economy or socialistic economic principles developed in the context of Western society and Western culture.* But this universalistic belief implies, by definition, another inadmissible error: *the exclusion of the possibility of emerging new phenomena and of emergent new problem solutions derived from diverging cultural foundations prevalent in other civilizations which are based on different, or even incommensurable, intentionalities, (background network beliefs) as well as on corresponding action-orientations.*

The universalistic belief meant that no effort was made to explore several factors, including: whether other features of human life closely correlated to the development of material civilization as produced in the West were really desired by the people living in non-Western cultures; and whether liberal-market economy or socialistic principles of economic growth, believed to be universally applicable, should or could be adapted in various regions of the world, taking into account the Popperian "situational logic," or, more simply, could or should they be adapted to the evolutionary context of those regions, and to the environmental and cultural conditioning of the peoples living there?[8]

The problems, therefore, of economic development in non-Western civilizations can be reduced to the following simple questions. Is the universalistic approach justified? Is the success of Western economic systems based on one of the great cognitive achievements of Western culture, its science and technology, universally valid for all peoples and for all ages without taking into account historical realities [Furtado 1964: 1-2], and, at the same time, ignoring irreversible historical processes? If the application of Western economic principles is the only way to obtain similar benefits of material civilization as those enjoyed in the richer countries of the West, is it not conceivable, or even unavoidable, to proceed before anything else with an examination of whether these principles can be simply and directly transplanted from one cultural world to another?[9]

The greater responsibility for neglecting these questions rests more with the thinkers and leaders of non-Western countries than with those who became the apostles of modernization in the West. No foreigner can undertake the selection of imported ideas, concepts, and processes capable for adaptation in a given cultural framework, that is, to adjust and harmonize them with the traditions, values, and worldview prevailing inside the boundaries of a specific cultural world. Only those born and socialized into these traditions, values, and worldviews are capable of carrying out such an endeavor. This, of course, does not mean that natives of a country could not incorporate in their economic design, what Kuznets called "the *transnational stock* of useful knowledge" available in a definite epoch of history [Kuznets 1966: 287; italics in original], and that foreign advisers could not be helpful in the transfer of this knowledge.

The relevance of the cultural foundation and ethical legitimation for economic life and action is now more and more widely accepted; it is admitted that "given cultural traditions have a coherent and distinctive character that can have important social and economic consequences" [Inglehart 1990: 61]. Among recent writers, Hayek emphasized particularly the role of tradition and culture in economic and social life. In his view, tradition is a process of selection, over successions of generations, from among irrational or apparently unjustified beliefs, which, once crystallized, shape custom and morality in a community. He affirms that traditions are "adaptations to the unknown in all communities life and in all segments of man's activities" [Hayek 1988: 76]. Frank Cancian gave the clearest expression of the recognition that cultural foundations of economics cannot be ignored:

> Economic man always operates within a cultural framework that is logically prior to his existence as economic man, and the cultural framework defines the values in terms of which he economizes. This is a platitude to anthropologists and economists alike. It is a simple restatement of the idea that the 'given' institutional framework of the economic system may vary. However, it can be transformed in the conclusion that there are no economic men; i.e., there are no men whose economic activities are free of culture [Quoted by: Poggie and Lynch 1974: 145].

Emerging new conceptions about the economy and its embeddedness in a cultural context are well reflected in one of the latest books by Lester C. Thurow. It is the first time that a mainstream American economist recognized an important difference between the "individualistic Anglo-Saxon British-American form of capitalism" and the "communitarian German and Japanese variants of capitalism" [Thurow 1992: 32]. In sum, the first version of capitalism recognizes only individual interests, where individual firms serve the interests of their shareholders; this is reflected in the profit-maximizing principle and in the almost complete neglect of all aspects of human relationships, implying a lack of any kind of ties, such as loyalty, between employees and their firms or organizations. In Thurow's view, the communitarian variant of capitalism is based on team activity. Here, the individual identifies with a team, and the most important individual decision concerns what team he should join.[10] In this variant, the firm is oriented to the interests of all its "stakeholders;" among them, employees and workers, as well as customers, have more prominence than shareholders.

It is interesting to compare Thurow's conception of two types of capitalism with Bellah's description of the changing economic scene during the Togukawa period in Japan. Bellah sees the main characteristics of the Confucian doctrine in: first, the "unity of economy and polity," that is, a common direction of the two essential activities of society to safeguard order in the lifeworld; and, second, "'encourage production and discourage consumption," in conformity with Confucius' principles of frugality, through the limitation of desires and individual or collective spending. With reference to Thurow's assertion of German and Japanese communitarianism, it is remarkable that, since the Togukawa period, the Japanese did not embrace wholeheartedly economic competition, but had recourse to "all forms of association among producers" [Bellah 1985: 108-109].

4. *Modernization As Application of Economic Rationality*

The question concerning the much debated problem of *economic rationality* is whether there is such a thing as economic rationality, and, for that matter, whether there are rationality can be broken down by economic sub-sectors, such as the rationality of the productive sector or of the consumer's choices, or that there is no other rationality than a plain, *meaningful* human rationality? Economists such as Lord Robbins linked economic rationality to choosing, in full awareness, between ends, to know what one prefers of available alternatives [Robbins 1984: 152]. Martin Hollis believes in a relational concept of economic rationality, relations linking an agent's preferences, actions and consequences, in view of maximization of the satisfaction of his preferences [Hollis 1987: 16]. Sociologists, including Parsons and Smelser, recognized that there is a general value system in society that assigns relative importance to economic functions in the whole of a social action system, and considered economic rationality as the economic sector's proper value sphere. Economic rationality as value system controls individual behavior through motivation, through internalization of its tenets by members of the society, and through sanctions which contribute to the stabilization of these internalized orientations and to the adaptation of behavior to specific, changing circumstances. Parsons and Smelser also believed that there is a universal core of economic rationality independent of cultural and environmental variability, though they did not identify economic rationality with purposive rationality. In their view, purposive rationality belonged to society's general value system.

The problem of economic rationality is, therefore, the same as the problem of *economic man*, a theoretical creation satisfying computational and modeling needs of economists and statisticians. The whole idea of economic man reflects the absolute primacy assigned to the material development of human life, neglecting the embeddedness of economic phenomena in the total context of man's culture and society. This conceptualization even led to the devaluation of all other spheres of human existence compared to economic activities. And economic reductionism went much further. Not only was man reduced to economic man, and not only was meaningful and practical human rationality reduced to "economic rationality," but the latter was also postulated in narrow (and not always compatible) terms correlated with some specific economic or behavioral theories, such as profit maximization, preferred utilities, or consumer preferences.

A more tuned-down, probabilistic version of economic rationality called *rational expectations* does not take us much further, either. It consists of the supposition that people include in their previsions and predictions some kind of evaluation of what others expect in the future; thus, one can detect a sort of reflexivity in this approach, but, of course, a reflexivity derived from the belief in economic rationality and in the preference orderings of economic man. One must also take into account that one's own economic preferences change, sometimes substantially, even during short lapses of time; such changes are related to one's experiences, values, preferences and unattained expectations, as perspectives (if not life-chances) are invariably pluralistic.

Not economic or sectoral rationality governs human life, but a meaningful human rationality, a matter of environmental conditions and cultural belonging. If human reason is a universal faculty, rationality is culturally elaborated and transmitted; therefore, if methodologies and processes of modernization and economic development are not embedded in the world's various civilizations, economic rationality implanted from a foreign culture will never be an effective instrument.

5. *The International Dimension of Modernization and Economic Development*

Modernization and economic development became, over the course of the last thirty years, a major preoccupation on the international scene. Approaches to resolve problems in this domain were, unfortunately, confused and muddled because the whole question became politicized. Various pressure groups used it to promote their own political and economic agendas, not least the governments of many countries of Africa, Asia, and Latin America. These economies struggled for survival as the infusion of capital and technical assistance remained unsuccessful, and inefficiency, imprudent policies and sheer incompetence created in those countries explosive social situations.

Decolonization led to the creation of independent and sovereign states, most of which, though having abundant physical (even if agricultural) and human resources, were not economically viable in a modern economy. However, as Jackson wrote in a recent study, "The international change was essentially normative, and basically entailed abolishing international legal disabilities previously imposed on non-Western peoples" [Jackson 1990: 55];[11] the new states were incorporated in the Western-style international system of positive sovereignty with the presupposition that they possess all the prerequisites of such a status. This concerned also all necessary fundamentals for the desired rapid economic and social development, again, of course, in the Western-style.

As the transformation of international relations was made in a voluntarist and constructivist mode, the "removal of international legal disabilities" was completed by the egalitarian requirement of the right of emerging states to economic and social development. Sovereignty hitherto meant not only the right to political independence, but also to aid and assistance on behalf of the rich, industrialized countries because, so the argument goes, colonialism was the cause of the former colonies' economic and social backwardness, understood in terms of the Western cultural and civilizational framework. The sovereignty of newly independent countries was therefore conceived as having a negative and a positive side -- negative in excluding the interference of others, and positive in the form of a right to economic and financial aid and assistance. The second aspect of sovereignty can be expressed as the right to an equitable share of global resources and opportunities. All the efforts undertaken in the framework of international and bilateral cooperation (UNCTAD, UNDP, World Bank, OECD, the New International Economic Order, the Integrated Commodity Scheme, and so on) were conceived and carried out with the objective of endowing newly independent countries with the requisites of economic sovereignty.

This doubled-faced sovereignty which now governs international relations has several effects which gravely reduce prospects of modernization in a great number of non-Western countries. The first effect is that this type of deferred compensation for damages and sufferance endured by the former colonies creates a sentiment of dependence by the governments and people receiving economic and financial aid. There is an attitude and mentality of being condemned to assistance, perhaps for a long time to come. The so-called doctrine of collective self-reliance (the accent should be placed on self-reliance) remained but a slogan without any concrete effect, except political cooperation efforts at international gatherings. However, the psychological impact of present aid policies and technical assistance is one of the reasons no innovative action has been undertaken to discover new means, for promoting economic growth and social development in a manner sensitive to cultural differences in various regions.

Another one of the distorting effects of the new status of non-Western states in the international community is that all modernizing or developing countries are considered to have uniform characteristics, ignoring their wonderful human and environmental diversity, and also ignoring the differential impact of the civilizations and native cultures to which they belong. They are treated as a uniform, homogeneous mass, instead of emphasizing their differences due to their differential resource endowments and their varying human capabilities and possibilities; in fact, their complete Otherness in comparison to the Western universalistic typification is ignored. An approach taking into account human and civilizational diversity will, of course, have to deny the equality of man as economic performer precisely because of the differing environmental and cultural endowments mentioned above.

Policies in non-Western countries concurrently aim at the construction of a modern economy and a voluntaristic restructuring of the society. At the same time, these policies try, under the influence of the West, to promote equality and equity, imitating the welfare states of the industrialized world without having the means to implement it. In this way, incoming capital and assistance is wasted without creating a sustainable base for continued developmental-cum-welfare policies.

The effort of imitation eliminates all incentive for inventiveness and innovation which could take the form, if not of new devices to promote new economic or social policies, but at least of the adaptation to the cultural environment of the concepts and methods borrowed from abroad. In addition, as trade cannot supply the engine of growth (as was the case for Europe), developing countries have to look for other domestic resources by: emphasizing growth of agricultural production for foodstuffs without draining away all surpluses and profits, in order to cover the needs of the state budget overburdened by the cost of unnecessarily large administrative machinery; or promoting industrialization based on domestic raw materials and traditional skills which can only slowly enter into a more intense phase of industrialization.

Finally, the manner in which political sovereignty was transferred from metropolitan countries to their former territories led, in most non-Western states, to a situation in which the current governmental bureaucracy is exclusively in charge of all economic and social developmental policies. The result was the complete "politicization" of these societies in the sense that no effort was made to give opportunities to social forces other than the government and the parties supporting it to attain a well-established organizational existence and operational efficacy. It is natural that governments prefer, as a corollary to their policies at home, to imprint an orientation on international regimes and organizations in order to proceed with authoritative rather than market allocation of the world's resources, with authoritative rather than free changes in patterns of economic activities and in flows of trade, finances and invisibles. This orientation also represents a serious drawback to modernization efforts. Authoritative solutions only postpone the moment of real choices and decisions. Such tendencies, however, are understandable in most countries in the non-Western world. The fluctuations and shocks on the world market have resulted in severe economic dislocations, relative deprivation, corruption, or disappointment of rising expectations in these regions. These symptoms clearly show the underlying disparities in power relations.

One can conclude, having reviewed the international dimensions of economic development and the societal and cultural inertia in non-Western nations strongly linked to this international framework, that the development process, in reality, was forgotten by the extraneous bureaucracies: the governmental bureaucracy at home which looks after its own interest and the special interests it is linked to; the international bureaucracy that imposes doctrines without taking into account each country's specificity; and the bilateral, donor bureaucracies which act under the pressure of domestic public opinion, if not in the interest of their own governments. Few really care if the countries of Africa, Asia, and Latin America finally reach a true economic sovereignty.

CHAPTER NINE

CONCLUSIONS

The conclusions of these investigations follow in a natural fashion from the body of the preceding text, which reflects a coherent and realistic perspective. It is evident that the book and the conclusions here presented will disappoint some of the readers a contextual perspective in inter-civilizational relations, a turn qualified by many as relativistic but what I consider to be a pluralist worldview.

Conclusion One

The fundamental thesis on which this study is based, the disjunction between the Western civilization and the other great cultures of the world, is an undeniable, empirical fact; if it is not recognized as such, it is because most people, even the greatest part of the intelligentsia of non-Western countries, believe that we are marching forward towards a universal civilization which *must* be modeled on the Western culture, with its undeniable achievements and undeniable destructive forces as well. The disjunction between cultures (which is always judged from the Western point of view) appears as a necessary corollary of the period of transition to a universal civilization.

If one admits that there is a disjunction between Western and non-Western cultures and, consequently, between their respective social structures, technological and economic conditions of life, and their modes of thought construed in context-relative styles of reasoning, if one accepts that there are different "worlds of culture" or "lifeworlds" corresponding to various human groups' divergent evolutionary past, traditional beliefs, values and existential histories, then there can be no other point of departure in exploring the possibilities of a dialogue between these worlds of culture but the effort to reach a genuinely new intellectual and spiritual framework which accommodates the co-existence of these differing cultural worlds.

The review of the ontological/cosmic imagination and problem setting of various great civilizations or culture-areas of the world shows a basic disjunction in comparison to the modern Western outlook. Clearly stated, the worldviews of most non-Western cultures are largely transcendentally motivated or are, at least, dualistically shaped, in contradistinction to the West's physicalist or naturalist monism. This shows that we encounter different "patterns of reasoning" and that the (like the Einsteinian) "coordinate systems" of the various cultures of humanity are diverging and reaching a point of disjunction. *In consequence, the first obstacle to any inter-civilizational dialogue is constituted by belief and value systems that reflect a different, fundamental ontological/cosmic framework.*

An in-depth dialogue of different civilizations in the contemporary world, and this is the most promising approach for the future, could lead to their mutual enrichment through an exchange of their specific ontological and cosmic views. The outcome of such a dialogue may be, on the one hand, an attenuation of the universalizing, ahistorical, and transcultural as well as epistemological (at the expense of the ontological) and scientific-technological tendencies of the Western civilization. The result may be a reestablishment of the sense of community between man and nature and the renascent and genuine solidarity between human communities. On the other hand, such a dialogue may produce a partial acceptance of the West's epistemic-scientific-technological outlook, based on the primacy of the immanent world, by other cultures, as far as such an outlook can be harmonized with their respective fundamental belief and value systems. An understanding achieved between various civilizations in a common ontological-cosmic framework could then lead to the disappearance of the disjunction between different cultures and culture-areas of the globe, and could contribute in the future to the elaboration of a shared and common lifeworld. This could and should never be universally identical in every civilization, but based on the reciprocal understanding of the particularity of each cultural world.

The description of different cultural characteristics of the uniqueness of man plays a crucial explanatory role. First, it shows that the transcendence of man, the fundamental structure and integrative power of the human mind, produces similar ideas, thoughts, and mental processes in persons belonging to different cultures with different belief and value systems. This proves the possibility of a dialogue between people of different civilizations. Second, the review also demonstrates the enormous diversities in "patterns of reasoning" despite the similarity of mental processes and evolutionary developments because of different human contexts, different interaction-patterns with the environment, and different historical heritage and social conventions. However, it is evident that the most fundamental difference is the one concerning the all embracing, ontological/cosmic framework that unavoidably conditions worldviews of men in all cultures. From this fundamental disjunction follow the next three conclusions in respect of reality, rationality and the ethical perspective.

The first major conclusion, therefore, is *the necessity to return to the ontological/cosmological basis of human existence and formulate a worldview which*, through the re-affirmation of the preeminence of the ontological-existential condition of man (as opposed to the primordiality of the Cartesian epistemological position), and the embedding of every cultural phenomenon into nature (understood as the totality of physical and non-physical phenomena) while emphasizing man's unique position in the evolutionary context, *acknowledges, in consequence, the necessity of a relativistic reading of realism, rationality and all other aspects of the lifeworld, a multiple, pluralistic ordering of reality.*

Conclusion Two

The dialogue of cultures presupposes the existence of other beings and of the world as it is experienced. Reality encompasses the physical world — organic and inorganic — as well as the mental and cultural worlds, the latter cognitively grasping, emotionally appropriating, and artistically expressing the shared experiences of a community. The realism underlying the dialogue of cultures refers to a reality conceptualized, felt, normatively organized, and expressed by particular types of symbolism. This is essential in founding the possibility of cultural dialogue. *Dasein-within-the-world, Dasein-with-other-beings shares this reality with others, who are members of other cultural groups possessing different genetic endowment and living in different environments than him.* The reason is that all members of the species commonly perceive reality, through man's belonging to the cosmos and evolving in the bosom of nature.

The facts which are invariably real in man's existence include concepts such as father, mother and child figures, the environment, trees, stones, clouds, and stars. And not only such basic features of the lifeworld but also the emotions related to them, or to any other human beings, and the concern about nature itself. Beyond such invariant realities which may vary in intensity, direction, or shades as historically institutionalized, reality for man also includes basic human desires not related to strictly biological, existential, or emotional necessities, but to what I call the transcendence in man. For example, the urge to express the world and the self in artistic forms is one such desire.

Though the underlying reality is shared by all members of the human species due to the evolutionary development of man, which entails the same fundamental experiences to all human beings, *this same reality is seen differently by each man.* Having recourse to the philosophical implications of the Einsteinian relativity, it can be said that each culture, each particular "pattern of reasoning" is like a different system of coordinates which unavoidably leads to differing visions, to different worldviews; this is *dialectical realism.* It is consistent with the cosmic-evolutionary framework to conceive cultural differences, i.e. the diversities of "seeing as," as positions referring to varying systems of coordinates. Coordinates vary between cultures, between individuals, during a man's lifetime, in accordance with a human being's transcendence as well as his dialogic, symbolic communications and relations with his community. The reference to different *patterns of reasoning* or *systems of coordinates* defined synchronously and diachronically by the interaction of various physical, environmental and cultural factors, also indicates the importance of the intentionality of man's nature. Intentionality presupposes its own rationality, interlinked with rationality criteria at other levels. Individual intentionality and reflexivity as well as cultural conditioning are thus the three crucial elements which make it impossible to infer, as in the natural sciences, invariant regularities and laws from human action, behavior, and thought processes. Therefore, there can be no characterization of man's lifeworld in deterministic terms, indeterminism is the only way to seek to understand and interpret human and cultural phenomena.

Reality and truth are closely interdependent. The truth of the sciences depends on their one-world concept (that is, the one physical world) while the correspondence of knowledge to this world constitutes, in this perspective, truth. In the great religions, truth cannot but correspond to the teachings of God, or to the founder of a religion; in fact, truth is identity or quasi-identity with God. In the ontological/cosmic worldview, on the other hand, which admits the co-existing human, cultural worlds, truth, as well as reality, cannot but be read relativistically, because they are culturally conditioned although ontologically correlated. The relativistic reading of truth and reality should not be interpreted as if it would concern the reality of the external world and the truth of knowledge about it. Instead, it asserts that the human perspective is relativized through cultural conditioning and interaction with the environment: the real meaning of contextuality. What are conditions of truth or falsity, what are truth-conditions of linguistically expressed truths, if not underlying beliefs, values and customs, habits, which all in all, are the systems of cultural coordinates in which a man lives? Many post-analytic thinkers accepted the idea that truths professed by scientists of the past cannot be judged and evaluated from the standpoint of today's scientific theories, but in comparison to the best available information and knowledge of the age. In the same vein, it should be possible to say that in each culture, the truth-and-falsity of statements and beliefs has to be measured against the stock of information possessed in respect of the universe while taking into account the different cultures' own norms, expressions and assessments of human and social conditions.

The second major conclusion, therefore, is the imperative of a relativistic reading of realism. Reality, or *the common core of actual and potential human experience which is at the basis of all worldviews in worlds of culture, remains the only solid foundation for sharing judgements about some truths-and-falsities in diverse cultural beliefs, values, attitudes which reflect the varying systems of cognitive, ethical and aesthetic coordinates. The relativistic reading of realism thus corresponds to the different "patterns of reasoning," culturally conditioned, but ontologically correlated; it is a feature of co-existing cultural lifeworlds. This difference in perspective related to truth and truth-conditions therefore constitute a strong version of relativism.*

Conclusion Three

The inapplicability of the Western *rationality concept* in other culture-areas is closely interwoven with problems of reality perception and must be dealt with separately, as it relates to an essential aspect of human existence. Each "pattern of reasoning" defines its own rationality in a regulatory role; its products, thought, behavior, and action, are rational because consistent with the pattern and coherent with itself. No rationality independent of the "pattern of reasoning," of the genetically- and culturally- conditioned worldview exists. Rational criteria are internalized in mental structures as norms; therefore, it is more correct to speak instead of different types of rationality -- such as scientific, instrumental, or value rationality -- that is, of *meaningful* rationality. These criteria of rationality pretended to be universal are but hypostatized rational criteria of particular visions or "patterns of reasoning." However, the underlying fundamental realities of the lifeworld impose certain aspects of reasonableness, for example, the respect of human life, or the awareness of death, the inexorable passing away of human time. In fact, in our contemporary culture, there is no universally valid concept of rationality either; the rationality of everyday action is purposive-instrumental in a very simple sense, without even being thought of as a basic principle of existence. People simply act in accordance with what they want to achieve or what they are ordered to do. But, and here is the substantial difference with the philosophers' and sociologists' purposive-instrumental rationality, one always acts in the framework of the culturally transmitted goal definitions, values and ways of acting. *Zweckrationalität* serves *Wertrationalität*; action and interaction are instrumental in the realization of certain purposes that are themselves, with the exception of routine actions, guided by beliefs, values and cultural orientations.

If the concept of rationality as *meaningful rationality*, not a formal, empty, or uniquely methodological concept, is admitted, then all other civilizations are rational in terms of their cultural heritage, traditions, and environmental conditions. For rationality to be meaningful, it has to be contextual in the same way as the perception of reality and the disclosure of truth. Consequently, every culture area of the world possesses its own substantial rationality that may or may not be subject to such formal norms as coherence and consistency.

Thus, our third major conclusion concerns rationality: *the existence of different "patterns of reasoning" and the corresponding relativistic reading of reality leads us to affirm that each civilization has its own meaningful rationality. Thus, no dialogue between various co-existing civilizations is possible without the mutual acknowledgement of their respective, authentic rationality.*

Conclusion Four

In the sphere of ethical-moral considerations it again became evident that the great difference in "patterns of reasoning" in specific cultural worlds produced an important divergence of ethical systems and practical morality; except in the case of the late Neo-Confucian Japanese thinkers, in whose pronouncements quite a number of similarities with the modern, Western moral approaches arose. In general, however, it is also clear that between the Western culture and all other civilizations, there is a significant disjunction in the ethical-moral domain, though these differences are much less clear-cut than in the case of the ontological/cosmic worldview. The absolute division is between the ethics of world-renunciation or world-distanciation and the immanent normative system of the West; but the basic trends of thinking between, for example, the Confucian ethics and its successive schools of practical learning, and the modern ethical thinking in our culture are much more convergent. In a way, they can be seen as if they were shading into each other.

Consequently, the lesson of the inter-civilizational comparison in the ethical-moral field is that, *with the exception of other-worldly ethics on either side, there is a "common core" in all ethical systems and moral attitudes, a core which is the treasure of all humanity and which reflects fundamental givens in man's biological constitution, as well as in his adaptive endeavors to his environment.* The common core, of course, is based on man's characteristics, such as his transcendence, his integrative power of the mind, and his symbolic capabilities that allow the formulation of ethical, normative standards to proceed. These impregnate the lifeworld with moral coherence and a practical moral vision.

Emergent reality in experience is all the more decisive in that there is no absolute ranking of high-order principles (for example, utility or universalizability); moral judgement therefore has to be formulated with reference to the particular context. Morality is an autonomous, *sui generis* domain of value, though our deepest moral commitments are *a priori* in the species' perspective. However, the existence of this common core does not imply that there are no substantial differences in ethical-moral rules and behavior in various cultures. This difference in everyday moral attitudes, i.e., between a free lifestyle verging on libertinism, and a traditional and strictly regulated way of life based on strong family ties, represents the greatest ethical-moral divergence between Western culture and all other contemporary civilizations. Societies exposed to the pervasive influence of Western mores and media feel themselves to be on the road toward an unrecoverable loss of their identity sustained by proper ethical principles and moral behavior: they feel themselves to be condemned to total perdition.

In consequence, our fourth conclusion is that *ethical and moral trends in the Western-style modernization processes entail, in the eyes of people belonging to non-Western civilizations, an erosion of traditional family values, of social mores, and of communal solidarity which endanger existing social structures and provoke resistance in large segments of the population.*

Conclusion Five

Social structures in a given cultural area are among the most important factors exerting influence on approaches to other civilizations. The overwhelming difference between Western and non-Western societies is the degree of functional differentiation (some such differentiation can be found everywhere), and the acceptance of the newly differentiated roles which are copied from abroad and are not brought forth naturally from the social tissue. A gradually but increasingly differentiated social structure is thus superimposed on the indigenous, segmented, or stratified structure; even worse, institutions presupposing the existence of a highly differentiated society and the corresponding differentiated roles, are grafted onto a traditional society, one which witnesses a very slow mutation of social structures. The worst possible scenario is thus produced, as inherited symbolic systems and cultural predispositions shaped by the prevailing worldview are unchanged or undergoing an extremely slow, gradual modification.

Finally, new power structures are also imposed through the creation of Western-type popular mass movements in politics and the extensive bureaucratization of the newly established state mechanisms, which replace or entirely marginalize the former power establishments.

The ensuing crisis of society and the feeling of loss of collective identity are only natural, but it is totally ignored by the ruling elite in non-Western countries, as well as by the representatives of industrialized countries or officials from international organizations. The fifth conclusion of our inquiry, then, is that *in each non-Western culture or civilization: traditional social structures may be the best, at least for the time being, in order to absorb the shocks of modernization; the Western-type differentiation of society is not necessarily the best solution to sustain modernization efforts; and there may be a possibility to integrate, at least partially, differentiated social roles and functions with traditional social structures which reflect the specific worldviews and inherited cultural predisposition of the population.*

Conclusion Six

The great error of modern Western, universalizing ideologies, condemning nationalism, tribalism or other blood and socially specific ties, is now fully revealed. The sense of community based on the belief of common origins and substantiated principally by common cultural heritage, symbolic expressions, and ways of life is among the strongest and profoundest ontological relatedness among human beings. Ethnic and national, as well as tribal forces must be acknowledged today as much as yesterday, especially in the non-Western civilizations of the contemporary world. Our sixth conclusion therefore requires *the acceptance of ethnic and national particularities of people living in the orbit of non-Western culture areas and the facilitation of their efforts toward economic and social development in the proper ethnic or communal framework they wish to maintain, without imposing our ideas of universal brotherhood in the form of Westernization of their lifeworld.*

Conclusion Seven

As Winston Churchill once said, participatory democracy may not be the best possible political regime, but it is the only acceptable one available to us. However, ideologists of modernism contend that democracy is the panacea for all of humanity's problems, in whatever context and under all conditions. This, of course, is a great exaggeration. Even if it is recognized that democracy is, in principle, the only known political regime corresponding to modernity and our contemporaries' aspirations, it must be considered with nuances and qualifications as to its possible function and advantages in varying human and historical situations. It has to be acknowledged that there may be political regimes in other civilizations substantially different from participatory democracy, but which correspond more to the given context, environment, symbolic, and cultural backgrounds of the people. It would therefore be hazardous to rigidly state that participatory democracy would automatically bring with it the blessings of modernization in all contexts and under all conditions.

The seventh conclusion, in consequence, affirms that *contextuality with all its aspects must be taken into account when considering the suitability of any political regime in the non-Western world. The realization of popular participation in governing the collectivity's life and in regulating its own affairs should certainly be kept as the final objective. But the democratization process, which presupposes a modification in people's belief and value systems and overall worldviews, as well as considerable educational advances in the Western sense, should only be gradually introduced, once sacrifices, necessary for the attainment of economic and social modernization, are accepted and sustained.*

Conclusion Eight

Closely related to the problem of political regimes in non-Western civilizations are the perspective of decentralization and the presence of an ever-expanding bureaucracy. Henry Kissinger once wrote that decentralization is the highest form of democracy. Indeed, decentralization versus bureaucratization is one of the most essential dilemmas facing countries outside the Western cultural orbit; it seems today that bureaucracy undoubtedly won out in all such countries. Due to forces inherent in modernization, and contrary to what the theory of functional differentiation foresees, bureaucratization in impoverished countries became the most important job-creation device of the governments. They were under pressure to create public administration or public sector employment not only for the intelligentsia, the governing group's *clientèle* but to all people who were in need and represented for any reason (ethnic or tribal affiliation, trade union adherents, etc.), a pressure group with which the government had to contend with. This trend produced such results that in some of the poorest countries, the payroll of public administration and of public-sector employment reached eighty percent of the national budget. The sad story of the last thirty five years' developmental and modernization efforts is too well known and need not be stressed here; the lack of success of these efforts is due, in great part, to the interaction and complementarity of: the national bureaucracies; the bureaucracies of the countries giving bilateral assistance to governments in non-Western culture areas; and, bureaucracies of multilateral, international or regional organizations.

Therefore, our eight conclusion relates *to the absolute necessity to decentralize the public administration and the public sector in countries of non-Western heritage, if needed through the revival of traditional local authorities and systems of governance, in order to revitalize participatory efforts for the enhancement of the country and its social and economic conditions. Decentralization is an essential prerequisite of modernization.*

Conclusion Nine

The overwhelming importance assumed by the ontological/cosmic framework, the crucial character of the relativistic reading of realism, rationality, and truth, the highly determinant role played by social structures and existing power relations, including the web of ethnic, national, or tribal forces, as well as the integrating or dominating role of the state and political institutions — all these conclusions necessitate a thorough adaptation of transplanted concepts, ideas, and notions, borrowed from any other culture than the one in which they have to be adapted.

Expressed in one word, contextuality has to be taken into account whenever a solution of problems in non-Western culture-areas is to be found. The dual nature of economies in non-Western civilizations and the unavoidable character of unbalanced growth meaning non-proportionality in the sequential changes of various economic and social sectors, represent the main elements of contextuality. As a result, a ninth conclusion can be formulated as follows: *All economic and social development programs must only be undertaken on the basis of a conceptualization which encompasses the local, social-cum-economic-cum-cultural realities and which adapts any idea or notion borrowed from abroad; if such adaptation does not seem possible, then the given culture's innovative, creative capabilities must be left free in order to find the "contextually correct" solution.*

NOTES

Introduction

1. "The uniqueness of the world hinges on its diversity, the nonuniversality of man. There is one world only, there are many men; and just because there are many kinds of men, there is one world. For the unique world is the achievement of *some* men only; and had men and cultures not been diversified, the single world might never have emerged, for social forms would not have differed enough to hit on this special one; and all this is of the essence of the thing." (Gellner, [1984]: 186; italics in original).

2. An earlier version of this study appeared under the title "Language, Truth and Reason," in (Hollis and Lukes, eds., [1984]: 48-66).

3. Both descriptions are better than the word scientism, widely used in a way which does not correspond to the point of view on science's role in modernity presented in this study.

4. See (Shils, [1974]) on a well-balanced appraisal of science. As an amusing reminder of how some great men saw science in the nineteenth century, one may look to Victor Hugo, who said that "science searches for perpetual motion. It has found it; it is itself." Hugo, Victor, *William Shakespeare*, part one, book 3, sec. 4. Transl. by M.B. Anderson. [Chicago: A. McClury, 1911]: 105); in (Blumenberg [1983]: 231).

5. John Dewey succinctly expressed the danger of selective treatment of subjects related to human affairs: "The case of astronomy is typical of physical science in general as compared with knowledge of human affairs. The essence of the latter is that we cannot indulge in the selective abstractions that are the secret of the success of physical knowing. When we introduce a like simplification into social and moral subjects we eliminate distinctively the

human factors: - reduction to the physical ensues... *Artificial simplification or abstraction is a necessary precondition of securing ability to deal with affairs which are complex in which there are many more variables and where strict isolation destroys the special characteristics of the subject-matter.* This statement conveys the important distinction which exists between physical and social and moral objects. The distinction is one of methods of operation not of kinds of reality... Objection comes in, and comes in with warranted force, when the results of an abstract operation are given a standing which belongs only to the total situation from which they have been selected." (Dewey, [1980]: 216-217; italics in original).

6. I certainly think that the methods employed in the natural sciences are justified and useful on the condition that the boundaries of their applicability are clearly traced, and the evaluation of background information and the definiton of initial conditions are more rigorously undertaken in order to limit the pre-suppositions underlying the hypotheses tested through trial-and-error experiments. One should not forget the warning of Heisenberg that in the twentieth century "confidence in the scientific method and rational thinking replaced all other safeguards of the human mind." (Heisenberg, [1958]: 198).

7. Schroedinger notes: "One can say in a few words why our perceiving and thinking self is nowhere to be found within the world picture, because it itself is this world picture," (quoted by Gantt, W.H. "The Sciences of Behavior and the Internal Univers" in Eccles, ed., [1985]: 116).

Chapter One

1. This is a reference to the so-called *law of evolutionary potential* formulated as early as 1884 by the paleontologist E.D. Cope who called it the Law of the Unspecialized. According to Cope's phylogenetic law only relatively unspecialized animal species were likely to survive throughout different geological epochs and to develop essentially new and advanced structural types. (Cope, E.D. *Progressive and Regressive Evolution Among Vertebrates*, quoted in Rensch, [1972]: 21-22). See also Huxley, [1943] and Sahlin-Service, [1982].

2. There is a beautiful text from Schroedinger on the interrelation of the evolution of the individual and of the species: "We are evolving. In every day of our life there occurs in us something of that evolution of our species which is still in full career. In fact every individual life, indeed every day in the life of an individual, *has* to represent a part, however small, of this evolution, a

chisel-stroke, however insignificant, on the eternally infinished statue of our species. For the whole of its tremendous evolution consists of myriads of such insignificant chisel-strokes. And so at every step we have to change, overcome, destroy the form which we have had hitherto. The resistance of our primitive desires, which we encounter at every step, seems to me to have its physical correlate in the resistance of the existing form to the shaping chisel. For we are at once both chisel and block, overcoming and overcome -- there is a real, continuous self-contest." (Schroedinger, [1983]: 54; italics in original).

3. Hebb, D.O. "The Problem of Consciousness and Introspection," in (Adrian, E. et al. eds., *Brain Mechanics and Consciousness.* [Oxford, Oxford University Press]: 402-417, quoted in Geertz, [1973]: 71). See also Eccles, John, *Cerebral Activity and the Freedom of Will,* in (Eccles, [1985]: 162).

4. Geertz also compares the culture to computer-like programs: "... culture is best seen not as complexes of concrete behavior patterns -- customs, usages, traditions, habit clusters -- as has, by and large, been the case up to now, but as a set of control mechanisms -- plans, recipes, rules, instructions (what computer engineers call 'programs') -- for the governing of behavior." (Geertz, [1973]: 44). Schroedinger expresses this in a transparent way: "It is only the individual peculiarities in any one ontogenesis which become conscious... Becoming is conscious, being is unconscious." (Schroedinger, [1983]: 51).

Chapter Two

1. (G. Hoffmeister, *Goethe und der deutsche Idealismus.* [Leipzig, 1932]: 10).

2. The *Kena Upanishad* (II. 3) gives a marvelous description of the inscrutability of Brahman:

"It is conceived of him by whom It is not conceived of,
He by whom It is conceived of, knows It not.
It is not understood by those who [say they] understand It.
It is understood by those who [say they] understand It not."
(Radhakrishnan, S.S. and Moore, Ch. A. eds. [1957]: 42).

3. Ravindra, Ravi, "Death and the Meaning of Life -- A Hindu Response," in (Eccles, ed. [1985]: 333).

4. (Nakamura, Hajime, *A History of the Development of Japanese Thought*. [Tokyo, 1977]: 61).

5. Ray, Benjamin, "The Story of Kintu: Myth, Death, and Ontology in Buganda," in (Karp-Bird, eds. [1987]: 60-82).

6. "Only a being that could have conscious intentional states could have intentional states at all, and every unconscious intentional state is at least potentially conscious... there is a conceptual connection between consciousness and intentionality that has the consequence that a complete theory of intentionality requires an account of consciousness." (Searle, [1992]: 132).

7. Sperry, Roger, "Bridging Science and Values: A Unifying View of Mind and Brain," in (Eccles, [1985]: 296). See also Eccles, John, "A Critical Appraisal of Brain/Mind Theories," (ibid. 51-57).

8. (Sperry, op. cit. 299).

9. (Bohr, Niels, *Atomic Physics and Human Knowledge*. [New York: Wiley]: 92-93).

10. Both of these men advanced propositions I willingly accept, though in respect to the thinking of both, I have important reservations.   These reservations concern in Heidegger's philosophy the unnecessary nebulousness and complication of expression, leading in some cases, to confusion and in others to a quasi-intelligibility. Concerning Dewey's philosophy, I cannot agree with the views and propositions referring to a certain kind of physicalism, that is, I find in him an evident oscillation between physicalism and holistic, ontological views of nature. Further, in respect to Heidegger, I do not take into account in the present inquiry aspects of Heidegger's political engagement or activities. Although his attitude and public positions were not only objectionable, but definitely condemnable at the beginning of the Nazi era, I am mainly concerned here with the ontological conceptual elaborations of Heidegger's philosophy, and would consider it unacceptable to ignore his innovating and all-embracing reflections. However, the discrepancy between his thought and acts, in a certain period of his life, is evident.

11. In Heidegger's theory the ontological refers to the "world" of Being, as opposed to the world of entities and beings, -- a "world" without extension in space and time, an opposite to the everyday world and, therefore, ultimately elusive. In contrast, the ontic means this everyday world in which we all live, what common sense takes as *the* world, in which we all locate ourselves at a point in history and in a particular geographical position.

12. For George Herbert Mead, the objective world and our world of experience are separate, and for Mead this dividing line is bridged by meanings the mind gives to objects of the physical world in accordance with the characteristics these objects acquire for humans in the course of experience. External and internal experiences are distinguished by the fact that the latter are constituted by meanings given to physical objects by the mind. (Mead, [1934]: 131, note 35).

Chapter Three

1. However, one category of entities is mentioned by Heidegger for which intraworldliness is wholly determinating for its existence, namely what he calls "historical" entities, the culture and works of man. In the Heideggerian dialectical phenomenology this is the main difference between culture and nature: works of culture are born under quite different ontological conditions than the conditions which underlie their decay, even if they survive their creator; whereas nature is extant, or extra-worldly, and becomes an intraworldly entity inasmuch as it is apprehended by *Dasein* which makes it part of its world. (Heidegger, [1962]: 169).

2. Bergson's theory was, in a way, preceded by the Indian Buddhist *Vaibhasika* school, which already contended that "a person simply is a continuum (*samtana*) of events - where an event is a *dharma* and every *dharma* is a uniquely individuated momentary existent -- connected by (theoretically) specifiable causal connections and capable of individuation from other such continua by (largely) empirical criteria." (Griffiths, [1986]: 71).

3. Dilthey's conception of consciousness or mind shows some similarity with that of the Buddhist *Yogacara* thinkers, especially *Vasubandu*. They considered that only mind (or consciousness) exists because the entire cosmos is nothing but representation (*vijnapti*). Consciousness is conceived entirely as an intentional phenomenon, to be conscious is to be conscious of something. Mental events all have intentional objects and are, without exception, representations. Thus, representation and sense-perception are coincidental. Beside consciousness, Theravada Buddhism also maintains the existence of a "subliminal consciousness" which is permanently present in the individual even when empirically observable mental events (in fact, the mind) disappear from the continuum of his life. This theoretical subterfuge was invented to avoid the difficulties originating from the identification of consciousness with empiricaly perceptible mental events, and of mental events with intentionality — though in many psychic states there is no mental phenomenon involved. The concept of "subliminal consciousness" was also useful in explaining the process of death

followed by rebirth — *karma* — in which this consciousness assures continuity; in addition, it made it possible for *Buddhagosa* and his followers to avoid the abandonment of the most sacred doctrine, the attainment of a mindless state in which a complete cessation of consciousness occurs. See (Lévy, Sylvain, ed. *Vijnaptimatratasiddhi: Deux traités de Vasubandhu: Vimsatika et Trimsika.* Bibliothèque de l'Ecole de Hautes Etudes, Sciences historiques et philologiques, Fasc. 245. [Paris, Honoré Champion, 1925]: 12ff).

4. Campbell here refers to (Lorenz, Konrad, "Kant's Doctrine of the A Priori in the Light of Contemporary Biology," in Bertalanffy, L.V. and Rapoport, A., eds. *General Systems. Yearbook of the Society for General Systems Research* [1962]: 26-47; quoted in (Campbell, [1987a]: 84).

5. A good example of the interplay of genetic disposition, that is, the potentiality of acquiring cultural capabilities, and of culture as human initiative, is given by Dobzhansky and Boesiger: "Human genes are indispensable for learning human languages, but they do not determine which of the many existing languages a person will learn, let alone what the person will choose to say in that language." (Dobzhansky-Boesiger, [1983]: 64).

6. "Rites, designs, patterns are all charged with a significance which we may call mystique" — says Dewey — "but which is immediate and direct to those who have and celebrated them. Be the origin of the totem what it may, it is not a cold, intellectual sign of social organization; it is that organization made present and visible, a centre of emotionally charged behavior." (Dewey, [1958]: 82).

7. (Rousseau, Jean-Jacques, *A Preface to Narcisse: or the Lover of Himself.* Trans. by B.R. Barber and J. Forman, in *Political Theory*, Vol. 6. [1978]: pp. 550-551). Does this reservation of Rousseau not remind us of the situation prevailing in today's Western world? See also (Hiley, [1988]: 74), and (Gillespie, [1984}: 29).

8. Evans-Pritchard's narrative concerning the Nuer's sense of the temporal shows with great clarity how non-modern cultures differ from the modern extension of the time-concept -- as described by— Luhmann. In the world of the Nuer, the daily tasks are the points of reference for each day; otherwise time is constituted by reference to recurrent activities or seasonal movements, that is, large periods are conceived in a structural way. "The passage of time is the succession of activities and their relations to one another"; as they do not have an abstract system of time-reckoning, they do not coordinate activities in accordance with an "abstract passage of time". (Evans-Pritchard, [1962]: 103)

9. All quotes are taken from (Weil, Eric, "Science and Modern Culture," in Holton, ed. [1965]: 199-217).

Chapter Four

1. (Locke, John, *Essay*, IV, 19, 4 and 14, quoted in Wolterstorff [1983]: 182).

2. Montaigne already remarked that "each man calls barbarism whatever is not his own practice... for we have no other criterion of reason than the example and the idea of the opinions and customs of the country we live in." (Montaigne, Michel, *Les essais de M. Montaigne*. Ed. P. Villery. [Paris, Presses Universitaires de France, 1978]: 205; English translation from René Dubos' article in Holton, ed. [1965]: 260).

3. A good practical example of the interlinkage of social institutions and moral principles is given by Fortes in his analysis of kinship among the Tallensi: "To study Tale kinship institutions apart from the religious and moral ideas and values of the natives would be as one-sided as to leave out the facts of sex and procreation. On the other hand, our analysis has shown that it is equally impossible to understand Tale religious beliefs and moral norms, apart from the context of kinship. A very close functional interdependence exists between these two categories of social facts. The relevant connecting link, for our present problem, is the axiom implicit in all Tale kinship institutions, that kinship relations are essentially moral relations, binding in their own right. Every social system presupposes such basic moral axioms." (Fortes, M. *The Web of Kinship Among the Tallensi*. [London, 1949]: 344-346).

4. For a definition of welfarist consequentialism, I quote from Sen and Williams: "Utilitarianism, in its central forms, recommends a choice of actions on the basis of consequences, and an assessment of consequences in terms of welfare. Utilitarianism is thus a species of *welfarist consequentialism* -- that particular form of it which requires simply *adding up* individual welfares or utilities to assess the consequences, a property that is sometimes called *sum-ranking*." (Sen and Williams, eds. [1982]: 4).

5. Rawls seems to have retreated from his "original" position a decade later, when he says in his Dewey Lectures that "we are not trying to find a conception of justice suitable for all societies regardless of their particular social and historical circumstances." (Rawls, John, "Kantian Constructivism in Moral Theory: The Dewey Lectures 1980." *The Journal of Philosophy*. Vol. XXVII. No. 9. [1980], 518).

Chapter Five

1. In respect of the relation between religion and society in Africa, MacGaffey writes that: "Religion may be a set of representations of the social structure, but it is certainly also a part of social relations as they are lived... Religion is an intrinsic element of social reality, neither an influence on it nor a reflection of it. To treat it as an independent set of symbols, values, and beliefs impinging on people's real lives in some way is to trivialize it." (MacGaffey, Wyatt, "African Religions: Types and Generalizations," in Karp and Bird, eds. [1987]: 322-323).

2. "For the relation between universal and particular is now transformed into the relations between (universal) subjects - each ontologically self-contained and existing in a state of 'metaphysical' equality." (Seligman, [1990]: 124).

3. A Chinese description of social stratification, from almost one and a half thousand years ago, is worth quoting here: "As the days have their divisions in periods of ten each, so man have their ten ranks. It is by these that inferiors serve their superiors, and that superiors perform their duties to the spirits. Therefore the king has the ruler [of each feudal states] as his subject; the rulers have the great prefects as their subjects; the prefects have their officers; the officers have their subalterns; the subalterns have their multitude of petty officers; the petty officers have their assistants; the assistants have their employees; the employees have their menials. For the menials there are helpers, for the horses there are grooms, and for the cattle there are cowherds. And thus there is provision of all things." From the *Tso Chuan*, written probably during the third century, concerning the social situation in the year 535 B.C. (Fung-Yu-Lan, [1983]: Vol. 1, 9).

4. (Giesen, Bernard, "The Temporalization of Social Order: Some Theoretical Remarks on the Change in 'Change'" in Haferkampf and Smelser, eds. [1992]: 308).

5. (Parsons, Talcott, "Evolutionary Universals in Society." *American Sociological Review*, Vol. XXIX, [1964], No. 3.

Chapter Six

1. (Mayo, Patricia, *The Roots of Identity: Three National Movements in Contemporary European Politics.* [London, Allen Lane, 1974]: 156).

2. (Lewis, Bernard, "Europe, Islam et société civile," in *Le Débat*. No. 62. November-December [1990}: 131).

3. (Sir Isaiah Berlin's interview with Nathan Gardel on *Two Concepts of Nationalism*, in *The New York Review of Books*. Vol. XXXVIII. No. 19. [21 November 1991]: 19-23).

4. (Hauser, Henri. *Le principe des nationalités*: Ses origines historiques. [Paris, Alcan, 1916]: 7).

5. (Renan, Ernest, *Qu'est ce qu'une nation?* [Paris, Calmann-Lévy, 1882]: 27).

6. (Meinecke, Friedrich, *Weltburgertum und Nationalstaat*. 6. ed. [1922]: 15, quoted in Cobban, [1969]: 108).

7. (List, Friedrich, *The National System of Political Economy*. [London, 1885]: 174, quoted in Hobsbawm, [1990]: 29-30).

8. Quoted in (Shafer, [1972]: 460, note 11).

9. (*Al-Manar*, Vol. XX, [1917-1918]: 33, quoted in Hourani, [1983]: 301).

10. See also (Steppat, F. "Nationalismus und Islam bei Mustafa Kamil." *Die Welt der Islam*. Vol. IV. [1956], 241-341).

11. (Abd al-Rahman al-Bazzaz, "Islam and Arab Nationalism" [1952], in Haim, ed. [1962]: 173-174 and 181).

12. As Ricoeur stated a quarter of a century ago "meeting other traditional cultures is a serious test and, in a way, totally novel for European culture. The fact that universal civilization has for a long time originated from the European center has maintained the illusion that European culture was, in fact and by right, a universal culture. Its superiority over other civilizations seemed to provide the experimental verification of this postulate... It is not easy to remain yourself and to practice tolerance toward other civilizations." (Ricoeur [1965]: 277). He recognized as well that not every culture can "sustain and absorb the shock of modern civilization. There is the paradox: how to become modern and to return to sources; how to revive an old, dormant civilization and take part in universal civilization." (ibid. 278).

Chapter Seven

1. (Habermas, Jürgen, *Toward a Rational Society: Student Protest, Science, and Politics*. Trans. by J.J. Shapiro. [London, Heinemann, 1971]: 105).

2. It is an extremely important insight of Etzioni that the "mass element" in society is apparent when the state and organizations deal with the individual directly, rather than as members of collectivities or sub-collectivities; such an effort of deliberate mobilization of individuals, or direct access to them by the state or any other organization then supposes the destruction of the collective entities to which they belong, or an indirect control, through the elites, of these collectivities. (Etzioni, [1968]: 441 and 443).

3. This expression was used by Peter Sugar in *Southeastern Europe Under Ottoman Rule, 1354-1804*, quoted by (Ash, Timothy Garton, *The New York Review of Books*, Vol. XXXV, No. 14, [29 September 1988]: 56).

4. In opposition to the holistic view, the figure of *Abd al-Raziq* stands alone who affirmed that "Islam did not determine a specific regime, nor did it impose on the Muslims a particular system according to the requirements of which they must be governed; rather it has allowed us absolute freedom to organize the State in accordance with intellectual, social and economic conditions in which we are found, taking into consideration our social development and the requirements of the times." (Binder, [1988]: 131).

5. (Mawlana al-Mawdudi, *Political Theory in Islam*, quoted by Ahmad, Kh. ed., *The Islamic Law and Constitution*. 6. ed. [Lahore, Islamic Publications, 1977]: 159).

Chapter Eight

1. See among these outstanding critics: Professor Ragnar Frisch in his contribution to: *Induction, Growth and Trade. Essays in Honour of Sir Roy Harrod*. Ed. by W.A. Eltis, M.FG. Scott and J.N. Wolfe. [London, Clarendon Press]: 163; another Nobel Laureate, Professor Wassili Leontief, in his 1970 Presidential Address of the American Economic Association, published in the *American Economic Review*. Vol. 61. [1971]: 1-7; Sir Phelps Brown, President of the Royal Economic Society at the beginning of the seventies whose address was reproduced in the *Economic Journal*. [March 1972]: 3; Professors Fritz Machlup (Machlup, [1978]) and (Kenneth Boulding, *History of Political Economy*. Vol. 3. [1971]: 233).

2. (Albert, H. "Modellplatonismus: Der neoklassische Stil des oekonomischen Denkens," in Topitsch, E. *Logik der Sozialwissenschaften. [Köln*, 1965]: 406ff, quoted by Habermas, [1988]: 49).

3. Speaking of laws in economics, Samuelson wrote: "If these be Laws, Mother Nature is a criminal by nature." (Samuelson, [1966]: 1539).

4. (Mill, John Stuart, *Collected Works: Essays on Economy and Society*. Ed. J.M. Robson. [Toronto, University of Toronto Press, 1967]: 21).

5. "We need not worry about exhaustible resources because they will always have prices which ensure their proper use." (Hahn, H. *On the Notion of Equilibrium in Economics*. [1973]: 14). This assumption is evidently untrue, as our contemporary environmental problems prove. A good example of economic forecasters' failure, based on statistical assumptions, is given by Thurow: "During the 1950s, the Russian growth rate was much higher than ours. If the two growth rates were plotted, the Russian economy surpassed the American economy in 1984 -- a year with a certain literary significance." (Thurow, [1983]: 127).

6. I think that it would be a mistake to identify methodological individualism in economics with philosophical nominalism as Popper promoted it recently; the nature of the error implied by the first is evident and simple, while the problems of philosophical nominalism and universalism are much more complicated. It can be noted here that the so-called "institutional individualism" of Popper and his followers do not really improve questions related to methodological individualism.

7. I am using the two terms of growth and development in the following sense: growth denotes increases of economic magnitudes, differentiation of structures in the economic sector and formation or modification of economic institutions. Development concerns, in addition to the above, the integrated process of changing the mental and social patterns of a people; i.e., a *proportional* change between the various social sectors which is realized in their dynamic interaction.

8. One exception, just after the Second World War, was Oscar Lange who recognized the importance for economic science, "the science of administration of scarce resources," of the fact that people living in various historical civilizations experience various needs. Therefore, he wrote: "Statements enunciating the patterns of uniformity are referred to as *economic laws*. Economic laws are, like all other scientific laws, conditional statements. They assert that such and such happens regularly whenever such and such conditions are satisfied... No scientific law applies when its prerequisite conditions do not

occur. Since the administration of scarce resources is influenced by social organizations and institutions, such organizations and institutions are among the conditions implied in economic laws. Consequently, economic laws which hold under one type of social organization may fail to do so under another type. Most economic laws are thus limited historically to certain given types of social organization and institutions." (Lange [1945/1946]: 20).

9. I found, for example, that in several countries in Africa, national investment plans were prepared on the basis of the Incremental Capital/Output Ratio (ICOR), a practice which appeared to me completely ridiculous. What could this ratio mean in, let's say, the Senegalese context? See (Bauer, [1981]: 251-252) as well as Paul Streeten's "A Critique of the 'Capital/Output Ratio' and its Application to Development Planning" in (Streeten [1972]: 71-116).

10. "The Anglo-Saxon model is not wrong. Individualism and the desire for consumption and leisure are all parts of human nature. Business firms can be based on the historical, psychological and sociological fact that individuals are also social builders who want to belong to empires that expand. Man is a consumer, but he is also a tool-using animal. As a tool-using animal, work is not a disutility. It determines who one is. Belonging, esteem, power, building, winning, and conquering are all human goals just as important as maximizing consumption and leisure. Work is where one achieves such goals." (Thurow, [1992]: 118).

11. Further, he explains that the doctrine of self-determination, expressed in the 1960 *Declaration on the Granting of Independence to Colonial Countries and Peoples*, "changed the definition of both the collective 'self' and political 'determination'. The self was no longer either historical or ethnic 'nations' but artificial ex-colonial 'jurisdictions' which were multi-ethnic entities in most cases and ironically reminiscent of the old multinational empires of Europe. The 'nation' was now merely all who had been subjects of a particular colonial government and were of different race from their alien rulers. Indigenous successors to those rulers were by definition legitimate whether or not they expressed the popular will. Their rights as sovereigns and the human rights of their subjects to self-determination were one and the same... self-determination was de-colonization." (Jackson, [1990]: 77).

BIBLIOGRAPHY

'ABDUH, Muhammad. 1966. *The Theology of Unity*, trans. from the Arabic by I. Musa'ad and K. Cragg. London: George Allen & Unwin.

Alexander, Jeffrey C. and Seidman, Steven ed. 1990. *Culture and Society: Contemporary Debates*. Cambridge: Cambridge University Press.

Alland, Alexandre Jr. 1972. *The Human Imperative*. New York: Columbia University Press.

---. 1973. *Evolution and Human Behavior: An Introduction to Darwinian Anthropology*. 2. rev. and exp. ed. New York: Anchor Press/Doubleday.

Allinson, Robert E. ed. 1989. *Understanding the Chinese Mind: The Philosophical Roots*. Oxford: Oxford University Press.

Almond, Gabriel A. and Verba, Sidney. 1989. *The Civic Culture: Political Attitudes and Democracy in Five Nations*. Newbury Park, Cal.: SAGE Publications.

Apter, David A. 1987. *Rethinking Development: Modernization, Dependency, and Postmodern Politics*. Newbury Park, Cal.: SAGE Publications.

Arab Nationalism: An Anthology. 1962. Selected and ed., with an Introd. by S.G. Haim. Berkeley, Cal.: University of California Press.

Archer, Margaret S. 1988. *Culture and Agency: The Place of Culture in Social Theory*. Cambridge: Cambridge University Press.

Archibald, G.C. 1959a. "The State of Economic Science." *British Journal of the Philosophy of Science*, Vol. 10. pp. 64-65.

---. 1959b. "Welfare Economics, Ethics, and Essentialism." *Economica*. Vol. 26. pp. 316-327.

Arendt, Hannah. 1951. *The Origins of Totalitarianism*. New York: Harcourt, Brace, Jovanovich.

---. 1959. *The Human Condition: A Study of the Central Dilemma Facing Modern Man*. Garden City, N.Y.: Anchor Books.

Arens, W. and Karp, I. eds. 1989. *Creativity of Power: Cosmology and Action in African Societies*. Washington: Smithsonian Institution Press.

Arnason, Johann P. 1990. "Nationalism, Globalization and Modernity," in Featherstone, Mike. ed. pp. 207-236.

Aron, Raymond. 1962. *Dix-huit lecons sur la société industrielle*. Paris: Gallimard.

---. 1965. *Essai sur les libertés*. Paris: Calmann-Lévy.

---. 1984. *La lutte des classes: Nouvelles lecons sur les sociétés industrielles*. Paris: Gallimard.

Arrington, Robert C. 1989. *Rationalism, Realism, and Relativism: Perspectives in Contemporary Moral Epistemology*. Ithaca, N.Y.: Cornell University Press.

Arrow, Kenneth J. 1951. *Social Choice and Individual Values*. New York: John Wiley & Sons.

---. 1967. "Values and Collective Decision-Making," in Hahn, Frank and Hollis, Martin eds. 1979. pp. 110-126.

BAKHTIN, M.M. 1981. *The Dialogic Imagination: Four Essays*. Ed. by M. Holquist. Trans. by C. Emerson and M. Holquist. Austin: University of Texas Press.

Barber, Benjamin. 1984. *Strong Democracy: Participatory Politics For a New Age*. Berkeley, Cal.: University of California Press.

Barber, Bernard and Inkeles, Alex. eds. 1971. *Stability and Social Change*. Boston: Little Brown.

Barnett, H.G. 1953. *Innovation: The Basis of Cultural Change*. New York: McGraw-Hill.

Bary, Wm. Theodore de (with the Conference on Seventeenth-Century Chinese Thought), 1975. *The Unfolding of Neo-Confucianism*. New York: Columbia University Press.

---. 1981. *Neo-Confucian Orthodoxy and the Learning of the Mind-and-Heart*. New York: Columbia University Press.

--- and Bloom, Irene. eds. 1979. *Principle and Practicality: Essays in Neo-Confucianism and Practical Learning*. New York: Columbia University Press.

Bateson, Gregory. 1980. *Mind and Nature: A Necessary Unity*. New York: Bantam Books.

Bauer, Peter T. 1971. *Dissent on Development: Studies and Debates in Development Economics*. London: Weidenfeld & Nicholson.

Bauman, Zygmunt. 1976. *Towards a Critical Sociology: An Essay on Commonsense and Emancipation*. London: Routledge & Kegan Paul.

---. 1978. *Hermeneutics and Social Science*. New York: Columbia University Press.

---. 1992. *Intimations of Postmodernity*. London: Routledge.

Beattie, J.H.M. 1984. "On Understanding Ritual," in Wilson, Bryan R. ed. pp. 240-268.

Beck, Ulrich. 1992a. *Risk Society: Towards a New Modernity*. Trans. by M. Ritter. Newbury Park, Cal.: SAGE Publications.

---. 1992b. "From Industrial Society to Risk Society: Questions of Survival, Social Structure and Ecological Enlightenment," in Featherstone, Mike. ed. pp. 97-123.

Beetham, David. 1987. *Bureaucracy*. Minneapolis: University of Minnesota Press.

Bell, Cathrine. 1992. *Ritual Theory, Ritual Practice*. Oxford: Oxford University Press.

Bell, Daniel. 1960. *The End of Ideology: On the Exhaustion of Political Ideas in the Fifties*. Glencoe, Ill.: Free Press.

---. 1965. "The Disjunction of Culture and Social Structure," in Holton, Gerald. ed. pp. 236-250.

---. 1978. *The Cultural Contradictions of Capitalism*. New York: Basic Books.

Bellah, Robert N. 1970. *Beyond Belief: Essays on Religion in a Post-Traditional World*. New York: Harper & Row.

---. 1971. "Continuity and Change in Japanese Society," in Barber Bernard and Inkeles, Alex. eds. pp. 377-404.

---. 1979. "New Religious Consciousness and the Crisis in Modernity," in Rabinow, Paul and Sullivan, William M. eds. pp. 341-363.

---. 1985. *Tokugawa Religion: The Cultural Roots of Modern Japan*. New York: The Free Press.

Bendix, Reinhard. 1977. *Nation-Building and Citizenship; Studies of Our Changing Social Order*. New enlarged ed. Berkeley, Cal.: University of California Press.

Benedict, Ruth. 1959. *Patterns of Culture*. New York: Mentor Books.

Benn, S.O. and Mortimore, G.W. eds. 1976. *Rationality and the Social Sciences: Contributions to the Philosophy and Methodology of the Social Sciences*. London: Routledge & Kegan Paul.

Berger, P. L. and Luckmann, Th. 1966. *The Social Construction of Reality: A Treatise on the Sociology of Knowledge*. New York: Doubleday.

278

Bergson, Henri. 1946. *The Creative Mind: An Introduction to Metaphysics*.
New York: The Wisdom Library.

---. 1977. *The Two Sources of Morality and Religion*. Trans. by R. A. Audra
and C. Brereton with the assistance of W.H. Carter. Notre Dame, Ind.:
Notre Dame University Press.

---. 1991. *Matter and Memory*. Trans. by N.M. Paul and W.S. Palmer.
New York: Zone Books.

Binder, Leonard. 1964. *The Ideological Revolution in the Middle East*.
New York: John Wiley & Sons.

---. 1988. *Islamic Liberalism: A Critique of Development Ideologies*. Chicago:
University of Chicago Press.

Blau, Peter M. and Meyer, Marshall W. eds. 1971. *Bureacracy in Modern
Society*. 2nd ed. New York: Random House.

Blaug, Mark. 1980. *The Methodology of Economics, or How Economists
Explain*. Cambridge: Cambridge University Press.

Blumenberg, Hans. 1983. *The Legitimacy of the Modern Age*. Trans. by R.M.
Wallace. Cambridge, Mass.: MIT Press.

---. 1985. *Work on Myth*. Trans. by R. M. Wallace. Cambridge, Mass.: MIT
Press.

Boeke, J.H. 1953. *Economics and Economic Policies in Dual Societies*. Glencoe,
Ill.: Free Press.

Bohm, David. 1957. *Causality and Chances in Modern Physics*. Foreword by
Louis de Broglie. Philadelphia: University of Pennsylvania Press.

Bohr, Niels. 1958. *Atomic Physics and Human Knowledge*. New York: Wiley.

Boland, Lawrence A. 1982. *The Foundations of Economic Method*. London:
George Allen & Unwin.

Boullata, Issa J. 1990. *Trends and Issues in Contemporary Arab Thought*.
Albany, N.Y.: State University of New York Press.

Borkenau, Franz. 1981. *End and Beginning: On the Generations of Cultures and
the Origins of the West*. Ed. with an introduction by R. Lowenthal.
New York: Columbia University Press.

Bourdieu, Pierre. 1977. *Outline of a Theory of Practice*. Cambridge: Cambridge
University Press.

Bowles, Samuel and Gintis, Herbert. 1987. *Democracy and Capitalism.
Property, Community, and the Contradictions of Modern Social Thought*.
With a New Introduction by the Authors: The Politics of Capitalism and the
Economics of Democracy. New York: Basic Books.

Boyd, Robert and Richerson, Peter J. 1985. *Culture and the Evolutionary
Process*. Chicago: University of Chicago Press.

Brown, Harold I. 1990. *Rationality*. London: Routledge.

Buchanan, James. 1975. *The Limits of Liberty: Between Anarchy and Leviathan*.
Chicago: University Press of Chicago.

CALDWELL, Bruce J. 1982. *Beyond Positivism: Economic Methodology in the Twentieth Century*. London: Allen & Unwin.

Campbell, Donald T. 1987a. "Rationality and Utility from the Standpoint of Evolutionary Biology," in Hogarth, Robin M. and Reder, Melvin W. pp. 171-180.

---. 1987b. "Evolutionary Epistemology," in Radnitzky, Gerard and Bartley, W.W. III. eds. pp. 47-89.

---. 1987c. "Blind Variation and Selective Retention in Creative Thought as in Other Knowledge Processes," in Radnitzky, Gerard and Bartley, W.W. III. eds. pp. 91-114.

Cassirer, Ernst. 1944. *An Essay on Man*. New Haven, Conn.: Yale University Press.

---. 1946. *The Myth of the State*. New Haven, Conn.: Yale University Press.

---. 1955. *The Philosophy of Symbolic Forms*. New Haven, Conn.: Yale University Press. Trans. by R. Manheim. Preface and Introd. by Ch. W. Hendel.

Vol. 1. *Language*.

Vol. 2. *Mythical Thought*.

Vol. 3. *The Phenomenology of Knowledge*.

Chan, Wing-tsit. 1973. *A Source Book in Chinese Philosophy*. Trans. and compiled by Wing-tsit Chan. Princeton, N.J.: Princeton University Press.

Chung-Ying Cheng. 1975. "Reason, Substance, and Human Desires in Seventeenth-Century Confucianism," in de Bary, Wm. Theodore de. ed. pp. 469-509.

Chung-Ying Cheng 1979. "Practical Learning in Yen Yuan, Chu Hsi, and Wang Yang-ming," in de Bary, Wm. Theodore de and Bloom, Irene. eds. 1979. pp. 37-67.

Chung-Ying Cheng. 1989. "Chinese Metaphysics as Non-metaphysics: Confucian and Daoist Insights Into the Nature of Reality," in Allinson, Robert E. ed. pp. 167-208.

Churchland, Paul. 1988. *Matter and Consciousness: A Contemporary Introduction to the Philosophy of Mind*. Rev. ed. Cambridge, Mass.: MIT Press.

Connor, W. 1972. "Nation-building or Nation-destroying?" *World Politics*. Vol. 24. pp. 319-355.

---. 1973. "The Politics of Ethnonationalism." *Journal of International Affairs*. Vol. 27. pp. 1-21.

---. 1978. "A Nation is a Nation, is a State, is an Ethnic Group, is a..." *Ethnic and Racial Studies*. Vol. 1. pp. 377-400.

Coulson, Noel J. 1969. *Conflicts and Tensions in Islamic Jurisprudence*. Chicago: University of Chicago Press.

Crozier, Michel. 1963. *Le phénomène bureaucratique. Essai sur les tendances bureaucratiques des systèmes d'organisation modernes et sur leurs relations en France avec le système social et culturel*. Paris: Seuil.

Cua, Antonio S. 1989. "The Concept of Li in Confucian Moral Theory," in Allinson, Robert E. ed. pp. 209-235.

Cusa, Nicholas de. 1962. *Unity and Reform: Selected Writings*. Ed. by J. P. Dolan. Notre Dame, Ind.: University of Notre Dame Press.

DAHL, Robert A. 1982. *Dilemmas of Pluralist Democracy: Autonomy Versus Control*. New Haven, Conn.: Yale University Press.

---. 1989. *Democracy and Its Critics*. New Haven, Conn.: Yale University Press.

Dallmayr, Fred R. 1984. *Polis and Praxis: Exercises in Contemporary Political Theory*. Cambridge, Mass.: MIT Press.

Davidson, Donald 1980. *Essays on Actions and Events*. Oxford: Clarendon Press.

---. 1984. *Inquiries Into Truth and Interpretation*. Oxford: Clarendon Press.

---. 1989. "The Myth of the Subjective," in Krausz, Michael ed. pp. 159-172.

Dennett, Daniel C. 1981. *Brainstorms: Philosophical Essays on Mind and Psychology*. Cambridge, Mass.: MIT Press.

Dewey, John. 1922. *Human Nature and Conduct: An Introduction to Social Psychology*. New York: Random House.

---. 1939. *Freedom and Culture*. New York: G.P. Putnam's Sons.

---. 1948. *Reconstruction in Philosophy*. Boston: Beacon Press.

---. 1958. *Experience and Nature*. New York: Dover.

---. 1965. *The Influence of Darwin on Philosophy and Other Essays in Contemporary Thought*. Bloomington, Ind.: Indiana University Press.

---. 1969. *Outlines of a Critical Theory of Ethics*. New York: Greenwood Press.

---. 1980. *The Quest for Certainty: A Study of the Relation of Knowledge and Action*. Gifford Lectures 1929. New York: G.P. Putnam's Sons.

The Dhammapada. 1987. Trans. with general introd. by E. Easwaran. With chapter introductions by S. Ruppenthal. London: Arkana.

Diesing, P. 1971. *Patterns of Discovery in the Social Sciences*. Chicago: Aldine Atherton.

Dilthey, Wilhelm. 1961. *Pattern and Meaning in History: Thoughts on History and Society*. Ed. and Introd. by H.P. Rickmann. New York: Harper & Row.

---. 1989. *Selected Works*. Vol. I. *Introduction to the Human Sciences*. Ed. with and Introd, by R.A. Makkreel and F. Rodi. Princeton, N.J.: Princeton University Press.

Dilworth, David A. 1979. "*Jitsugaku* as an Ontological Conception: Continuities and Discontinuities in Early and Mid-Tokugawa Thought," in de Bary, Wm. Theodore and Bloom, Irene eds. pp. 471-514.

Djait, H. (1974), *La personnalité et le devenir arabo-islamique*. Paris: Le Seuil.

Dobzhansky, Theodosius. 1962. *Mankind Evolving: The Evolution of the Human Species*. New Haven, Conn.: Yale University Press.

--- and Boesiger, Ernst. 1983. *Human Culture: A Moment in Evolution*. Ed. and completed by B. Wallace. Illustrations by H. Erni. New York: Columbia University Press.

Donohue, John J. and Esposito, John L. eds. 1982. *Islam in Transition: Muslim Prespectives*. New York: Oxford University Press.

Dumont, Louis. 1980. *Homo Hierarchicus: The Caste System and Its Implications*. Complete rev. English ed. Chicago: University of Chicago Press.

---. 1986. *Essays on Individualism: Modern Ideology in Anthropological Perspective*. Chicago: University of Chicago Press.

Dunn, John. 1979. *Western Political Theory in the Face of the Future*. Cambridge: Cambridge University Press.

Dupré, Louis. 1993. *Passage to Modernity: An Essay in the Hermeneutics of Nature and Culture*. New Haven, Conn.: Yale University Press.

ECCLES, Sir John. ed. 1985. *Mind and Brain: The Many-Faceted Problems*. New York: Paragon House.

Eckstein, Harry. 1979. "On the 'Science' of the State." *Daedalus*. Vol. 108. No. 4. Fall 1979. pp. 1-20.

---. 1988. "A Culturalist Theory of Political Change." *American Political Science Review*. Vol. 82. pp. 789-804.

Einstein, Albert. 1961. *Relativity: The Special and General Theory*. Trans. by R.W. Lawson. New York: Bonanza Books.

---. 1985. *Ideas and Opinions*. Based on *Mein Weltbild*. Ed. by C. Seelig, and other sources. New trans. and revisions by S. Bargmann. New York: Crown Publishers.

Eisenstadt, Shmuel N. 1977. "Sociological Theory and an Analysis of the Dynamics of Civilizations and of Revolutions." *Daedalus*. Vol. 106. No. 4. Fall 1977. pp. 59-78.

---, ed. 1987. *Patterns of Modernity*. Vol. 2. *Beyond the West*. London: Frances Pinter.

Eliade, Mircea. 1971. *The Myth of the Eternal Return or, Cosmos and History*. Trans. from the French by W.R. Trask. Princeton, N.J.: University Press of Princeton.

---. 1975. *Myth and Reality*. Trans. from the French by W.R. Trask. New York: Harper & Row.

Elias, Norbert. 1978. *What Is Sociology?* Trans. by S. Mennell and G. Morrissey. With a Foreword by R. Bendix. New York: Columbia University Press.

Ellul, Jacques. 1964. *The Technological Society*. With and introd. by R. K. Merton. New York: Vintage Books.

Esposito, John. 1984. *Islam and Politics*. 3. ed. Syracuse, N.Y.: University of Syracuse Press.

Etzioni, Amitai. 1968. *The Active Society: A Theory of Societal and Political Processes*. New York: Free Press.

Evans-Pritchard, E.E. 1962. *Social Anthropology and Other Essays*. New York: Free Press.

FAIRBANK, John K. 1987. *The Great Chinese Revolution: 1800-1985*. New York: Harper & Row.

Featherstone, Mike. ed. 1990. *Global Culture: Nationalism, Globalization and Modernity*. /Theory, Culture and Society Special Issue./ Newbury Park, Cal.: SAGE Publications.

---. ed. 1992. *Cultural Theory and Cultural Change*. Newbury Park, Cal.: SAGE Publications.

Feyerabend, Paul. 1978. *Against Method: Outline of an Anarchistic Theory of Knowledge*. London: Verso.

---. 1981. *Philosophical Papers*. Cambridge: Cambridge University Press.
Vol. 1. *Realism, Rationalism & Scientific Method*.
Vol. 2. *Problems of Empiricism*.

Fine, Arthur. 1984. "The Natural Ontological Attitude," in Leplin, Jarrett. ed. pp. 83-107.

---. 1986. *The Shaky Game: Einstein, Realism and the Quantum Theory*. Chicago: University Press of Chicago.

---. 1990. "Causes of Variability: Disentangling Nature and Nurture," in French, P.A.; Uehling, Th.E. and Wettstein, H.K. eds. pp. 94-113.

Forde, Daryll 1991. *African Worlds: Studies in the Cosmological Ideas and Social Values of African Peoples*. Oxford: Oxford University Press.

Foucault, Michel. 1973. *The Order of Things: An Archaeology of the Human Sciences*. New York: Vintage Books.

French, P.A.; Uehling, Th. E.; and Wettstein, H. K. eds. 1980. *Studies in Ethical Theory*. /Midwest Studies in Philosophy. III/ Minneapolis: University of Minnesota Press.

---. eds. 1988. *Realism and Anti-Realism*. /Midwest Studies in Philosophy. XII/ Minneapolis: University of Minnesota Press.

---. eds. 1990. *The Philosophy of the Human Sciences*. /Midwest Studies in Philosophy. XV/ Notre Dame, Ind.: University of Notre Dame Press.

Freud, Sigismund. 1961. *Civilization and Its Discontents*. The Standard Edition. Trans. by J. Strachey. New York: W.W. Norton.

Friedman, Milton. 1953. *Essays in Positive Economics*. Chicago: University Press of Chicago.

Fung Yu-lan. 1983. *A History of Chinese Philosophy*. Princeton: N.J.: Princeton University Press.

    Vol. 1. *The Period of the Philosophers (from the beginnings to circa 100 B.C.)*.

    Vol. 2. *The Period of Classical Learning (from the Second Century B.C. to the Twentieth Century A.D.)*.

Furtado, Celso 1964. *Development and Underdevelopment*. Trans. by R.W. de Aguiar and E.C. Drysdale. Berkeley, Cal.: University of California Press.

---. 1976. *Le mythe du développement économique*. Paris: Anthropos.

GADAMER, Hans-Georg. 1976. *Philosopghical Hermeneutics*. Trans. and ed. by D.A. Linge. Berkeley, Cal.: University of California Press.

---. 1979. "The Problem of Historical Consciousness," in Rabinow, Paul and Sullivan, William M. eds. pp. 103-160.

---. 1985. *Truth and Method*. New York: Crossroad.

---. 1986. *Reason in the Age of Science*. Cambridge, Mass.: MIT Press.

Gardet, Louis. 1961. *La cité musulmane: Vie sociale et politique*.

    2. ed. augmentée. Paris: J. Vrin.

Geertz, Clifford. 1971. "After the Revolution: The Fate of Nationalism in the New States," in Barber, Bernard and Inkeles, Alex. eds. pp. 357-376.

Geertz, Clifford. 1973. *The Interpretation of Cultures: Selected Essays*.

    New York: Basic Books.

---. 1983. *Local Knowledge: Further Essays in Interpretive Anthropology*.

    New York: Basic Books.

Gellner, Ernest. 1983. *Nations and Nationalism*. Ithaca, N.Y.: Cornell University Press.

---. 1984. "Relativism and Universals," in Hollis, Martin and Lukes, Steven. eds. pp. 181-200.

---. 1985. *Relativism and the Social Sciences*. Cambridge: Cambridge University Press.

---. 1992. *Reason and Culture: The Historic Role of Rationality and Rationalism*. Oxford: Blackwell.

284

Gert, Bernard. 1988. *Morality: A New Justification of the Moral Rules*.
New York: Oxford University Press.

Giddens, Anthony. 1976. *New Rules of Sociological Method: A Positive Critique
of Interpretative Sociologies*. London: Hutchinson.

---. 1977. *Studies in Social and Political Theory*. New York: Basic Books.

---. *A Contemporary Critique of Historical Materalism*. Berkeley, Cal.:
University of California Press.
Vol. 1. 1981. *Power, Property and the State*.
Vol. 2. 1985. *The Nation-State and Violence*.

---. 1984. *The Constitution of Society: Outline of the Theory of Structuration*.
Berkeley, Cal.: University of California Press.

---. 1990. *The Consequences of Modernity*. Stanford, Cal., Stanford University
Press.

---. 1991. *Modernity and Self-Identity: Self and Society in the Late Modern Age*.
Stanford, Cal.: Stanford University Press.

Gillespie, Michael A. 1984. *Hegel, Heidegger and the Ground of History*.
Chicago: University Press of Chicago.

Girard, René. 1977. *Violence and the Sacred*. Trans. by P. Gregory. Baltimore:
John Hopkins University Press.

Goodman, Nelson. 1985. *Ways of Worldmaking*. Indianapolis, Ohio: Hackett.

Gouldner, Alwin W. 1970. *The Coming Crisis of Western Sociology*. New York:
Basic Books.

---. 1976. *The Dialectic of Ideology and Technology: The Origins, Grammar,
and Future of Ideology*. New York: Oxford University Press.

Griffiths, Paul J. 1986. *On Being Mindless: Buddhist Meditation and the
Mind-Body Problem*. La Salle, Ill.: Open Court.

HABERMAS, Jürgen. 1971. *Knowledge and Human Interests*. Trans. by
J.J. Shapiro. Boston, Mass.: Beacon Press.

---. 1973. *Theory and Practice*. Trans. by J. Viertel. Boston, Mass.: Beacon
Press.

---. 1975. *Legitimation Crisis*. Trans. by Th. McCarthy. Boston, Mass.: Beacon
Press.

---. *The Theory of Communicative Action*. Trans. by Th. McCarthy. Boston,
Mass.: Beacon Press.
Vol. 1. 1984. *Reason and Rationalization of Society*.
Vol. 2. 1989. *Lifeworld and System: A Critique of Functionalist Reason*.

---. 1987. *The Philosophical Discourse of Modernity: Twelve Lectures*. Trans.
by F. Lawrence. Cambridge, Mass.: MIT Press.

285

---. 1988. *On the Logic of the Social Sciences*. Trans. by S.W. Nicholsen and J.A. Stark. Cambridge, Mass.: MIT Press.

---. 1990. *Moral Consciousness and Communicative Action*. Trans. by Ch. Lenhardt and S.W. Nicholsen. Cambridge, Mass.: MIT Press.

Hacking, Ian. 1975. *Why Does Language Matter to Philosophy?* Cambridge: Cambridge University Press.

---. ed. 1981. *Scientific Revolutions*. Oxford: Oxford University Press.

---. 1983. *Representing and Intervening: Introductory Topics in the Philosophy of Natural Science*. Cambridge: Cambridge University Press.

---. 1985. "Styles of Scientific Reasoning," in Rajchman, John and West, Cornel. eds. pp. 145-165.

Haferkampf, Hans and Smelser, Neil J. eds. 1992. *Social Change and Modernity*. Berkeley, Cal.: University of California Press.

Hahn, Frank and Hollis, Martin. eds. 1979. *Philosophy and Economic Theory*. Oxford: Oxford University Press.

Hampshire, Stuart. 1977. *Two Theories of Morality*. Oxford: Oxford University Press.

---. 1982. "Morality and Convention," in Sen, Amartya K. and Williams, Bernard. eds. pp. 145-157.

---. 1983. *Thought and Action*. Notre Dame, Ind.: University of Notre Dame Press.

Hansen, Chad. 1989. "Language in the Heart-mind," in Allinson Robert E. ed. pp. 75-124.

Hanson, Norwood R. 1958. *Patterns of Discovery: An Inquiry Into the Conceptual Foundations of Science*. Cambridge: Cambridge University Press.

Hardin, Russell 1988. *Morality Within the Limits of Reason*. Chicago: University Press of Chicago.

Hare, R. M. 1982, "Ethical Theory and Utilitarianism," in Sen, Amartya K. and Williams, Bernard. eds. pp. 23-38.

---. 1989. *Essays in Ethical Theory*. Oxford: Clarendon Press.

Harman, Gilbert. 1977. *The Nature of Morality; An Introduction to Ethics*. Oxford: Oxford University Press.

Harré, Rom. 1989. "The 'Self' As a Theoretical Concept," in Krausz, Michael. ed. pp. 387-417.

Harsányi, John C. 1982. "Morality and the Theory of Rational Behavior," in Sen, Amartya K. and Williams, Bernard. eds. pp. 39-62.

Hayek, Friedrich, A. v. 1941. "The Counter-Revolution of Science." *Economica*. Vol. 8. Part I. February. pp. 9-36; Part II. May. pp. 119-150; Part III. August. pp. 281-320.

286

---. 1942-44. "Scientism and the Study of Society." *Economica*. Vol. 9. Part I.
No. 9, August 1942. pp. 267-291; Part II. No. 10, February 1943.
pp. 34-63; Part III. No. 11, February 1944. pp. 27-39.

---. 1944. *The Road to Serfdom*. Chicago: University Press of Chicago.

---. 1960. *The Constitution of Liberty*. Chicago: University Press of Chicago.

---. 1988. *The Fatal Conceit: The Errors of Socialism*. /The Collected Works
of F.A. Hayek. Vol. I. Ed. by W.W. Barthley III./ Chicago: University
Press of Chicago.

Heesterman, J.C. 1985. *The Inner Conflict of Tradition: Essays in Indian Ritual,
Kingship, and Society*. Chicago: University of Chicago Press.

Hegel, F.W. 1967. *The Phenomenology of Mind*. Trans. with an Introd. and
Notes by J.B. Baillie. Introd. to the Torchbook ed. by G. Lichtheim.
New York: Harper & Row.

---. 1977. *Phenomenology of Spirit*. Trans. by A. Miller. Oxford: Oxford
University Press.

Heidegger, Martin. 1959. *An Introduction to Metaphysics*. Trans. by
R. Manheim. New Haven, Conn.: Yale University Press.

---. 1962. *Being and Time*. Trans. by J. Macquarrie and E. Robinson.
New York: Harper & Row.

---. 1970. *Hegel's Concept of Experience*. New York: Harper & Row.

---. 1982. *The Basic Problems of Phenomenology*. Trans. with an Introd., and
Lexicon by A. Hofstaedter. Bloomington, Ind.: Indiana University Press.

---. 1985a. *History of the Concept of Time: Prolegomena*. Trans. by Th. Kisiel.
Bloomington, Ind., Indiana University Press.

---. 1985b. *Schelling's Treatise on the Essence of Human Freedom*. Transl. by
J. Stambaugh. Athens, Ohio: Ohio University Press.

Heisenberg, Werner. 1958. *Physics and Philosophy: The Revolution in Modern
Science*. Introd. by F.S.C. Northrop. New York: Harper & Row.

---. 1979. *Philosophical Problems of Quantum Physics*. Woodbridge, Conn.,
Ox Bow Press.

Held, David. 1989. *Political Theory and the Modern State: Essays on State,
Power, and Democracy*. Stanford, Cal.: Stanford University Press.

Herder, Johann G. v. 1968. *Reflections on the Philosophy of the History of
Mankind*. Abridg. and with an introd. by F.E. Manuel. Chicago: University
of Chicago Press.

Herrick, Bruce and Kindelberger, Charles P. 1983. *Economic Development*.
4. ed. New York: McGraw-Hill.

Herskovits, Melville J. 1948. *Man and His Works: The Science of Cultural
Anthropology*. New York: Alfred A. Knopf.

---. 1952. *Economic Anthropology: A Study in Comparative Economics*.
New York: Alfred A. Knopf.

Hicks, John R. 1965. *Capital and Growth*. New York: Oxford University Press.

---. 1974. *The Crisis in Keynesian Economics*. New York: Basic Books.

---. 1979. *Causality in Economics*. New York: Basic Books.

Higgins, Benjamin J. 1956. "The 'Dualistic Theory' of Underdeveloped Areas." *Economic Development and Cultural Change*. Vol. 4. January 1956. pp. 99-115.

---. 1968. *Economic Development: Principles, Problems and Policies*. New York: W.W. Norton.

Hiley, David R. 1988, *Philosophy in Question: Essays on a Pyrrhonian Theme*. Chicago: University Press of Chicago.

Hill, Polly. 1986. *Development Economics on Trial: The Anthropological Case for Prosecution*. Cambridge: Cambridge University Press.

Hinsley, F.H. 1986. *Sovereignty*. 2. ed., Cambridge: Cambridge University Press.

Hirsch, Fred. 1976. *Social Limits to Growth*. Cambridge, Mass.: Harvard University Press.

Hirschman, Albert O. 1958. *The Strategy of Economic Development*. New Haven, Conn.: Yale University Press.

Hobsbawm, Eric. 1990. *Nations and Nationalism Since 1780: Programme, Myth, Reality*. Cambridge: Cambridge University Press.

---. and Ranger, Terence eds. 1983. *The Invention of Tradition*. Cambridge: University of Cambridge Press.

Hodgson, David. 1991. *The Mind Matters: Consciousness and Choice in a Quantum World*. Oxford: Clarendon Press.

Hogarth, Robin M. and Reder, Melvin W. eds. 1987. *Rational Choice: The Contrast Between Economics and Psychology*. Chicago: University Press of Chicago.

Hollis, Martin. 1977. *Models of Man: Philosophical Thoughts on Social Action*. Cambridge: Cambridge University Press.

---. 1984a. "The Limits of Irrationality," in Wilson, Bryan R. ed. pp. 214-220.

---. 1984b. "Reason and Ritual," in Wilson, Bryan R. ed. pp. 221-239.

---. 1984c. "The Social Destruction of Reality," in Hollis, Martin and Lukes, Steven. eds. pp. 67-86.

---. 1987. *The Cunning of Reason*. Cambridge: Cambridge University Press.

---. and Nell, Edward J. 1975. *Rational Economic Man: A Philosophical Critique of Neo-Classical Economics*. Cambridge: Cambridge University Press.

---. Lukes, Steven eds. 1984. *Rationality and Relativism*. Cambridge, Mass.: MIT Press.

Holton, Gerald. ed. 1965. *Science and Culture: A Study of Cohesive and Disjunctive Forces*. Boston-Cambridge, Mass.: Houghton Mifflin-Riverside Press.

---. 1973. *Thematic Origins of Scientific Thought. Kepler to Einstein.* Cambridge, Mass.: Harvard University Press.

Horkheimer, Max and Adorno, Theodor W. 1972. *Dialectic of Enlightenment.* Trans. by J. Cumming. New York: Continuum.

Horton, Robin. 1967. "African Traditional Thought and Western Science." *Africa.* Vol. XXXVII. pp. 50-71, 155-187.

Hourani, Albert. 1983. *Arabic Thought in the Liberal Age, 1798-1939.* Cambridge: Cambridge University Press.

Hübner, Kurt. 1983. *Critique of Scientific Reason.* Trans. by P.R. Dixon and H.M. Dixon. Chicago: University Press of Chicago.

---. 1985. *Die Wahrheit des Mythos.* München: C.H. Beck.

Hume, David. 1966. *An Enquiry Concerning the Principles of Morals.* With an introd. by J.B. Stewart. 2. ed. La Salle, Ill.: Open Court.

---. 1988. *An Enquiry Concerning Human Understanding.* Buffalo, N.Y.: Prometheus Books.

Huntington, Samuel P. 1968. *Political Order in Changing Societies.* New Haven, Conn.: Yale University Press.

---. 1996. *The Clash of Civilizations and the Remaking of World Order.* New York: Simon & Schuster.

---. and Nelson, Joan M. 1976. *No Easy Choice: Political Participation in Developing Countries.* Cambridge, Mass.: Harvard University Press.

Husserl, Edmund. 1964. *The Phenomenology of Internal Time-Consciousness.* Ed. by M. Heidegger. Trans. by J.S. Churchill. Introd. by C.O. Schrag. Bloomington, Ind.: Indiana University Press.

---. 1970. *The Crisis of European Sciences and Transcendental Phenomenology: An Introduction to Phenomenological Philosophy.* Trans. with an Introd. by D. Carr. Evanston: Northwestern University Press.

Hutchison, T.W. 1965. *The Significance and Basic Postulates of Economic Theory.* New York: Augustus M. Kelley.

---. 1977. *Knowledge and Ignorance in Economics.* Oxford: Blackwell.

---. 1978. *On Revolutions and Progress in Economic Knowledge.* Cambridge: Cambridge University Press.

Huxley, Julian. 1943. *Evolution: The Modern Synthesis.* New York: Harper.

---. 1989. *Evolution and Ethics. With New Essays on Its Victorian and Sociobiological Context.* Ed. and introd. by J. Paradis and G.C. Williams. Princeton, N.J., Princeton University Press.

The I Ching or Book of Changes. 1967. The Richard Wilhelm trans. rendered into English by C.F. Baynes. Foreword by C.G. Jung. Preface to the third edition by H. Wilhelm. /Bollingen Series XIX./ Princeton, N.J.: Princeton University Press.

Ibn Khaldun. 1967. *The Muqaddimah: An Introduction to History*. Trans. from the Arabic by F. Rosenthal. Abridged and ed. by N.J. Dawood. /Bollingen Series./ Princeton, N.J.: Princeton University Press.

Inglehart, Ronald. 1990. *Culture Shift In Advanced Industrial Society*. Princeton, N.J.: Princeton University Press.

JACKSON, Robert H. 1990. *Quasi-States: Sovereignty, International Relations, and the Third World*. Cambridge: Cambridge University Press.

James, William. 1975. *Pragmatism: A New Way for Some Old Ways of Thinking*, and *The Meaning of Truth: A Sequel To Pragmatism*. Introd. by A.J. Ayer, Cambridge, Mass.: Harvard University Press.

Jargy, Simon. 1981. *Islam et Chrétienté: Les fils d'Abraham entre la confrontation et le dialogue*. Genève: Labor et Fides.

Jaspers, Karl. 1933. *Man in the Modern Age*. Transl. by E. and C. Paul. New York: Henry Holt.

---. 1971. *Philosophy of Existence*. Transl. and with an Introd. by R.F. Grabau. Philadelphia: University of Pennsylvania Press.

KALDOR, Nicholas. 1982. "The Irrelevance of Equilibrium Economics." *The Economic Journal*. Vol. 82. pp. 1237-1252.

Kant, Immanuel. 1964. *Groundwork of the Metaphysic of Morals*. 1785. Transl. by H.J. Paton. New York: Harper & Row.

---. 1966. *Critique of Pure Reason*. Trans. into English by F.M. Muller. Garden City, N.Y.: Doubleday.

---. 1985. *Critique of Practical Reason*. Transl. with an introd. by L.W. Beck. New York: Macmillan.

---. 1987. *Critique of Judgment*. Including the First Introduction. 1790. Trans. with an Introd. by W.S. Pluhar. With a foreword by M.J. Gregor. Indianapolis, Ind.: Hackett.

Kaplan, Abraham. 1964. *The Conduct of Inquiry: Methodology for Behavioral Science*. San Francisco: Chandler.

Kapp, William K. 1963. *Hindu Culture, Economic Development and Economic Planning in India*: A Collection of Essays. London: Asia Publishing House.

Karp, Ivan and Bird, Charles S. eds. 1987. *Explorations in African Systems of Thought*. Washington: Smithsonian Institution Press.

Kedourie, Elie. 1960. *Nationalism*. London: Hutchinson.

Kelley, Allen C. et al. 1972. *Dualistic Economic Development: Theory and History*. Chicago: University Press of Chicago.

Keynes, John M. 1963. *Essays in Persuasion*. New York: W.W. Norton.

---. 1964. *The General Theory of Employment, Interest, and Money*. New York: Harcourt Brace Jovanovich.

King, Winston L. 1964. *In the Hope of Nibbana: Theravada Buddhist Ethics*. LaSalle, Ill.: Open Court.

Kohli, Atul 1990. *Democracy and Discontent: India's Growing Crisis of Governability*. Cambridge: Cambridge University Press.

Kohn, Hans. 1944. *The Idea of Nationalism: A Study in Its Origins and Background*. New York: Macmillan.

Kolakowski, Leszek. 1989. *The Presence of Myth*. Trans. by A. Czerniawski. Chicago: University Press of Chicago.

Kolb, David. 1986. *The Critique of Pure Modernity: Hegel, Heidegger and After*. Chicago: University Press of Chicago.

Koselleck, Reinhart. 1985. *Futures Past: On the Semantics of Historical Time*. Trans. by K. Tribe. Cambridge, Mass.: MIT Press.

Krausz, Michael. ed. 1989. *Relativism: Interpretation and Confrontation*. Notre Dame, Ind.: University of Notre Dame Press.

---. and Meiland, Jack W. eds. 1982. *Relativism: Cognitive and Moral*. Notre Dame, Ind.: University of Notre Dame Press.

Krishna, Daya. 1991. *Indian Philosophy: A Counter Perspective*. New-Delhi-Oxford: Oxford University Press.

Kroeber, Alfred L. 1963. *Anthropology: Culture Patterns and Processes*. New York: Harcourt, Brace, Jovanovich.

---. and Kluckhohn, Clyde. 1963. *Culture: A Critical Review of Concepts and Definitions*. New York: Vintage Books.

Kuhn, Thomas 1970. *The Structure of Scientific Revolutions*. 2. ed. enlarged. Chicago: University Press of Chicago.

---. 1977. *The Essential Tension: Selected Studies in Scientific Tradition and Change*. Chicago: University Press of Chicago.

Kuznets, Simon. 1965. *Economic Growth and Structure: Selected Essays*. New York: W.W. Norton.

---. 1966. *Modern Economic Growth: Rate, Structure and Spread*. New Haven, Conn.: Yale University Press.

---. 1972. "Modern Economic Growth: Findings and Reflections." /Acceptance Speech for the Nobel Prize in Economic Science, Stockholm, December 1971/. *American Economic Review*. Vol. 63. pp. 247-258.

LAKATOS, Imre and Musgrave, Alan. eds. 1970. *Criticism and the Growth of Knowledge*. /Proceedings of the International Colloquium in the Philosophy of Science. 1965./ Cambridge: Cambridge University Press.

Lange, Oscar. 1945/1946. "The Scope and Method of Economics." *The Review of Economic Studies*. Vol. XIII. No. 33. pp. 19-32.

Lao-tzu. 1985. *Tao Te Ching: The Book of Meaning and Life*. Trans. and commentary by R. Wilhelm. Trans. into English by H.G. Ostwald. London: Arkana.

La Palombara, Joseph. ed. *Bureaucracy and Political Development*. Princeton, N.J.: Princeton University Press.

Lapidus, Ira. 1988. *A History of Islamic Societies*. Cambridge: Cambridge University Press.

Larmore, Charles E. 1987. *Patterns of Moral Complexity*. Cambridge: Cambridge University Press.

Laroui, Abdallah. 1967. *L'idéologie arabe contemporaine: essai critique*. Paris: Maspero.

---. 1974. *La crise des intellectuels arabes: Traditionalisme ou historicisme?* Paris: Maspero.

Lash, Scott. 1990. *Sociology of Postmodernism*. London: Routledge.

Laudan, Larry. 1984. *Science and Values: The Aims of Science and Their Role in Scientific Debate*. Berkeley, Cal.: University of California Press.

---. 1990. *Science and Relativism: Some Key Controversies in the Philosophy of Science*. Chicago: University Press of Chicago.

Laue, Theodore H.v. 1987. *The World Revolution of Westernization. The Twentieth Century in Global Perspective*. New York: Oxford University Press.

Lawson, Hilary. 1985. *Reflexivity: The Post-Modern Predicament*. La Salle, Ill.: Open Court.

Leplin, Jarrett. ed. 1984. *Scientific Realism*. Ed. with an introd. by J. Leplin. Berkeley, Cal.: University of California Press.

Leontief, Wassily. 1971. "Theoretical Assumptions and Nonobserved Facts." *American Economic Review*. Vol. 61. pp. 1-7.

Lerner, Daniel et al. 1958. *The Passing of Traditional Society: Modernizing the Middle East*. Glencoe, Ill.: Free Press.

Levenson, Joseph R. 1958. *Confucian China and its Modern Fate*. London: Routledge & Kegan Paul.

Levy, Marion. 1966. *Modernization and the Structure of Societies. A Setting for International Affairs*. Princeton, N.J.: Princeton University Press. Vols. 1-2.

Lévy-Brühl, L. 1975. *The Notebooks on Primitive Mentality*. Preface by M. Leenhardt. Trans. by P. Riviere. New York: Harper & Row.

Lewis, Bernard. 1988. *The Political Language of Islam*. Chicago: University Press of Chicago.

Lewis, William A. 1955. *The Theory of Economic Growth*. London: Allen & Unwin.

---. 1982. *The Theory and Experience of Economic Development*. Boston, Houghton Mifflin.

Lindberg, R. et al. eds. 1975. *Stress and Contradiction in Modern Capitalism*. Lexington, Mass.: Lexington Books.

Little, Ian M.D. 1982. *Economic Development: Theory, Policy, and International Relations*. New York: Basic Books.

Lloyd, G.E.R. 1990. *Demystifying Mentalities*. Cambridge: Cambridge University Press.

Loasby, Brian J. 1976. *Choice, Complexity and Ignorance: An Enquiry Into Economic Theory and the Practice of Decision-Making*. Cambridge: Cambridge University Press.

Locke, John. 1967. *Two Treatises Of Government*. A Critical Edition with an Introd. and apparatus criticus by A. Laslett. Cambridge: Cambridge University Press.

Logue, John. 1979. "The Welfare State: Victim of Its Success." *Daedalus*. Vol. 108. No. 4. pp. 60-87.

Lorenz, Konrad. 1987. *The Waning of Humaneness*. Trans. from the German by R.W. Kickert. Boston: Little Brown.

Luhmann, Niklas. 1991. *Zweckbegriff und Systemrationalität: Über die Funktion von Zwecken in sozialen Systemen*. 5. Aufl. Frankfurt am Main: Suhrkamp.

---. 1982. *The Differentiation of Society*. Trans. by S. Holmes and Ch. Larmore. New York: Columbia University Press.

---. 1987. "The Representation of Society Within Society." *Current Sociology*. Vol. 35. No. 2. pp. 101-108.

---. 1990. *Die Wissenschaft der Gesellschaft*. 1. Aufl. Frankfurt am Main: Suhrkamp.

---. 1992. "The Direction of Evolution," in Haferkampf, Hans and Smelser, Neil. eds. pp. 279-293.

---. 1993. *Soziale Systeme. Grundriß einer allgemeinen Theorie*. 4. Aufl. Frankfurt am Main: Suhrkamp.

---. 1995. *Social Systems*. Transl. by J. Bednarz Jr. Foreword by Eva M. Knodt. Stanford, Cal., Stanford University Press.

Lukes, Stephen. 1970. "Some Problems About Rationality," in Wilson, Bryan R. ed. pp. 194-213.

---. 1984. "Relativism in Its Place," in Hollis, Martin and Lukes, Steven. eds. pp. 261-305.

Lyotard, Jean-Francois. 1988. *The Differend: Phrases in Dispute*. Trans. by G. Van Den Abbeele. Minneapolis: Minnesota University Press.

MACHLUP, Fritz. 1978. *Methodology of Economics and Other Social Sciences*. New York: Academic Press.

MacIntyre, Alasdair. 1984. *After Virtue: A Study in Moral Theory*. 2. ed. Notre Dame, Ind.: University of Notre Dame Press.

---. 1988. *Whose Justice? Which Rationality?* Notre Dame, Ind.: University of Notre Dame Press.

---. 1989. "Relativism, Power, and Philosophy," in Krausz, Michael. ed. pp. 182-204.

Mannheim, Karl. 1948. *Ideology and Utopia: An Introduction to the Sociology of Knowledge*. London: Routledge and Kegan Paul.

---. 1982. *Structures of Thinking*. Text ed. and introd. by D. Kettler, V. Meja and N. Stehr. Trans. by J.J. Shapiro and S.W. Nicholsen. London: Routledge & Kegan Paul.

Margolis, Howard. 1987. *Patterns, Thinking, and Cognition: A Theory of Judgement*. Chicago: University Press of Chicago.

Margolis, Joseph. 1986. *Pragmatism Without Foundations: Reconciling Realism and Relativism*. Oxford: Blackwell.

---. 1990. "The Methodological and Metaphysical Peculiarities of the Human Sciences," in French, P.A.; Uehling, Th.E.; and Wettstein, H.K. eds. pp. 167-182.

---. 1991.*The Truth About Relativism*. Oxford: Blackwell.

Matilal, Bimal K. 1989. "Ethical Relativism and Confrontation of Cultures." in Krausz, Michael. ed. pp. 339-362.

Maund, J.B. 1976. "Rationality of Belief -- Intercultural Comparisons," in Benn, S.O. and Mortimore, G.W. eds. pp. 34-57.

Mayr, Ernest. 1982. *The Growth of Biological Thought: Diversity, Evolution, and Inheritance*. Cambridge, Mass.: Belknap Press/Harvard University Press.

---. 1988. *Toward a New Philosophy of Biology: Observations of an Evolutionist*. Cambridge, Mass.: Harvard University Press.

Mbiti, John S. 1969. *African Religions and Philosophy*. London: Heinemann.

McNeill, William H. 1991. *The Rise of the West: A History of the Human Community*. With a Retrospective Essay. Chicago: University Press of Chicago.

Mead, George H. 1934-1938. *Works*. Chicago: Chicago University Press.

Vol. 1. *Mind, Self, and Society from the Standpoint of a Social Behaviorist*. Ed. and with an introd. by Ch.W. Morris.

Vol. 2. *Movements of Thought in the Nineteenth Century*. Ed. and with an introd. by M.H. Moore.

Vol. 3. *The Philosophy of the Act*. Ed. and with an introd. by Ch.W. Morris.

294

---. 1980. *The Philosophy of the Present*. Ed. by A.E. Murphy. With prefatory remarks by J. Dewey. Chicago: University Press of Chicago.

Meier, Gerald M. and Seers, Dudley eds. 1984. *Partners in Development*. Washington/New York: World Bank/Oxford University Press.

Melitz, J. 1965. "Friedman and Machlup on the Significance of Testing Economic Assumptions." *Journal of Political Economy*. Vol. 73. pp. 37-61.

Mencius. 1970. *The Works of Mencius*. Transl. and with critical and exegetical notes, prolegomena, and copious indexes by J. Legge. New York: Dover.

Merton, Robert K. 1957. *Social Theory and Social Structure*. Rev. and enl. ed. Glencoe, Ill.: Free Press.

Mill, John Stuart. 1974. *Utilitarianism. -- On Liberty. -- Essay on Bentham*. Together with selected writings of Jeremy Bentham and John Austin. Ed. by M. Warnock. New York: New American Library.

Mises, Ludwig v. 1962. *The Ultimate Foundation of Economic Science: An Essay on Method*. Princeton, N.J.: Van Nostrand.

---. 1970. *Bureaucracy*. New Rochelle: Arlington House.

---. 1981. *Epistemological Problems of Economics*. Transl. by G. Reisman. New York: New York University Press.

Mohanty, Jitendra N. 1989. "Phenomenological Rationality and the Overcoming of Relativism," in Krausz, Michael ed. pp. 326-338.

Monod, Jacques. 1971. *Chance and Necessity*. New York: Vintage Books.

Morin, Edgard. 1968. "Pour une sociologie de la crise." *Communications*. Vol. 12. pp. 2-16.

Mynt, Hla. 1967. "Economic Theory and Development Policy." *Economica*. Vol. 34. pp. 117-130.

---. 1971. *Economic Theory and the Underdeveloped Countries*. New York: Oxford University Press.

Myrdal, Gunnar. 1957. *Economc Theory and the Underdeveloped Regions*. London: Duckworth.

---. 1958. *Value in Social Theory: A Selection of Essays on Methodology*. Ed. by P. Streeten. London: Routledge and Kegan Paul.

---. 1972. "How Scientific Are the Social Sciences?" /The Gordon Allport Memorial lecture. Harvard University, 4 November 1971/. *Economies et sociétés*. T. 7. No. 18. pp. 1473-1495.

---. 1973. *Against the Stream; Critical Essays on Economics*. New York: Pantheon Books.

NAGEL, Ernest. 1963. "Assumptions in Economic Theory." *American Economic Review*, Papers and Proceedings. Vol. 53. pp. 211-219.

Naraghi, Ehsan. 1977. *L'Orient et la crise de l'Occident*. Paris: Ed. Entente.

Nash, Manning. ed. 1977. *Essays on Economic Development and Cultural Change*. In honor of Bert F. Hoselitz. Chicago: Chicago University Press.

Nelson, Benjamin. 1981. *On the Roads to Modernity. Conscience, Science, and Civilizations: Selected Writings*. Ed. by T.E. Huff. Totowa, N.J.: Rowman and Littlefield.

Newton-Smith, W.H. 1981. *The Rationality of Science*. London: Routledge and Kegan Paul.

---. 1984. "Relativism and the Possibility of Interpretation," in Hollis, Martin and Lukes, Steven. eds. pp. 106-122.

Nisbet, Robert. 1990. *The Quest for Community: A Study in the Ethics of Order and Freedom*. San Francisco: Institute for Contemporary Studies.

Niskanen, William A. 1973. *Bureaucracy: Servant or Master?* London: Institute of Economic Affairs.

O'DONNELL, Guillermo. 1973. *Modernization and Bureaucratic Authoritarianism*. Berkeley, Cal.: University of California Press.

Offe, Claus. 1975. "The Theory of the Capitalist State and the Problem of Policy Formation," in Lindenberg, R. et al. eds.

---. 1984. *Contradictions of the Welfare State*. Ed. By J. Keane. Cambridge, Mass.: MIT Press.

---. 1985. *Disorganized Capitalism: Contemporary Transformations of Work and Politics*. Ed. by J. Keane. Cambridge, Mass.: MIT Press.

Olson, Mancur. 1965. *The Logic of Collective Action: Public Goods and Theory of Groups*. Cambridge, Mass.: Harvard University Press.

Olson, Mancur. 1982. *The Rise and Decline of Nations: Economic Growth, Stagflation, and Social Rigidities*. New Haven, Conn.: Yale University Press.

PAAUW, Douglas S. and Fei, John C.H. 1973. *The Transition in Open Dualistic Economies*. New Haven, Conn.: Yale University Press.

Parsons, Talcott. 1951. *The Social System*. Glencoe, Ill.: Free Press.

---. 1954. *Essays in Sociological Theory*. Rev. ed. Glencoe, Ill.: Free Press.

---. 1968. *The Structure of Social Action: A Study in Social Theory With Reference to a Group of Recent European Writers*. With a new Introduction. New York: Free Press.

Vol. 1 *Marshall, Pareto, Durkheim*.

Vol. 2. *Weber*.

---. 1977. *The Evolution of Societies*. Ed. and with an Introd. by J. Toby. Englewood Cliffs, N.J.: Prentice-Hall.

---, Bales, Robert F. and Shils, Edward A. 1953. *Working Papers in the Theory of Action*. New York: Free Press.

--- and Shils, Edward A. eds. 1951. *Toward a General Theory of Action*. Cambridge, Mass.: Harvard University Press.

--- and Smelser, Neil J. 1984. *Economy and Society: A Study in the Integration of Economic and Social Theory*. London: Routledge and Kegan Paul.

Paz, Octavio. 1985. *One Earth, Four or Five Worlds: Reflections on Contemporary History*. Trans. by H.R. Lane. New York: Harcourt, Brace, Jovanovich.

Piscatori, James P. 1986. *Islam in a World of Nation-States*. Cambridge: Cambridge University Press.

Plamenatz, John. 1970. *Ideology*. New York: Praeger.

Plantinga, Alvin and Wolterstorff, Nicholas eds. 1983. *Faith and Rationality: Reason and Belief in God*. Notre Dame, Ind.: University of Notre Dame Press.

Poggie, John. J. and Lynch, Robert, N. eds. 1974. *Rethinking Modernization; Anthropological Perspectives*. Westport, Conn.: Greenwood Press.

Popper, Karl R. 1952. *The Open Society and its Enemies*. 2. rev. ed. 2 vols. London: Routledge and Kegan Paul.

---. 1965. *Conjectures and Refutations. The Growth of Scientific Knowledge*. New York: Harper & Row.

---. 1968. *The Logic of Scientific Discovery*. New York: Harper & Row.

---. 1979. *Objective Knowledge: An Evolutionary Approach*. Rev. ed. Oxford: Clarendon Press.

---. 1987a. "Campbell on the Evolutionary Theory of Knowledge," in Radnitzky, Gerard and Bartley, W.W. III. eds. pp. 115-120.

---. 1987b. "Natural Selection and the Emergence of 'Mind'," in Radnitzky, Gerard and Bartley, W.W. III. eds. pp. 139-155.

--- and Eccles, John C. 1983. *The Self and Its Brain: An Argument for Interactionism*. London: Routledge and Kegan Paul.

Putnam, Hilary. 1978. *Meaning and the Moral Sciences*. London: Routledge and Kegan Paul.

---. 1979. *Philosophical Papers*. 2. ed. Cambridge: Cambridge University Press.

Vol. 1. *Mathematics, Matter and Method*.

Vol. 2. *Mind, Language and Reality*.

---. 1981. *Reason, Truth, and History*. Cambridge: Cambridge University Press.

---. 1987. *The Many Faces of Realism*. The Paul Carus Lectures. La Salle, Ill.: Open Court.

---. 1988. *Representation and Reality*. Cambridge, Mass.: MIT Press.

QUINE, Willard v.O. 1980. *From a Logical Point of View: Logico-Philosophical Essays*. 2. rev. ed. Cambridge, Mass.: Harvard University Press.

---. 1983. *Word and Object*. Cambridge, Mass.: Harvard University Press.

RABINOW, Paul and Sullivan, William M. eds. 1979. *Interpretive Social Science: A Reader*. Berkeley, Cal.: University of California Press.

Radhakrishnan, S.S. 1989. *Eastern Religions and Western Thought*. New Delhi-London: Oxford University Press.

---. and Moore, Ch.A. eds. 1957. *A Sourcebook in Indian Philosophy*. Princeton, N.J.: Princeton University Press.

Radnitzky, Gerard and Bartley, W.W. III eds. 1987. *Evolutionary Epistemology, Rationality, and the Sociology of Knowledge*. La Salle, Ill.: Open Court.

Rae, Douglas. 1979. "The Egalitarian State: Notes on a System of Contradictory Ideals." *Daedalus*. Vol.108. No.4. pp.37-54.

Rajchman, John and West, Cornel eds. 1985. *Post-Analytic Philosophy*. New York: Columbia University Press.

Rangel, Carlos. 1982. *L'Occident et le Tiers-Monde: De la fausse culpabilité aux vraies responsabilités*. Traduit de l'espagnol par G. Liebert. Préface de J-F. Revel. Paris: Robert Laffont.

Rappaport, Roy A. 1971. "Nature, Culture, and Ecological Anthropology," in Schapiro, Harry. ed. pp. 237-267.

Rasmussen, David. 1990. ed. *Universalism Versus Communitarianism: Contemporary Debates in Ethics*. Cambridge, Mass.: MIT Press.

Rawls, John. 1971. *A Theory of Justice*. Cambridge, Mass.: Belknap Press.

---. 1985. "Justice As Fairness: Political Not Metaphysical." *Philosophy and Public Affairs*. Vol. 14. No. 3. pp. 223-251.

Rensch, Bernhard. 1972. *Homo Sapiens: From Man to Demigod*. Trans. by C.A.M. Sym. New York: Columbia University Press.

Ricoeur, Paul. 1965. *History and Truth*. Trans. with an Introd. by Ch.A. Kelley. Evanston: Northwestern University Press.

---. 1981. *Hermeneutics and the Human Sciences: Essays on Language, Action and Interpretation*. Ed., transl., and Introd. by John B. Thompson. Cambridge-Paris: Cambridge University Press/Ed. de la Maison des Sciences de l'Homme.

---. 1986. *Lectures on Ideology and Utopia*. Ed. by G.H. Taylor. New York: Columbia University Press.

Riepe, Dale. 1982. *The Naturalistic Tradition in Indian Thought*. Westport, Conn.: Greenwood Press.

Riesman, David. 1950. *The Lonely Crowd*. With N. Glazer and R. Denney. Abr. ed. with a 1969 preface. New Haven, Conn.: Yale University Press.

Robbins, Lionel Ch. 1984. *The Nature and Significance of Economic Science.* 3. ed. Foreword by W.J. Baumol. New York: New York University Press.

Robertson, Roland. 1992. *Globalization: Social Theory and Global Culture.* Newbury Park, Cal.: SAGE Publications.

Rorty, Richard. 1979. *Philosophy and the Mirror of Nature.* Princeton, N.J., Princeton University Press.

---. 1982. *Consequences of Pragmatism. (Essays: 1972-1980).* Minneapolis: University of Minnesota Press.

---. 1989a. *Contingency, Irony, and Solidarity.* Cambridge: Cambridge University Press.

---. 1989b. "Solidarity or Objectivity?" in Krausz, Michael. ed. pp. 35-50.

Rosen, Stanley. 1989. *The Ancients and the Moderns: Rethinking Modernity.* New Haven, Conn.: Yale University Press.

Rosenberg, Nathan and Birdzell, L.E. Jr. 1986. *How the West Grew Rich: The Economic Transformation of the Industrial World.* New York: Basic Books.

Rosenthal, Erwin I.J. 1965. *Islam in the Modern National State.* Cambridge: Cambridge University Press.

Rostand, Jean. 1960. *Error and Deception in Science: Essays on Biological Aspects of Life.* Trans. by A.J. Pomerans. London: Hutchinson.

Rostow, W.W. 1960. *The Process of Economic Growth.* Oxford: Clarendon Press.

Rougemont, Denis de. 1962. *Pour un dialogue des cultures.* Genève: Payot.

Russell, Bertrand. 1952. *The Impact of Science on Society.* London: Unwin.

---. 1962. *The Scientific Outlook.* New York: W.W. Norton.

Ryan, Alan. 1970. *The Philosophy of the Social Sciences.* London: Macmillan.

Ryle, Gilbert. 1949. *The Concept of Mind.* Chicago: University Press of Chicago.

Ryoen, Minamoto. 1979. "Jitsugaku and Empirical Rationalism in the First Half of the Tokugawa Period," in de Bary, Wm. Theodore and Bloom, Irene. eds. pp. 375-469.

Ryuji, Yamashita. 1979. "Religious Thought and Its Relation to Jitsugaku," in de Bary, Wm. Theodore and Bloom, Irene. eds. pp. 307-335.

SAHLINS, Marshall D. 1976. *Culture and Practical Reason.* Chicago, University Press of Chicago.

---, and Service, Elman R. eds. 1982. *Evolution and Culture.* Ann Arbor, Mich.: University of Michigan Press.

Samuelson, Paul A. 1966. *The Collected Scientific Papers.* Ed. by Joseph E. Stiglitz. Vols. 1-3. Cambridge, Mass.: MIT Press.

---. 1983. *Foundations of Economic Analysis.* Enlarged ed. Cambridge, Mass.: Harvard University Press.

Sandel, Michael J. 1982. *Liberalism and the Limits of Justice.* Cambridge: Cambridge University Press.

Saussure, Ferdinand. 1964. "Signs and Language." Excerpts from: *Course in General Linguistics.* New York: McGraw-Hill, pp. 9-17, 65-76, reprinted in Alexander, Jeffrey S. and Seidman, Steven. eds. 1990. pp. 55-63.

Scheler, Max. 1973. *Formalism in Ethics and Non-Formal Ethics of Values: A New Attempt Toward the Foundation of an Ethical Personalism.* Evanston: Northwestern University Press.

Schluchter, Wolfgang. 1981. *The Rise of Western Rationalism: Max Weber's Developmental Theory.* Trans. with Introd. by. G. Roth. Berkeley, Cal.: University of California Press.

Schroedinger, Erwin. 1983. *My View of the World.* Trans. from the German by C. Hastings. Woodbridge, Conn.: Ox Bow Press.

Schumpeter, Joseph A. 1961. *The Theory of Economic Development: An Inquiry Into Profits, Capital, Credit, Interest and the Business Cycle.* Cambridge, Mass.: Harvard University Press.

---. 1976. *Capitalism, Socialism and Democracy.* With a new Introd. by T. Bottomore. New York: Harper & Row.

Schutz, Alfred. 1967. *The Phenomenology of the Social World.* Trans. by G. Walsh and F. Lehnert. Introd. by G. Walsh. Evanston: Northwestern University Press.

Searle, John R. 1983. *Intentionality: An Essay in the Philosophy of Mind.* Cambridge: Cambridge University Press.

---. 1984. *Minds, Brains, and Science.* Cambridge, Mass.: Harvard University Press.

---. 1992. *The Rediscovery of the Mind.* Cambridge, Mass.: MIT Press.

Segesvary, Victor. 1968. *Le réalisme khrouchtchévien: La politique soviétique à l'égard du nationalisme arabe, 1953-1960.* Neuchâtel: Ed. La Baconnière.

---. 1978. *L'Islam et la Réforme: Etude sur l'attitude des réformateurs zurichois envers l'Islam (1510-1550).* Lausanne: Ed. L'Age d'Homme.

---. 1995. "Group Rights: The Definition of Group Rights in the Contemporary Legal Debate Based on Socio-Cultural Analysis." *International Journal on Group Rights.* Vol. 3. No. 2. pp. 89-107.

---. 1999. *From Illusion to Delusion : Globalization and the Contradictions of Late Modernity.* San Francisco: International Scholars Publications.

---. 1999. *Existence and Transcendence : An Anti-Faustian Essay in Philosophical Anthropology.* San Francisco: International Scholars Publications.

---. 2000. *Dialogue of Civilizations : An Introduction to Civilizational Analysis.* Lanham, MD: University Press of America.

Seligman, Adam B. 1990. "Towards a Reinterpretation of Modernity in an Age of Postmodernity," in Turner, Bryan S. ed. 1990a. pp. 117-135.

Sen, Amartya K. 1979a. "Rational Fools," in Hahn, Frank and Hollis, Martin. eds. pp. 87-109.

---. 1979b. "Utilitarianism and Welfarism." *Journal of Philosophy*. Vol. 76. No. 9. pp. 463-489.

---. Williams, Bernard. eds. 1982. *Utilitarianism and Beyond*. Cambridge-Paris: Cambridge University Press/Editions de la maison des sciences de l'homme.

Shafer, Boyd C. 1972. *Faces of Nationalism: New Realities and Old Myths*. New York: Harcourt Brace Jovanovitch.

Shapere, Dudley. 1977. "Scientific Theories and Their Domains," in Suppe, Frederich. ed. pp. 518-565.

---. 1984. *Reason and the Search for Knowledge: Investigations in the Philosophy of Science*. Dordrecht: D. Reidel.

Shapiro, Harry. ed. 1971. *Man, Culture and Society*. Rev. ed. Oxford: Oxford University Press.

Sharabi, Hisham B. 1966. *Nationalism and Revolution in the Arab World*. New York: Van Nostrand Reinhold.

Sherrington, C.S. 1951. *Man on His Nature*. 2. ed. Cambridge: Cambridge University Press.

Shils, Edward. 1974. "Faith, Utility, and the Legitimacy of Science." *Daedalus*. Vol. 103. No. 3. pp. 1-15.

---. 1981. *Tradition*. Chicago: University Press of Chicago.

Simmel, Georg. 1971. *On Individuality and Social Forms: Selected Writings*. Ed. and with an introd. by D.N. Levine. Chicago: University Press of Chicago.

---. 1977. *The Problems of the Philosophy of History: An Epistemological Essay*. Transl. and ed., with an Introd. by G. Oakes. New York: Free Press.

---. 1980. *Essays on Interpretation in Social Science*. Trans. and ed. with an Introd. by G. Oaks. Totowa, N.J.: Rowan and Littlefield.

---. 1990. *The Philosophy of Money*. Ed. by D. Frisby. Trans. by T. Bottomore and D. Frisby from a first draft by K. Mengelberg. London: Routledge.

Simon, Herbert A. 1976. "From Substantive to Procedural Rationality," in Hahn, Frank and Hollis, Martin. eds. 1979. pp. 65-86.

---. 1986. "Rationality in Psychology and Economics," in Hogarth, Robin M. and Reder, Melvin W. eds. pp. 25-40.

Simon, Lawrence H. 1990. "Rationality and Alien Cultures," in French, P.A.; Uehling, Th.E.; and Wettstein, H.K. eds. pp. 15-43.

Singer, Milton. 1956. "Cultural Values in India's Economic Development." *Annals of the American Academy of Political and Social Science*. Vol. 305. May 1956, pp. 81-91.

---. 1966. "Religion and Social Change in India: The Max Weber Thesis, Phase Three." *Economic Development and Cultural Change*. Vol. XIV. No. 4, July 1966, pp. 497-505.

Singh, Balbir. 1987. *Indian Metaphysics*. Atlantic Highlands: Humanities Press.

Skorupski, John. 1978. "The Meaning of Another Culture's Belief," in Hookway, Christopher and Pettit, Phillip. eds. pp. 83-106.

Smith, Anthony D. 1981. *The Ethnic Revival*. Cambridge: Cambridge University Press.

---. 1983. *Theories of Nationalism*. 2. ed. New York: Holmes & Meyer.

---. 1986. *The Ethnic Origins of Nations*. Oxford: Blackwell.

Sperber, Dan. 1984. "Apparently Irrational Beliefs," in Hollis, Martin and Lukes, Steven eds. pp. 149-180.

Spengler, Oswald. 1986. *The Decline of the West*. Auth. trans. with notes by Ch. F. Atkinson. New York: Alfred. A. Knopf.

Vol. 1. *Form and Actuality*.

Vol. 2. *Perspectives of World-History*.

Srinivas, S.M. 1967. *Social Change in Modern India*. Berkeley, Cal.: University of California Press.

Staal, Frits. 1988. *Universals: Studies in Indian Logics and Linguistics*. Chicago: University Press of Chicago.

Stcherbatsky, F.Th. 1962. *Buddhist Logic*. Vol. 1. New York: Dover.

Steward, Julian H. 1972. *Theory of Culture Change: The Methodology of Multilinear Evolution*. Urbana, Ill.: University of Illinois Press.

---. 1977. *Evolution and Ecology: Essays on Social Transformation*. Ed. by J. C. Steward and R. F. Murphy. Urbana, Ill.: University of Illinois Press.

Strawson, Peter F. 1959. *Individuals: An Essay in Descriptive Metaphysics*. London: Methuen.

Strayer, Joseph. 1970. *On the Medieval Origins of the Modern State*. Princeton, N.J. University of Princeton Press.

Streeten, Paul. 1950. "Economics and Value Judgements." *Quarterly Journal of Economics*. Vol. LXIV, pp. 583-595.

---. 1959. "Unbalanced Growth." *Oxford Economic Papers*. New Series. Vol. 11. No. 2, pp. 167-190.

---. 1972. *The Frontiers of Development Studies*. New York: John Wiley.

---. 1974. "The Limits of Development Research." *World Development*. Vol. 2, Nos. 10-12, pp. 11-34.

Suppe, Frederich. ed. 1977. *The Structure of Scientific Theories*. Ed. with a critical Introd. and an Afterword. 2. ed. Urbana, Ill.: University of Illinois Press.

TAMBIAH, Stanley J. 1990. *Magic, Science, Religion, and the Scope of Rationality*. Cambridge: Cambridge University Press.

Taylor, Charles. 1979a. *Hegel and Modern Society*. Cambridge: Cambridge University Press.

---. 1979b. "Interpretation and the Sciences of Man," in Rabinow, Paul and Sullivan, William M. eds. pp. 25-71.

---. 1982. "The Diversity of Goods," in Sen, Amartya K. and Willams, Bernard. eds.

---. 1984. "Rationality," in Hollis, Martin and Lukes, Steven eds. pp. 87-105.

---. 1985. *Philosophy and the Human Sciences*. /Philosophical Papers. 2/ Cambridge: Cambridge University Press.

Tenbruck, Friedrich H. 1990. "The Dream of a Secular Ecumene: The Meaning and Limits of Policies of Development," in Featherstone, Mike. ed. pp. 193-206.

Thompson, John B. 1990. *Ideology and Modern Culture*. Stanford, Cal.: Stanford University Press.

Thurow, Lester C. 1981. *The Zero-Sum Society: Distribution and the Possibilities for Economic Change*. New York: Penguin.

---. 1983. *Dangerous Currents. The State of Economics*. New York: Random House.

---. 1992. *Head To Head: The Coming Economic Battle Among Japan, Europe, and America*. New York: William Morrow.

---. 1996. *The Future of Capitalism: How Today's Economic Forces Shape Tomorrow's World*. New York: Penguin Books.

Tibi, Bassam 1990. *Islam and the Cultural Accomodation of Social Change*. Boulder, Col.: Westview Press.

Tilly, Charles. ed. 1975. *The Formation of National States in Western Europe*. Princeton, N.J.: Princeton University Press.

Tönnies, Ferdinand. 1957. *Community and Society (Gemeinschaft und Gesellschaft)*. Trans. and ed. by Ch.P. Loomis. New York: Harper.

---. 1971. *On Sociology: Pure, Applied, and Empirical. Selected Writings*. Ed. and with an Introd. by W.J. Cahman and R. Heberle. Chicago: University Press of Chicago.

Toulmin, Stephen. 1972. *Human Understanding: The Collective Use and Evolution of Concepts*. Princeton: Princeton University Press.

---. 1982. *The Return to Cosmology: Postmodern Science and the Theology of Nature*. Berkeley, Cal.: University of California Press.

Touraine, Alain. 1990. "The Idea of Revolution," in Featherstone, Mike. ed. pp. 121-141.

---. 1992. "Two Interpretations of Contemporary Social Change," in Haferkampf, Hans and Smelser, Neil J. eds. pp. 55-77.

---. 1995. *Critique of Modernity*. Trans. by D. Macey. Oxford: Blackwell.

Turner, Bryan S. ed. 1990a. *Theories of Modernity and Postmodernity*. Newbury Park, Cal.: SAGE Publications.

---. 1990b. "The Two Faces of Sociology: Global or National?" in Featherstone, Mike. ed. pp. 343-358.

Turner, Jonathan H. 1988. *A Theory of Social Interaction*. Stanford, Cal.: Stanford University Press.

VATTIMO, Gianni. 1988. *The End of Modernity: Nihilism and Hermeneutics in Postmodern Culture*. Trans. and with an Introd. by J.R. Snyder. Baltimore: John Hopkins University Press.

Viner, Jacob. 1958. *The Long View and the Short: Studies in Economic Theory and Policy*. Glencoe, Ill.: Free Press.

WALLERSTEIN, Immanuel. 1991. *Geopolitics and Geoculture: Essays on the Changing World-System*. Cambridge-Paris: Cambridge University Press/ La Maison des Sciences de l'Homme.

Walzer, Michael. 1983. *Spheres of Justice: A Defense of Pluralism and Equality*. New York: Basic Books.

Waterston, A. 1965. *Development Planning; Lessons of Experience*. Baltimore: John Hopkins University Press.

Weber, Max. 1946. *From Max Weber: Essays in Sociology*. Trans. ed., with an Introd. by H.H. Gerth and C.W. Mills. New York: Oxford University Press.

---. 1947. *The Theory of Social and Economic Organization*. Trans. by A.M. Henderson and T. Parsons. Ed. with an Introd. by T. Parsons. New York: Free Press.

---. 1949. *Max Weber on the Methodology of the Social Sciences*. Trans. and ed. by E. A. Shils and H. A. Finch. Foreword by E.A. Shils. Glencoe, Ill.: Free Press.

---. 1958. *The Protestant Ethic and the Spirit of Capitalism*. Trans. by T. Parsons. Introd. by A. Giddens. New York: Charles Scribner's Sons.

---. 1964. *The Sociology of Religion*. Trans. by E. Fischoff. Introd.Parsons. Boston: Beacon Press.

---. 1978. *Economy and Society. An Outline of Interpretive Sociology*. Ed. by G. Roth and C. Wittich. Vols. 1-2. Berkeley, Cal.: University of California Press.

Weil, Eric 1965. "Science in Modern Culture," in Holton Gerald. ed. pp. 199-217.

Weisskopf, Walter A. 1979. "The Method Is Ideology: From a Newtonian to a Heisenbergian Paradigm in Economics." *Journal of Economic Issues*. Vol. XIII. No. 4. pp. 869-884.

Whitrow, G.J. 1988. *Time in History: The Evolution of Our General Awareness of Time and Temporal Perspective*. Oxford: Oxford University Press.

Whorf, Benjamin L. 1956. *Language, Thought, and Reality*: Selected Writings. Ed. and with an Introd. by J.B. Carroll. Foreword by S. Chase. Cambridge, Mass.: MIT Press.

Wigner, Eugene P. 1979. *Symmetries and Reflections: Scientific Essays*. Woodbridge, Conn.: Ox Bow Press.

Wilber, Charles K. and Harrison, Robert A. 1978. "The Methodological Basis of Institutional Economics: Pattern Model, Storytelling, and Holism." *Journal of Economic Issues*. Vol. 12. pp. 61-89.

Wilson, Bryan R. ed. 1970. *Rationality*. Oxford: Blackwell.

Winch, Peter. 1958. *The Idea of Social Science and Its Relation to Philosophy*. London: Routledge and Kegan Paul.

---. 1970. "Understanding a Primitive Society," in Wilson, Bryan R. ed. pp. 78-111.

Wittgenstein, Ludwig. 1989. *Philosophical Investigations*. Trans. by G.E.M. Anscombe. 3. ed. New York: Macmillan.

Wolff, Robert P. 1990. "Narrative Time: The Inherently Perspectival Structure of the Human World," in French, P.A.; Uehling, Th. E.; and Wettstein, H.K. eds. pp. 210-223.

Wrong, Dennis H. 1988. *Power: Its Forms, Bases, and Uses*. Chicago: University Press of Chicago.

Wuthnow, Robert. 1987. *Meaning and Moral Order: Explorations in Cultural Analysis*. Berkeley, Cal.: University of California Press.

YOUNG, J.Z. 1988. *Philosophy and the Brain*. Oxford: Oxford University Press.

ZIMMER, Heinrich. 1974a. *Philosophies of India*. Ed. by J. Campbell. /Bollingen Series. XXVI./ Princeton, N.J.: Princeton University Press.

---. 1974b. *Myths and Symbols in Indian Art and Civilization*. Ed. by Joseph Campbell. /Bollingen Series. VI./ Princeton, N.J.: Princeton University Press.

INDEX

ABOUT THE AUTHOR

Victor Segesvary was born in Hungary, country he left after the 1956 Revolution, and worked during 25 years with the United Nations in the field of economic and social development. His experiences in Asia and Africa familiarized him with the existence of different human worlds and taught him the necessity of understanding and tolerance in human relations. He obtained a Ph.D. in Political Science and International Relations from the Graduate School for International Studies, and a D.D. from the Faculty of Protestant Theology, both at the University of Geneva (Switzerland). His vast knowledge covers such diverse fields as sociology, economics, history and philosophy as well as the "new" science of comparative analysis of civilizations. He published many books and articles, among them *Inter-Civilizational Relations and the Destiny of the West: Dialogue or Confrontation?* and *From Illusion to Delusion : Globalization and the Contradictions of Late Modernity.* The latter links the phenomenon of globalization to the dialogue of civilizations. Victor Segesvary is chronicled in Marquis' WHO IS WHO IN AMERICA and WHO IS WHO IN THE WORLD.